STROLL ON

STROLL ON

Tony Booth

SIDGWICK & JACKSON
LONDON

First published in Great Britain in 1989 by Sidgwick & Jackson Limited

ISBN 0–283–99790–7

Phototypeset by Input Typesetting Ltd, London
Printed and bound in Great Britain by
Mackays of Chatham PLC, Chatham, Kent

for Sidgwick & Jackson Limited
1 Tavistock Chambers, Bloomsbury Way
London WC1A 2SG

For the women in my life –
especially Cherie, Lyndsey, Jenia, Bronwen, Sarah, Emma
and Nancy –
with my love
and hopes for their forgiveness.

Contents

'Life's but a walking shadow, a poor player,
That struts and frets his hour upon the stage,
And then is heard no more; it is a tale
Told by an idiot, full of sound and fury,
Signifying nothing.'

Macbeth, V.v. 24–28

Preface

Actors aren't often expected to present a one-man show in their otherwise deserted living room. If acting has any purpose at all, it is to communicate at least an aspect of the truth to an audience. That is why the better actors are able to adjust their performance according to the responses they receive.

Writing a book is a very different kettle of fish. Writers work alone and have no immediate response from the people with whom they are trying to communicate.

Like the earliest actors, I am but a storyteller who performs best for a live audience, welcoming their laughter and tears. I am grateful, therefore, for the help I have received from my friend, the biographer Sydney Higgins. He has encouraged me to keep on when I faltered and to reveal in my story the darkest as well as the sunniest moments.

Now that my work has been completed, I hand it over to you, the reader, and invite you to share my laughter and my tears.

Tony Booth

Prologue

I screamed and screamed and screamed so loud that my voice broke. I'd never known such agony. To escape the unbearable pain, I felt myself leaving my body and I passed out.

Somebody was gently shaking my shoulder. I opened my eyes. Leaning over me was a woman in white, wearing a surgical mask.

'Quick, quick. Wake up. Wake up,' she said softly. 'You're on the news.'

I looked across the room at a flickering television set and saw a photograph of myself. A voice was saying: 'TV actor Tony Booth was seriously burned in a mystery fire at his Hampstead home late last night. Tony Booth, who is forty-eight, won fame in the series *Till Death Us Do Part*. A spokesman for Mount Vernon Hospital described Mr Booth's condition as being "very serious".'

The pain hit me again. I tried to scream, but no sound came and I passed out.

What seemed to be the very next second, I was awakened by the same nurse, saying, 'Quick. Quick, Mr Booth. You're on the BBC as well!'

If the news that I'd been rushed into hospital was on both ITV *and* BBC, then I really was in trouble!

1

Family Matters

I look like my mother's father. He was over six foot tall and weighed fifteen stone – an Irish-Yorkshireman with a shock of blond hair who loved his drink. His wife, my grandmother, was just five foot – a tiny, irascible Irishwoman with red hair.

I was born on 9 October 1931, in their two-up and two-down house in Jubilee Road, Liverpool, where my parents had lodged since their marriage.

The street, like many others then surviving in the inner cities of the industrial north, had been built in the mid-nineteenth century. The houses formed a long terrace of 'back-to-backs', with their backyards separated only by a narrow alley from those of the houses in the parallel street behind. It was a close, overcrowded, but extremely friendly community where everybody knew each other's business. For the most part, the people were Roman Catholic and of Irish descent.

One day, when I was about four, my grandfather went off to Chester races. I was playing happily in the street when a copper came along and asked me where I lived. I told him and he walked back with me to the house. Everybody seemed very shocked when we arrived and I was shut away inside.

It turned out that my grandfather had won some money at the races and got paralytically drunk. He'd been arrested and thrown into Chester Gaol. The local policeman had come round to see if there was cash to bail him out, but my grandmother had replied, 'No, bugger him! Let him stay there!' So the copper had said that grandfather would be kept in overnight and then released in the morning.

The next day, I was told, 'You play in the street. When you see your grandfather turn the corner come in and tell us.'

I was having a game with my friends when one of the kids said, 'Here he is!' I looked up and saw my grandfather at the corner a-wet sail. He was not just pissed, but pissed off. I dashed into the house, shouting, 'Granddad's coming! Granddad's coming!'

'All right,' they said. 'Get out of the way.'

The house had a small hallway that led into the kitchen. My grandmother stood on a chair behind the kitchen door and said to my mother, 'Give me the frying pan.' She was handed one of those huge cast-iron jobs.

My grandfather came crashing through the front door, bellowing, 'Where is she? Where is she, the bitch?'

'I'm in here, luv,' she cooed.

'Don't you give me "luv",' he said.

As he walked into the kitchen, my grandmother smashed him on the back of the head with the frying pan. She poleaxed him, but before he hit the deck, he groaned, 'She loves me!'

While he was out cold on the ground, my gran and my mother were going through his pockets to see if there was anything left of his winnings.

Shortly afterwards, just before my sister was born, my parents managed to pay the deposit on a house in Ferndale Road, which was two quid upmarket. Then I went to St Edmund's Infant School. The boys there belonged to gangs but I didn't join one. I'd never been in a gang – I've never been that sort of guy and, for Christ's sake, we were only five.

Just after I'd started at the school, I saw a kid I was quite friendly with being beaten up by a gang in the playground. I went to pull the lads off, but they all rounded on me. 'No, no, no,' they said. 'You're the one we really want,' and they beat the shit out of me. To this day I don't really know why. But it taught me one thing – 'Not everybody out there loves you, Tony!'

Coming from my background, it was assumed that, as I was the eldest son and the eldest grandson, it was my destiny to be a priest. To make sure I got off to a flying start, I began to learn Latin when I was six. Three times a week I was sent to Park House, a woman's nursing home run by nuns, where the old priest who was the chaplain gave me lessons. I wasn't allowed to use the front door. I had to knock on the garden gate and the priest would smuggle me into his little room. He was obviously afraid that in my short trousers I would be a definite temptation to the nuns!

I'd been going there about a year and hadn't clapped eyes on a nun. Then one night the priest said to me, 'You know Reverend Mother died? Well, we're going to the chapel and we'll say a prayer together for her – in Latin.'

We went to the tiny chapel in the grounds. It was a chilly winter night. The door creaked slowly open. Inside, candles were burning. There, in the glim flickering light, I could see in front of the small altar an open coffin laid on a lace-covered table.

I was terrified. I'd never seen a dead body before and there was no way I wanted to set foot in the chapel.

'Come with me, boy,' the priest said and went in. I loitered behind. 'Come on. Come on, boy,' he insisted. Then he knelt by the coffin. I knelt down about a yard behind him. In the cold, echoing chapel we said the prayers in Latin. At last we finished.

Just as I stood up, he turned round, swept me up from the floor, and said, 'You have the privilege to kiss the Reverend Mother goodbye.' Then he lifted me right over the coffin and on to this old woman's wizened face which was framed by a black cowl. I'd never seen her alive and in death, with her sunken eyes and the crinkled parchment of her skin, she was the witch of my childhood nightmares. I screamed; he dropped me; and one of the candles was sent flying.

I didn't stop running until I reached home!

Later that evening, the priest arrived at our house to say that the candle I'd knocked over had set fire to the altar cloth and it had only been because of his quick thinking that the chapel had been saved from going up in flames, causing the premature and unwanted cremation of the Reverend Mother's corpse. There was hell to pay and, after that, the priest refused to teach me any more Latin. Still, I'd learnt enough for them to stick me on the altar, serving mass. It didn't matter that there wasn't a surplice small enough to fit me. Mine had to be tucked up under my belt.

Just before the Second World War, when I was eight, there was a diphtheria epidemic in Liverpool. In those days, before the advent of the National Health Service, such epidemics were commonplace and caused the deaths of many children in over-crowded city areas.

One evening, I came home from school with swollen glands and couldn't swallow. The doctor from the old National Health

Insurance panel arrived eventually and diagnosed diphtheria. I was taken to Fazackerly Hospital and put in the isolation ward. They examined me and I didn't have diphtheria, but I'd already been admitted and so I was stuck there. Because it was the place to which children with every kind of infectious disease were sent, I managed while I was there to catch diphtheria, scarlet fever, mumps, and diphtheria again. You name it – I had it. In the end, I spent nearly a year in Fazackerly.

Being in hospital was the greatest thing for my education. As they thought I was dying, the nurses gave me anything I wanted. My mother had taught me to read before I started school and I loved books. When I said that the comics in the children's ward were boring, the staff said they'd bring me books from the hospital library. But any book brought into the isolation ward had afterwards to be burnt. So I was given books that nobody else wanted, like Jack London's novels and the great classics. *'War and Peace will keep him quiet!'* – that sort of thing.

I read Dostoevsky and Gibbon's *The Rise and Fall of the Roman Empire* when I was only nine years old. I didn't know how to pronounce any of the names or understand the deeper meanings, but I loved the stories. There was nothing else to do and so I read day in and day out. I could even read at night – 'What does it matter, lad? You'll probably be dead soon and this is what you'll be missing!'

They moved the kids up the isolation ward according to the state they were in. If you didn't get better, you reached the top bed and then there was only one place to go – through the door that led to the mortuary. On the other hand, if you started to recover, you were moved back down the ward on the other side. I did the trip twice, up and down that ward.

The first time I was in the bed next to the end, I saw a figure, with a face completely hidden by a pointed cowl, who suddenly appeared by the top bed. He dragged some form of ectoplasm out of the boy's body and then drifted out with it through the door. At the same time, a cry came from the body. The nurses came running down, pulled the curtains round the bed and the body was removed. 'Jesus, Mary and Joseph,' I thought. 'That was death.' Then they came to move my bed. 'I'm not going in that spot,' I shouted. 'You die if you go there and I'm not going to die.'

'OK, smart alec,' they said and moved me instead over to the other side.

When at last I was released from hospital, my parents had

4

prepared me a bedroom of my own. It couldn't have been easy for them. During the thirties, the country didn't need merchant seamen. So my father was out of work most of the time. He did various odd jobs, like window cleaning. Then when the Second World War came, merchant seamen were desperately wanted. At the beginning of 1940, my father got his first ship for nearly ten years. It was the SS *Montrose*, which was sailed up from Liverpool to Glasgow to be refitted as an armed merchant vessel. While this was going on, he travelled backwards and forwards between home and the ship – 'working-by' as they call it.

The ship was due to sail early one week. On the Friday before, my mother had a dream that the SS *Montrose* had gone down with the loss of all hands. She was so convinced that the ship was going to be torpedoed that she told my father.

At first, he said, 'Oh don't talk rubbish!' But then my grandmother joined in and it became like the gypsy's warning. In the end, my father went sick on the Monday, because he'd become convinced that something would happen. The *Montrose* sailed on the Tuesday and on the Friday it was torpedoed in the North Atlantic with the loss of all hands.

Afterwards, my father went to sea regularly. Because of that, I never developed a really close relationship with him. I ran wild while he was away and for the ten days or so he was home on leave I had to be on my best behaviour. The sooner he went back to sea the better, as far as I was concerned. When he got torpedoed, I thought, 'Coo, he won't be back for some time now!' Poor sod, while he was drifting in the South Atlantic, I was having a terrific time. Then he came home and the discipline started again.

I was really brought up by my mother. All the beliefs I have come from her. She was honest in everything. She wasn't afraid to speak her mind and I always knew that she would stand by me, providing I told the truth. Mind you, she also believed that if you spared the rod you spoiled the child – and I've still got the bruises to prove it!

Like most working-class women at the time, she wasn't political. She didn't have the time. She was too busy trying to bring her children up on nothing. What time did she have to be political?

My early political education came from my grandfathers. I was crazy about my mother's father. He was a great influence on my life. A soldier in the First World War, he deserted. He suddenly became very Irish, went over to Ireland, changed his name from Tankard to Thompson and met my grandmother. During the General Strike of 1925, he was involved with the dockers' trade union. As a result, he was blacked by all the employers. That was at a time when the number of unemployed was rising rapidly and the world economic depression was deepening. In Liverpool, it was impossible to find alternative employment.

My grandfather used to sit outside the dock gates with an orange box and cut the sailors' hair when they came out. In return, he often got paid in kind, rather than cash. He built up a huge collection of shrunken heads, African shields, parrots, a violin, monkeys and every kind of damn thing. My grandmother used to say, 'Why doesn't he take money instead of all this useless junk? He tells me he's got Umslopogaas's battle-axe. The stupid man doesn't even know that Umslopogaas is someone in a story!'

Eventually, in the late thirties, my grandfather scraped together enough cash to open a very tiny barber's shop. Previously it had been a baker's. Once, when I called there on my way home from school, the shop was empty and so he said he'd show me the cellar. He lit a candle and I followed him down the narrow stone stairs. In the dank gloom, I could make out the old bread ovens and piles of the junk my grandfather had been given by sailors.

As we stood there, he told me in graphic detail how Sweeny Todd, the Demon Barber, had, in a barber's just like the one upstairs, cut the throats of his clients and dispatched them through a trapdoor into the cellar below where the bodies were cut up, cooked and made into succulent meat pies. I was terrified!

Later, my grandfather often used to talk to me about socialism. Why should society be like this? Why do they have money and we don't? Why are there kids starving when there is plenty of money to go round? Why is it that the only time the working-class is valued is when war comes? 'You wait and see,' he used to tell me. 'There's a war coming and they'll need us. They'll ask us to go and fight – kids like you with their fathers out of work. You'll be doing the fighting yet again.'

My other grandfather – Grandfather Booth – used to talk to me about pacifism. He'd been a pacifist during the First World War and was put into prison. But after a while he couldn't stand it any more and went into the Army as a stretcher bearer. He was badly gassed at Mons. But he remained a pacifist all his life.

I remember sitting with him in the park, early in 1939. He told me that he had a service revolver and should war be declared he was going to kill both his sons rather than have them go to war. Like a fool, I went home and told my mother. All the women in the family got together to try and get him certified. But he managed to escape that.

In 1942, when I was ten, I was entered for the eleven-plus and passed, but because I was too young to go to the grammar school, I had to stay another year at St Edmunds – an all-age school. I'd done so well, however, that I was put in the top class with the fourteen-year-olds, who were in their last year at school.

This was at the time when the Yanks were over here and Liverpool was being regularly bombed. Everybody had an Anderson shelter which was used for all kinds of purposes – storing black-market food, a secret pigsty, and, most frequently, illicit sexual activities. The older boys in my class used to make me stand guard at the entrance to the school's shelter while they amused themselves with one of the girls, called Sally. When the scandal broke, I was incriminated because I'd been there keeping a lookout – even though I didn't know what the hell was going on!

The following year, I took the eleven-plus again and passed once more, even though I had an asthma attack in the middle of the examination. So in the autumn I went to St Mary's College, Crosby. It was run by the Christian Brothers – a bunch of Irish hooligans I came to believe were licensed to beat the hell out of kids in the name of God and the Republic.

Boys attending the school had to wear a uniform. Not only was money scarce in our family, but it was wartime and clothes were rationed. My mother used to clean the house of a local doctor and his wife, whose son was already at St Mary's and my mother managed to buy his second-hand blazer. On my first day at the school, who should be outside but this wretched youth who bellowed, 'Ah, you're wearing my old blazer, aren't you?'

At St Mary's, pupils had to buy their own books. Because of this, the only way I was allowed to go to the school was by striking a deal with my mother that I'd earn the money for these myself. The school did give some bursaries. It was agreed that I'd try for one of them, but meanwhile I'd have to deliver newspapers – morning and evening.

After I'd been at school six months, I was told that I'd been awarded one of the bursaries and that my books would be paid for during the rest of my time there. So I thought, My career as a newspaper boy is over! But was it hell! My mother reneged on the deal and made me carry on until I was fifteen! Of course, I knew she needed the money, but I wasn't too pleased at the time. Every morning, I used to get up at six, cycle about five miles delivering papers, return home for a buttie and tea, dash to church so I could serve mass and then pedal like a maniac to school. In the evening, I'd get on my bike, deliver papers and then return home to do my homework.

When I was twelve, Grandfather Thompson died. As with most Irish families, the body had to be laid out in the front room so that friends and relatives could pay their last respects. As my grandparents lived above the barber's shop, the body couldn't be viewed there in the upstairs room. The coffin was brought to our house and laid out in our front parlour. I kept well out of the way. My last experience of seeing a corpse in a coffin had been bad enough. There was no way I wanted to see another.

At this time, my dad was away at sea. Whenever that happened, my mother fluctuated between warning me, 'Just wait until your father gets home and finds out what you've been doing,' and, if anything went wrong, saying, 'You're the man of the house. Do something.'

Because of the presence of my grandfather's body, I was once again promoted to being man of the house. Whenever somebody arrived to view the body, I had to open the front door and let them in. But I never went with them into the front parlour. I was too scared even to look inside. I just opened the door, stared the other way, let them go in, and then listened to them saying, 'Oh, doesn't he look peaceful? Isn't he marvellous? Oh, lovely! Just see how they've made him look.' That went on for a couple of days.

As my grandmother had moved into our house, she was sleeping with my mother. My sister, who was nine, had taken over my room and I slept with Bob, my baby brother, in the back room. In those days, we didn't have two-way electric switches and so the light in the hall had to be turned off downstairs. Once upstairs, there was no way of having the light on again, unless you went back downstairs.

On the second night, we'd all gone to bed. The house was quiet. The Westminster chimes of my parents' clock had just struck midnight. Everybody but me had gone to sleep. I was under the bedcovers with a torch reading a book.

Suddenly I heard a drawn-out whoosh and then an almighty bang. The whole house shook. It was terrible. Frozen under the bedclothes, I thought, 'My God. What's happened?'

Then I heard my mother say, 'Toneee! Toneee!' in that voice that used to send shivers down my spine, because it always meant I'd got to do something so unpleasant that there was no way my mother was going to do it herself.

I copped a deaf 'un and thought, 'Forget this!'

Then I heard my grandmother wail, 'My God! It's your father.

I knew he wasn't dead. He's come to in the coffin. The shock of it has made him fall over!' Then she shouted, 'Don't worry, love! Help's on its way!'

I immediately put out the torch, stuck the book under the pillow, and curled up next to my brother.

Meanwhile, my sister had woken up and started to have hysterics: 'Oh God, I knew he wasn't dead. They're trying to bury him alive.'

By now, my sister and grandmother were on the landing, crying, wailing and causing a terrible ruckus while my mother comes into my room and says, 'Tony, Tony, get down there, you little bugger, and see what's happening.'

My sister's screaming, 'Help, help. Say he's a skeleton. Will he be just a skull? Will the pennies have fallen off his eyes?'

I'm terrified, shouting, 'Don't make me. Don't make me. I'm not going downstairs.'

Eventually, my mother dragged me apart from my brother, took me by the scruff of the neck, and flung me down the first three stairs on to the small landing. As she stood, peering through the stair-rails with the light from the bedroom behind her, she said, 'Get on, lad. Get down there and see if your grandfather's all right.'

I shouted back, 'Please don't make me. I beg you, mother, please don't make me go down there. I've never seen his dead body. I don't want to see his dead body.'

She ran down the three stairs and pushed me all the way down so that I landed in a heap at the bottom. By the time I picked myself up, they were all standing behind the stair-rails – my mother, my gran, my sister and my baby brother.

'Get in there! Get in there!' my mother's shouting.

'You'll be all right, luv,' my grandmother's saying. 'Help is on its way. Thank you, Jesus, for bringing him back! I knew my prayers would be answered.'

Both my sister and my brother were screaming and sobbing.

I switched on the light in the hall and then crept slowly along the wall. When I arrived at the parlour door, I stopped.

My mother and my gran were still shrieking, 'Get in there! Get in there!'

I looked quickly into the room and in one glance saw the coffin and what had happened. I screamed, ran straight upstairs, jumped into bed, and pulled the covers over my head.

They came rushing in. 'What's the matter? What's the matter?'

'It's the coffin-lid,' I sobbed. 'The coffin-lid fell down!'

My grandfather's body had been laid out in the open coffin so that visitors could pay their last respects. The undertakers had placed the coffin-lid against the wall and, for some reason, it had suddenly slipped down to the floor, making the almighty crash we'd all heard.

My mother shouted, 'Right! Go downstairs, pick up the lid, prop it back up against the wall, switch off the light and come back to bed.'

'I don't care what you do to me,' I said adamantly. 'You can kill me. But I'm not going downstairs again.'

For the first time in the history of our house, the lights in the hall and parlour were left on all night. None of us dared go downstairs to switch them off!

2

Sex and Strife

The first girl I fell in love with was Mary. She started on the same day as I did at infant school and I loved her straightaway. When I was eleven and went to St Mary's, she went to the Convent, just across the road. I was mad about her. She was the girl of my dreams.

Because I'd been an altar boy for so long, I could deal myself the masses I wanted to do. So I always used to pick those that Mary attended. When it came to the sermon, I could sit there, watch her and make her blush.

At one particular ten o'clock mass on a Sunday, I was sitting next to the old priest. The young priest was giving the sermon – he was very shy and boring. It was a spring day, it was very warm, and everybody in the church was thinking, 'Why doesn't he get on with it? Is he never going to finish?'

I was looking at Mary and suddenly I started to get an erection. I couldn't stop it. I shifted my legs beneath my cassock and surplice, but it didn't do any good. I was fully erect, sitting on the altar, lusting after Mary.

'At any moment,' I thought, 'the top of the church is going to open and this great shaft of light is going to come down and hit me. All my clothes are going to fall off. The whole congregation, including my mother, my grandmother, my sister and Mary are going to see that I'm sitting here with a hard on. I'm going to be finished for ever.'

But it didn't happen. Then I started to giggle and I thought, 'I'm going to get away with this! God must have a hell of a sense of humour. While the priest is boring the arse off everybody else, I've got a hard on!'

I never told Mary of my love for her. I used to follow her at a discreet distance and, when I'd finished my paper-round, I'd cycle miles out of my way to pass her house just in the hope of seeing her. But my love was unrequited.

My first sexual contact with a girl was for ever being postponed. I was one of a whole generation that spent its puberty in Anderson shelters during the bombing furtively wanking. 'Oh, God, please don't let the bomb drop until I've come!' Hitler's got a hell of a lot to answer for!

I soon discovered that wanking was a worry to many of the boys at St Mary's College. As my grandmother was distantly related to the Archbishop – who was called by all the kids in Liverpool 'the Archie Bishop' – I was thought to have a hotline to God. I totally abused my position by dispensing advice to my fellow pupils when they had any religious problems.

From my first day at the school and for the next three years, I sat in the next desk to this lad called Renno. One day, he asked me if I believed that wanking was a mortal sin.

'Don't be ridiculous,' I told him. 'Of course it's not.'

'Well,' he said, 'our parish priest told me that it was a mortal sin and you have to confess it every time, because wanking kills unborn babies.'

'Ah! Your parish priest doesn't know his arse from his elbow. Listen! My uncle is the Archie Bishop of Liverpool and he told me wanking isn't a mortal sin,' I said, lying through my back teeth.

'Really?'

'Look, I'm telling you,' I said. 'It's just a venal sin.'

'Oh,' he said. 'Do you confess it?'

'No! I don't confess it!'

'Well I'm not going to confess it either,' he said, 'because the parish priest always gives me a hell of a time. I'm in church for hours saying Hail Marys and everybody knows I've been wanking. It's only the wankers that stay there for ever doing their absolution.'

After that, every ten weeks or so, Renno would say to me, 'Are you certain?'

'For Christ's sake!' I'd tell him. 'It's all right. Believe me. Don't worry about it. If you go blind, you can always sell newspapers.'

For three years he was still mithering me about wanking. One day I said, 'OK, I'll tell you what we'll do. We'll go to St Peter and St Paul's. The old canon there is in his eighties. He's deaf and daft. Whatever you've done, he gives you three Hail Marys, three Our Fathers, a Glory-be and away you go. It doesn't matter whether it's murder, rape or pillage. So don't worry about it. On Saturday morning, I'll meet you at St Peter and St Paul's, we'll do a quick confession and then go and watch the girls play hockey.'

When we met that Saturday, I said to Renno, 'Now listen. Whatever you say, the old canon always replies, "That's terrible!" It's like a record stuck in the groove – "That's terrible! That's terrible! That's terrible!" First you confess a few little sins. Then you slip in "sins against impurity", followed quickly by stealing and missing mass. Then if he wakes up, the old canon'll say, "You missed mass. That's terrible!" And that'll be it.'

We had to wait a while in the church, because the old canon always had a big queue. All the sinners went to him. The younger priest never got any trade at all.

I was going to go in first, when Renno said, 'Are you going to confess to wanking?'

'Sure. Yes,' I lied.

I did my confession and came out. Renno went in and I waited outside. Standing by the side of the church, I lit up the first of a packet of five Woodbines. I was down to my last Woodbine when an ashen-faced Renno staggered out of the church. He sputtered out, 'The canon wants to see you. You're a fuckin' liar!'

A short struggle ensued, while I dragged out of him what the hell he'd done, dropping me in it with the canon.

Apparently, Renno had gone in and started, 'In the name of the Father, Son and Holy Ghost, pray, father, give me your blessing. It is two weeks since my last confession. I accuse myself of being disobedient. . . '

'That's terrible, terrible,' the canon had said.

'. . . fighting and quarrelling. . . '

'That's terrible. Oh, God, that's terrible.'

'. . . missing morning prayers. . . '

'That's terrible, terrible.'

'. . . missing evening prayers, sins against impurity, stealing, missing mass on Sunday, taking the name of the Lord in vain. . .'

'Just a minute, boy. What was that you said?'

'Taking the Lord's name in vain.'

'No, no, no! Before that. Before that.'

'Missing mass on Sunday.'

'No, boy. No, boy! What are you doing? Before that. Before that.'

'Stealing, father.'

'You know what I'm talking about, boy.'

'Sins against impurity, father.'

'That's right. Sins *of* impurity, boy. That's terrible. Was it by yourself?'

'Yes, father.'

'Oh, that's terrible. That's terrible! And how many times have you done this, boy, since last you confessed?'

Renno said, 'Seven hundred and eighty-nine times, father.'

There was a long pause. Then the veil was lifted back. The old canon peered at Renno and said, 'How long was it you said since your last confession?'

'Two weeks, father.'

'Good God, boy,' the canon shouted, 'you'll kill yourself at this rate!'

Renno explained that it had been over three years – not a fortnight – and that he hadn't confessed before because Tony Booth, who was related to the Archie Bishop of Liverpool, had told him that the Pope had said it didn't matter about wanking.

As soon as I heard all this, I scampered off home. I didn't have the balls to face the canon. And I never went again to confession at St Peter and St Paul's!

According to the other lads, I was the only one who never got anywhere with the girls. Everybody else said they'd made it. They seemed to have an encyclopaedic knowledge of the girls who were easy. I felt really deprived.

When I asked what I should do, all the guys said, 'Everybody, but everybody's been out with Lin. She's easy. If you want to try it, why not try Lin?'

At that time in Liverpool, every major thoroughfare had a Chinese laundry. There was one on the corner of the next street to ours and that was where Lin lived. She was the same age as me and went to the Protestant school. That made it all right. It was OK to go out with a Protestant girl as long as you weren't serious. 'Practise on the Protestants and marry a Catholic' was the motto.

The next time I took my dad's collars round to the Chinese laundry, I plucked up enough courage to ask the beautiful Lin if she'd go with me to the pictures. Eventually, I persuaded her.

That night, we were sitting in the back row of the Odeon. I figured that I might as well give it a go. I tried. She told me she wasn't that kind of girl and that I was an idiot.

I said, 'But that's not what Barry said.'

'What's he say?'

'He said he took your knickers off.'

'He's a bloody liar.'

'Well, what about Brendan?'

'He lies. They're all liars. Chinese girls not like that.'

It was only when Lin jumped up and ran out of the cinema that it dawned on me that the guys had been lying. The bastards had dropped me right in it. Lin wasn't that kind of girl and they knew it.

The next day, I'd finished my paper-round and had got off my bike at the corner of our road when I ran smack into Lin's three brothers. I didn't know anything at the time about Oriental martial arts. But I soon learnt. They threw me all over the place, bouncing me from one end of the road to the other. Then they told me to stay away from their sister.

That was the first time I realized that men in the main are a bunch of bullshitters, especially where women are concerned. I also discovered that women with brothers should be avoided like the plague!

Sisters, on the other hand, could be quite useful. I was talking one day to mine about girls and she said, 'Oh that Joyce. She'd show anybody her knickers if they asked her.' That was enough to have me swooning at the very possibility of it. I knew Joyce well. She lived in our street and went to the same convent school as my sister.

At that stage, I had to take my brother with me whenever I went out. One summer's evening, hoping to chat up Joyce, I dragged him off down the park with our dog. It was a Springer Spaniel, called Buster, that had been given to my mother by a woman whose house she cleaned. Now Buster was a bugger. He was always hungry and always trying to get at it.

As luck would have it, I bumped into Joyce who was with a friend. Eventually, I talked her into coming into the bushes with me. I told my brother to take Buster off and play.

Joyce was wearing a brand-new blazer, which she took off and laid among the bushes. We sat on it and started what is now called 'heavy petting'. Then I discovered that my sister was right. Joyce let me pull her knickers off!

At that very moment, my brother and Buster appeared through

the bushes. There I was, with Joyce's knickers in my hand. The dog grabbed them and rushed off. Joyce screamed, jumped up and chased after Buster. Then another dog joined in and started tearing away at the knickers. Buster gave up, ran back into the bushes and dragged off Joyce's blazer. I caught hold of it and we began a tug-of-war. The blazer ripped. Joyce started crying the place down. A crowd gathered. A woman came over and handed Joyce the torn knickers. 'I think these are yours,' she said. We both wanted to die!

How do you talk your way out of that? Fortunately, Joyce didn't have any brothers, but her father said he was going to kill me. I made up a hell of a story to tell my mother – about how the dog had peed on the ground, Joyce had sat in the puddle and so had to take her knickers off so they could dry. I didn't get any further. My mother just said, 'A likely tale! You bloody liar!' and beat the hell out of me.

For months afterwards, I was a sort of outcast. People used to drag their daughters off the street when I walked past. The story was that I'd ripped off Joyce's blazer and her knickers, that she'd fought valiantly for her honour, and I was lucky not to go to prison!

Things got even nastier at school. One of the conditions attached to my bursary was that I should help in the book room. The brother who ran it was a bit odd. We used to call him Dummo. In class, he'd suck pieces of chalk and then throw them so accurately that he could hit a kid at twenty yards – smack between the eyes. You always knew who were St Mary's boys. They had coloured chalk marks on their foreheads like Indian braves! If he really didn't like you, he could knock you out with a precision-thrown board-rubber.

Because of the wartime shortages, I continued wearing short trousers. As I grew, so they got shorter. This, I now know, must have inflamed Dummo beyond belief.

In the book room, there was a ladder that was pushed along so you could get the books on the top shelf. Dummo was always sending me up there.

One day, I was standing on the ladder, wearing as always what my mother called 'sensible' shoes. Dummo put his hand up the leg of my trousers. I was so surprised that I went, 'Aah-haa!' and lashed out with my foot, my heel smashing his glasses and breaking his nose. He was in a terrible state. He was screaming like a scalded pig with blood pouring down his face.

By the time I'd got down the ladder, some of the other brothers had come running in to see what had happened. Dummo told them that I'd hit him. I knew I was in trouble. It was my word against his.

I was taken straight to the deputy headmaster. I tried to tell him what had happened, but he wouldn't listen. 'How dare you strike one of the brothers?' he said. 'Get out of this school and never come back!'

It was about three o'clock in the afternoon. I wandered around for a while, but then had to go home.

'What are you doing here?' my mother asked.

'I've been expelled.'

'Why?'

So I told her.

My mother then said, 'This is very serious, but you know the rules. If you lie to me, you're in real trouble. Now tell me – is this the truth?'

'Honest to God, mum, that's the truth. That's what happened. I didn't do it deliberately. It was an accident.'

'Right,' she said. 'Get your coat. We're going up to the school.'

'Oh, no, no, no. Let's forget it. Oh, no. I've been expelled. I'll go back to St Eddy's and work out my passage there. I don't want to go back to them Christian Brothers.'

She dragged me up to the school. The brothers were all having their evening tea, but she barged in and said she wanted to see the deputy headmaster. They said she couldn't, but she said she wasn't leaving until she did. Now she had a little clout, because my uncle was then the parish priest and our relationship with the Archbishop didn't hurt.

Eventually, we went in to see the deputy headmaster and he said, 'What's all this about? He did a dreadful thing and we can't have hooligans like him in the school!'

My mother told him what had happened and assured him it was the truth.

Dummo had just come back from the hospital and the headmaster said that he would hear what he had to say. We were told to wait outside while they talked.

We sat there for a while, before my mother was called back in.

When she came out, she said, 'Come on. We're going!'

'But what happened?' I asked, as we marched down the corridor.

'You'll be back here at school tomorrow morning.' She never said anything else about the matter.

When I turned up the next day, the whole school thought that I was Little Caesar. I was the guy who had busted Brother

Dummo's nose, put ten stitches in his head, and so wasn't to be pissed around with. Not only that, but I'd got away with it.

I was told to go and see the deputy headmaster, who said, 'I'm very sorry about what happened, but the brother tells me that he thought you were falling off the ladder!'

It was a bloody lame excuse. Every boy in the school had been touched up by Dummo. The only difference with me was that he'd scored a direct hit!

The next lesson I had with Dummo, there he was – with his nose in plaster and two black eyes – desperately trying to ignore me.

He wasn't the only brother I fell foul of. Our history master was Irish and hated English history. He made it up to suit his own purposes as he went along. I loved history and, ever since I'd been in the isolation hospital, had read anything I could get my hands on – not just factual books but historical novels and romances as well.

In one lesson, the Irish brother was talking about the Civil War. Like most Irishmen, he had a blank about Cromwell and was saying how terrible the Levellers were. I got to the state where I couldn't let him go on. 'No, no. It's not like that,' I said. 'I've just read a book on the Levellers and what you're saying is wrong.'

We started to argue. Then he stopped the lesson and said, 'You, Booth, outside. That's the end for you. You'll never attend another of my history lessons.'

In that school, they used to beat us up and give us the strap, but stopping my history lessons was the most terrible punishment for me. Reluctantly, I left, went to the cloakroom and sat with my feet up reading a book.

The next history lesson, I went along to the classroom. Again he kicked me out. 'There's only one thing to do,' I thought. 'I'll bring along my own books and study history myself.'

A few weeks later, I was in the cloakroom during a history lesson. I was sitting there, reading a history book and smoking a fag, when the headmaster walked in. He asked me why I was there and I explained. He told me to wait where I was and went off to see the history master. When he returned, he said, 'You. Come with me.'

'This,' I thought, 'is real trouble. Now I'm going to get leathered by the head.'

When we got to his room, he told me to sit down and asked me to tell him about the Levellers. We discussed the subject for some time and then he said, 'You really like history.'

I said, 'I love it.'

'It's my subject,' he said.

I didn't know that. I didn't even know that headmasters had subjects. I just thought they were figures of authority.

'I'll tell you what I'll do,' he said. 'Every history lesson, you'll come up here and take history with me.'

From then on, I had the headmaster as my private history tutor. He lent me books and told me what I should borrow from the library. We discussed and argued. He loved teaching history just as much as I loved studying it. At the end of that year, I took the same history exam as all the other boys, even though I hadn't officially been to the lessons. It was a doddle and I came top.

Things generally got much better. The war ended and there were many celebrations – street parties, festivities and bunting round the Anderson shelters. A big dance was held at the Protestant school. Every time I got dragged on the floor, I had to leave in haste because I'd got an erection. I think the girls kept dragging me off to dance just to witness my discomfort!

Before long, my private life suddenly and unexpectedly improved. One morning, I was delivering papers around the avenues. I cycled up a drive just as a woman opened the door to pick up the milk. She was wearing a dressing-gown over her night-dress. I didn't know how old she was, but would guess in her mid-twenties. As she bent over, my eyes stood out on stalks. She said, 'Do you fancy a cup of tea?'

I was slightly taken aback, but I said, 'Thank you very much!'

She took me in, gave me a cup of tea, and talked to me. Then she said, 'If you fancy another cup of tea, call tomorrow.'

That went on for about ten days. By then, school had finished for the summer holidays and so she said to me, 'Why don't you finish off your round, come back and have your breakfast here?'

I returned later and she gave me breakfast. Afterwards she said, 'Do you want to see the rest of the house?'

I nodded and off we went.

She showed me a lot more than the house. I couldn't believe my luck!

She didn't have to do much to make me swear on a stack of Bibles that I'd never say anything. I was petrified anyway, in case anybody found out. What would have happened to me? I'd have been drummed out of the altar boys for a start.

My breakfast treats went on for some time. When term started again, I used to cycle from her place to school, so I could be taught far less exciting lessons by the Christian Brothers.

The lady's husband was much older than she was. When I first met her, he was away at sea. But then he got promoted to the admiralty and they both moved off to London.

My regular sex life suddenly came to an end and my troubles really began. It was a hell of a lot worse than before. Then I just went without. Now I knew what it was all about and was going short. That was a totally different game!

3

Scraps and Scrapes

Although my breakfast treats had come to an end, I continued delivering newspapers on my bike. One night in 1947, I came home after my round. As I walked through the front door, my grandmother – the most fantastic of actors – burst into tears and wailed, 'Aahhh! Oh, no! The poor child doesn't know what's happened!'

I realized at once something was seriously wrong. She'd called me a 'poor child', instead of, as usual, 'that idiot'. 'What's going on?' I asked.

'Oh, God, I can't tell you,' she blubbered through her tears. 'You know, you know. . . '

'No, I don't know. What's happened? What's happened?'

'Oh, your poor father has had an accident.'

'Oh, my God. Is it bad?'

'We don't know. But he's in hospital. Your mother's gone to his bedside.'

My Uncle Richard arrived to take me to the hospital, which was down by the docks. We took a bus and then a tram. When we arrived at the hospital, we walked to the intensive-care unit, which was in a Nissen hut. We both peered in through the glass door.

21

My uncle said, 'Look at that poor bugger over there! What chance has he got?'

I stared at the body lying in the bed, covered with blood-soaked bandages and with tubes stuck everywhere.

My uncle exclaimed, 'Holy Christ!' He'd just seen my mother and so he knew it was my father in the bed.

He'd been so badly injured that everybody assumed he'd die. At the time he'd been working-by, one of a shadow crew on a ship that had to be fumigated at Liverpool docks. My father had been looking down an empty hold to see if the ship had been cleared out, when a derrick swung, caught him and knocked him so violently that he ricocheted from one side to the other down the eighty foot of the hold. His pelvis, back, ribs, one leg and one arm were smashed. He was in such a hell of a mess that it was three weeks before they decided that he'd survive.

We were now a family where the money had suddenly been cut off. The shipping company stopped his wages straightaway. They even docked him half a day for the work he missed after the accident. The only source of income we had was my paper-round and what my mother earned charring.

After about a fortnight, it was obvious that there was only one solution. I had to be pulled out of school to get a job. My mother went to St Mary's College to see the headmaster. Instead of being delighted to get rid of such an unmanageable, disruptive pupil, he tried every way he could to keep me at school. He told my mother that I should go to university and then become a history lecturer. He said he'd try to obtain a grant. But it was to no avail. My mother needed my wage.

Then the question arose of where I was to work. I'd already had several Saturday jobs – but not for very long. My mother had once fixed me up as a butcher's boy, but after two weeks the butcher said to me, 'Sorry. Between you and me, you're temperamentally unsuited to this sort of work!'

'What does that mean?' I asked.

'It means you're sacked!'

'If I can't even hold down a job with a butcher,' I thought, 'what the hell am I going to do?'

At the time, I was nearly sixteen and the only guy in my class still wearing short pants. I told my mother that there was no way I was going to work in those. That was how I got my first pair of long trousers!

I went for an interview to a warehouse in the docks, called Arbuckle Smith's. They took me on as a junior clerk for 17s 6d

(75p) a week. That became the major part of the money coming into our house. Because my mother couldn't afford to give me the fare, I had to cycle every day the eight miles to and from work.

After I'd been working as a clerk for a couple of months, a vacancy came up at the American Consulate, where my uncle had a friend, and I went there as an office junior. I was put in charge of the fingerprinting in the immigration section – a job that nobody else wanted to do. It was incredibly busy. The war had finished and there were thousands trying to get into America – displaced people, misplaced people, GI brides and that sort of thing. Every day there were long queues outside the place.

In the Consulate, they had an enormous safe with a vast metal door. Inside, there was an upstairs where all the papers were kept. Every time a girl was sent in to look up some files, I had to go with her to help open the door. There was only a steel ladder going up to the top and, being a gentleman, I always said, 'After you!' to the girls and followed them up. Many a pleasant and passionate hour was spent inside the safe when we were supposed to be searching through the files!

Most of the guys working there had come back from the war and so were worldly-wise. I was the kid. They used to entertain me with their stories about life in the army and air force.

Jimmy, who'd been in the Commandos, used to say during the lunch hour, 'What d'you know about unarmed combat? When a fellow comes at you with a knife, what d'you do?'

'I don't know.'

'Well, I'll show you. You just grab hold of my arm.'

Then he'd throw me on the floor and have a good laugh. His version of teaching the kid was to hurl him all around the place. But I did learn a few moves from him.

Eventually, I got fed up with always ending up in a heap with his foot pressed on to my throat. One day he came back from lunch having had more than enough to drink. He was well pissed. I was sitting in the small fingerprint office next to the switchboard. He picked up a big pair of scissors and advanced towards me. 'All right, Boothie,' he said. 'On your feet. Come on.'

'You're really for it now,' I thought. 'Come on, Jimmy,' I shouted, and then without thinking I jumped up and hit him. Down he went, smashing his head against the desk. He fell unconscious on the floor. The switchboard girl was screaming. The Vice-Consul rushed in and saw me kneeling over Jimmy, holding the scissors in my hand.

'That's it,' I thought. 'I'm sacked.'

23

Then Jimmy came round. Being an old soldier, he moaned, 'Ahhh! My back! It's my old war wound.'

I was suspended and sent home in disgrace. Jimmy took a fortnight off – while he thought up a good story.

When he returned, I was called in to see the Vice-Consul. Jimmy was in the room and he said that, as I was being bullied by some of the other men in the office, he'd been teaching me some unarmed combat so that I could defend myself. During his demonstration, he'd slipped, banged his head and injured his back. It was accidental and so it was nobody's fault. I don't think they believed him, but his story got me off and I was reinstated.

A few months later, I received my call-up papers for National Service. I went to see the Vice-Consul who said, 'If you want, there's a way out of this. We can transfer you to Washington.' Perhaps they thought that because I'd beaten up an ex-Commando I was really heavy and could be useful for the CIA!

I went home and told my mother about the Vice-Consul's offer.

'Oh, no,' my mother said, 'I don't want you going to America. What's going to happen to us if you're there?'

We still didn't have much money. My father had only just come out of hospital. He'd been in there for nearly two years and was still learning to walk again. My parents didn't want me to go and I wasn't keen. I didn't fancy taking fingerprints all round the world.

So I had to go for my medical. As I'd had asthma all my life, I thought, 'When it comes my turn, I'll bring on a really bad asthmatic attack and there's no way they can pass me.' Also a guy told me that if I ate soap, I'd froth at the mouth. I did everything. I tried every sodding thing to get out of the Army. But they passed me A1. So I was in. I had to go to Catterick to join the Royal Corps of Signals.

In January 1950, I set off for the camp in the middle of a very bad winter. The train from Liverpool took a day and a half – one of those jobs. There were snow ploughs on the line. I had to change at York, at Darlington and at Richmond. Then the Army lorries picked us up. We didn't arrive at Catterick till late evening. I was the last one into the billet and so I was lumbered with the bed next to the frigging door.

At the time, I was only five foot seven and weighed nine and a half stone. Two years later, when I came out of the Army, I was six foot one and weighed thirteen and a half stone. Sheer fear made me shoot up!

I'll never forget my first morning in the Army. At half past five, the doors were flung open and this yard-dog of a corporal barges in and bellows, 'Hands off cocks. On socks.'

I hadn't had a wet dream in ages – I'd been able to make other arrangements! But on my first night in the Army, two minutes before that corporal threw open the door, I had a bloody wet dream. My bed was nearest to him and he dragged off the blankets! Oh God, what a great start to my Army career! The whole thing was a mess!

It was really unbelievable how we were treated. Recruits were beaten up every day. The NCOs did exactly what they wanted. They had you in there and that was that. One kid committed suicide; other kids ran away. It was just terrible. There we were in that bloody awful winter at Catterick – the arsehole of the country.

Very early on, I came to the conclusion that there was no way I could beat them. To survive in the army I either had to play them at their own game and say 'Yes, sir, no, sir,' or I had to try and vanish. Both were difficult. Also, Britain at that time was involved in every kind of crap around the world – Korea, Malaysia, Kenya, Cyprus, Aden. The guys who did most of the fighting were the National Servicemen – not the regulars. I'm a coward and I didn't want to get killed.

I soon discovered that the Army is a great respecter of athletes. If you're good at any sport, the Army will look after you. At school, I'd played rugby for Merseyside, cricket and had been given a trial by Lancashire, and football. So I volunteered for all the teams and very quickly got into the regimental sides. That was the way out of it for me.

After our basic training, we stayed on at Catterick to be taught all about signalling. I'd always had a good retentive memory and so when they issued us with a training manual I learnt it off by heart. It was all child's-play stuff, making it simple for National Service thickheads like me to understand what we were supposed to be doing. I knew it backwards and so, after six weeks, in the final test, I just typed it all out word for word.

When the results came out, I'd got such a high mark that there was an inquiry – they obviously thought I'd cheated. While all the other guys were being posted to the peacetime war zones, I had to stay behind for a week to take another test. That time, I made sure I knew everything, including every semi-colon and comma.

The test was marked the same afternoon. The officer called me

25

in and said, 'I don't know how you did it. But as you got full marks, you're posted here as an instructor.'

Stay in Catterick! Who wants to stay in Catterick?

But that was it – I had to stay there. They made me an instructor, but I wasn't interested in it. I was taken off that and stuck in the office. Fortunately, a lot of my time was spent in sports – I played cricket for the Signals with Brian Close, and football for the Northern Command with John Charles.

One day, somebody said to me, 'The best gag you can get on here is either to be a musician or an actor.' I couldn't play an instrument and so I went along to the theatre. The guy who ran it was Corporal Geoffrey Dench – brother of the actress Judi Dench. He told me that officers usually got the parts, but if I hung around I might get something.

And I did. I struck up a friendly relationship with an officer's wife. In those days it was almost a topping offence for a lower ranker to have it off with an officer's lady. Naturally I didn't want to get caught, but she confessed all to her husband. I was posted immediately – to the War Office in London.

I arrived at Cambridge Barracks in Woolwich with another kid who'd also been posted to the War Office. We were unpacking our kit, when a corporal marched in and snarled, 'Which one o' you's Booth?'

'I am.'

'You're from Liverpool.'

'Yes.'

'Red or blue?'

I said, 'Red, of course.'

'That's you finished,' he said and walked out.

His name was Jones and he was a regular who'd only got a couple of months to do before returning to Liverpool and his job in the docks.

The next morning, when we went out on parade, this Corporal Jones put me straight on fatigues. He had me cleaning out the lavatories. His favourite trick was to come in after I'd finished, throw things on the floor and tell me to do it again. I'd been in the army for nine months and was hardened to it. So I'd do it again.

This guy rode me. I was on guard duty, sentry duty, fatigues all the time. He really gave me a heavy time. After about ten days, I couldn't stand it any longer. I was cleaning the lavatories one day when Jones came in and started pissing all over the floor.

I got hold of him and banged him up against the wall. 'That's it! That's it!' I hissed at him. 'Just because you support Everton and I support Liverpool! Well you can go fuck yourself. You've been stupid enough to shout your mouth off to me. Now I'm going to tell you this. You're going back to Liverpool. One night, you'll be found floating in the fucking dock. I'm not fucking about. I'm going to kill you unless you get off my fucking back. So what's it going to be?'

He said, 'You fucking Liverpudlians are all fucking mad!' Then he walked off. I was shaking all over and sweat was pouring off me. But that was the end of the matter. Next day on parade, I wasn't put on fatigues. For the first time, I was sent off to work at the War Office.

They soon discovered what a useless operator I was and so I used only to be summoned in dire emergencies. I spent most of my time working in the office at the barracks.

I'd been there a couple of months, when it was announced that we were going to have posted back to us from the nick at Colchester a bloke called Frank Mitchell. He was later to become the famous villain of the fifties and sixties, known as the 'Mad Axeman', who was used by the infamous Kray brothers as a heavy.

I was in the company office when Mitchell walked in, ducking under the doorway. I've seen some big guys in my life, but Frank Mitchell was massive. He made Superman look like Twiggy. There wasn't an ounce of fat on him. He was six foot seven of muscle and bone – a magnificent specimen. Like a lot of big guys, he turned out to be gentle, mild-mannered and soft-spoken.

'For some reason,' I thought, 'Nobody understands this poor guy. They're treating him all wrong. He's a nice guy really. It's just because he's big, everybody picks on him. Then he snaps. If they left him alone, they could do something with Mitchell. He could have been the Army heavyweight champion – no danger!'

So Mitchell was all right with me. I didn't have too much to do with him – he was too big and too ugly for anybody. There was no messing – 'You want a pass from me? You've got it. No hassle!'

One morning parade, Mitchell was ninety seconds late, because he'd been on fatigues cleaning the latrines. He was immediately charged by a Major, who was the Acting CO. When a soldier is charged in the Army, he has two soldiers as escorts to march him in. But as soon as Mitchell was charged, everybody around the camp vanished. Cambridge Barracks was empty – apart from the guard on the gate.

I was sitting in the office in my suedes, when I was summoned with another clerk to be Frank Mitchell's escort. We marched him in. After the case had been heard, the Major said to Mitchell, 'Are you prepared to accept my punishment, or wait for the CO?'

'No, no,' Mitchell said. 'I'll take your punishment.'

His offence didn't deserve more than forty-eight hours, but the Major said, 'Twenty-eight days!' This meant he'd have to go back to Colchester.

We were then ordered to march him out. I only came up to Mitchell's waist and the other guy was up to his crutch!

Mitchell didn't move. 'Hang on, hang on! What did you say?' he asked.

'Twenty-eight days.'

'You gave me twenty-eight days for being ninety seconds late?'

'Yes.'

'You can't do that. You're not the CO.'

'Don't you tell me what I can do. I'm the Acting CO.'

'You're only a Major,' Mitchell said. 'You can't give me more than twenty-one days.'

'Don't you question me!' the officer shouted. 'Get out of here!'

'I'm not going. Forty-eight hours for this – fair. Twenty-eight days – no way. I'm not having it.'

The officer bellowed at us to quick march, but Mitchell didn't move. I was thinking, 'Oh, my God! This I really need!' Then Mitchell sat down on the floor – he was still about the same height as me and I was standing to attention!

The sergeant major shouted to me and the other clerk, 'Right, you two. Pick him up.'

We tried, but there was no way we could move him. He was a man-mountain. He just sat there laughing at us.

So we were all ordered out and there was a big pow-wow in the corridor. When we got back into the office, Mitchell was lying on the floor. Six big guys came in, carried him over to the guardroom and stuck him in a cell. Mitchell was in real trouble. They were obviously going to throw the book at him. The order was that he should be kept in the guardroom until the CO returned.

I never did guard duty – I was a sportsman. I mean, I played for London District against Blackheath on Saturday – how could I possibly do guard duty? But the Major called the other clerk and me into his office. He told us we were a disgrace to the uniform because we should have done something about Mitchell. As punishment, we were to be put on guard duty.

Of the guys on guard, the smartest one always got the softest job. Can you imagine? I was the smartest guy – it was a right scruffy crowd! I was made what was called 'stick-man'. He collected the food and the tea, read the newspaper and so on – easy. What I didn't know was that the 'stick-man' also exercised the prisoners. There was only one prisoner – Mitchell.

The time came for the half-hour exercise period. 'Right, Booth. Come here.' Then they slapped a handcuff on me.

'What you doing?'

'You're going to exercise Mitchell.'

The whole guard turned out with rifles loaded with live ammunition – no buggering about. They pushed me into the cell. Mitchell was on the floor in his vest and underpants doing pushups like a steamhammer.

'Hello, Boothie,' he said. 'All right?'

I was handcuffed to him and we were escorted out to the exercise-yard – a small place surrounded by a twenty-foot wall topped with barbed wire and broken glass. They slammed shut the steel door and we were out there – just the two of us.

'Come on, Boothie,' Mitchell said.

'What we going to do?'

'We're going to exercise, aren't we?'

Then he started sprinting round the yard, dragging me behind him, gasping, 'Just a sec, Mitchell. You daft bugger. Hold it, Mitch. Oh, bloody hell! What you doing this for?'

'I've only got half an hour. So come on, Boothie.'

Every so often he'd stop and do some push-ups and I'd have to get down on the ground with him. After all, I was handcuffed to him.

Then as we were running round, he said to me, 'You know? I could break your back just like that. D'you know what I mean?'

'Yer in no danger,' I panted. 'I'm... I'm really grateful... you're not going to break me back.'

'What you think about me being in here then?'

'It's... it's... so unjust.'

'You're all right you are, Boothie.'

After twenty minutes I was totally knackered. So, he picked me up, put me under his arm, and ran round carrying me!

All the time he was talking to me: 'I'm going to break out of here, you know. And you can tell 'em if you like.'

'No, no,' I gasped. 'I won't say a word.'

'Just tell 'em that, when I decide to go, if they get in my way, I'll kill 'em.'

When the exercise period was over, we went back to the cell, the handcuffs were unlocked and straightaway he started doing

29

press-ups. I was whacked – my legs had seized up, my heart was pounding and I was breathless.

Two days later, they went to open Mitchell's cell to take him out for exercise. This time he was fully dressed. He picked up one guy and threw him straight at the rest of the guards who collapsed in a pile. Then he walked out, jogged past the gate and down the road off to Woolwich Station.

The alarm bell was ringing and people were screaming, 'Mitchell's escaped. Get after him!' But nobody wanted to play the hero. Mitchell jumped off the platform at the station, ran into the tunnel and just disappeared to enter London underworld mythology as the 'Mad Axeman'.

Years later, I used to drink in a pub, run by a mate of mine, at Lisson Grove. I went in there one Monday and at the end of the bar was a little old fellow wearing a trilby and an overcoat that practically came down to the ground. There were a few guys standing by him. One of them came up to me and said, 'Hello, Tone. How you doing? The old man wants to buy you a drink.'

I went over to these blokes, who were clearly all hoods, with smashed-in faces and cauliflower ears.

The old man bought me a drink and we stood there talking for a while. Then I said, 'Let me buy you a drink.'

'No,' he said. 'That's all right.'

'Come on,' I said. 'You're an old-age pensioner, for Christ's sake.' I thought the guys there were just looking after him.

But one of them said, 'Don't you know who this is?'

'No,' I replied. 'Who is he?'

'This is Ron and Reggie's dad.'

'Hello, Mr Kray!'

We stood there drinking until it was almost closing time. The old man said, 'When they close the pub up, we'll 'ave a good drink, son.'

And we did. After a while I was in good order.

He was going on about 'my boys', how 'society's been cruel to my boys', and saying, 'My boys never done nothin' evil. They was performing a public service, really.'

By then, I was well gone. 'What happened to Frank Mitchell?' I said. 'I was in the Army with Frank Mitchell and he was all right.'

'Do you know what was wrong with Frank Mitchell?' he said.

'No. Tell us.'

'Well, my boys wanted Mitchell to do a job. So they sprung 'im from Dartmoor and fixed 'im up with a very nice place in

Plumstead – over a shop. When my Ronnie went down to see 'im, 'e said, "What d'you want, Frank?" Do you know the one thing what 'e wanted?'

'After five years in clink? A bit of crumpet!'

'Clever boy! 'E wanted a girl. My Ronnie said, "Of course. I'll arrange that for you. Don't worry about that, Frank. But it's a bit dodgy at the moment – because everybody's looking for you. We've got to make sure we get a brass that ain't goin' to talk and what will come and do the business. I mean," my Ronnie said to him, "you've got the reputation of being a fuckin' animal. You're the Mad Axeman." Every time Ronnie or Reggie went down to see 'im, Mitchell said, "Where's this woman you promised me?" Six days went by and Mitchell was getting more and more angry, because 'e wasn't allowed to leave the premises. But he was getting special attention. Somebody was wiv 'im all the time – 'cos 'e was an animal. You should 'ave seen the food that went into the flat.'

'So what happened?' I asked.

'Well, my Ronnie went in there and Mitchell said, "Where is this girl you promised me?" Ronnie said, "It's a bit difficult." Then Mitchell laid 'ands on my Ronnie – nobody lays 'ands on my boys. 'E lifted Ronnie up, held 'im against the wall and said, "Let's get this straight. If you ain't got a woman 'ere tomorrow for me to 'ave, I'm goin' to come round and I'm goin' to. . . fuck your mother."'

'What?'

'He said he was goin' to fuck mummy.'

At this, all the guys round him were saying, 'Oh, definitely out of order. Definitely out of order that is!'

'You mean to say,' I said, 'that you believed him?'

''E was a bloody lunatic,' old man Kray said. ''E would 'ave come round and done anythin'.'

4

Entente Cordiale

The Duty Officer's secretary at Cambridge Barracks was a very tasty young lady. I knew the Duty Officer fancied her, but she wasn't having any.

I've always been interested in horse-racing and I managed to get a forty-eight-hour pass over Derby Day. So I said to her, 'How would you like to go with me to the races?'

She thought that was a splendid idea. We had a great day. Afterwards we went back to her place and spent the night together. The next morning, she had to go to work at the barracks and so I said I'd walk there with her.

We woke up late. She didn't arrive till nearly midday and the daily orders didn't get typed – the first time it'd happened since the days of Wellington!

As I walked with her through the gates, the Duty Officer saw us through the office window. She went into work. I returned to the barracks. I was just getting changed when a corporal came in and said, 'Booth! The Duty Officer wants to see you. You're in real shit.'

As soon as I got into his room, he started: 'How dare you corrupt this young girl? That's it! You're finished here. You're off this camp, the first posting that comes into the War Office. I don't

32

care where it's for. Get packed and you'll be gone by tomorrow. Till then you're confined to barracks. Now get out.'

I'd only got about eleven months to do and so it was too late for them to send me to Korea or anywhere really dangerous. But I was on a loser. Postings came into the War Office every five minutes and I could still land up in the Orkneys or Greenland.

Later that afternoon, I was sitting on my bed when one of the guys came over from the office and said, 'You're wanted in the office.'

'What? The Duty Officer's office?'

'No, the orderly office. The Duty Officer has gone home.'

I went over and the guy said, 'Right, I've got your posting here. I've done what I was told. It was the first one through for an Operator A3. You jammy bastard! It's Paris. Here's your orders and your travel warrant. You'd better be out of here before the Duty Officer comes back tomorrow morning. You won't be bloody on it then, for frigging sake! He'll cancel it for sure!'

'Don't you worry,' I said, grabbing the papers. 'I'll be gone before he's out of his bed!'

The first thing I had to do was report to the stores and collect two pairs of grey flannels, a pair of shoes, two shirts, a Signal's tie and a blazer. British personnel working at SHAPE (Supreme Headquarters, Allied Powers, Europe) in Paris were not allowed to wear uniform at that time.

At nine o'clock the next morning, I was decked out in my new gear heading for France. When the Duty Officer arrived at the barracks, he must have really been sick!

I'd been given an address to go to in Paris. The Americans had their own barracks, the French did too – but we were also-rans and so we were stuck in a luxury hotel! I arrived there in the early evening and went to the reception desk.

'Zero four hundred Booth reporting,' I said.

'Pardonnez-moi?'

'Signalman Booth reporting.'

'Ah! Mr Booth. You're in Room 63. Here's your key. You share with Mr Atkins. He will tell you where you are to go. What time do you want a call in the morning?'

'What time is breakfast?'

'Breakfast is served from eight until ten. Do you wish to have it in the bedroom or in the dining room?'

'Well I'll have it at eight in my room.'

I went upstairs, but there was no sign of Mr Atkins. As I was starving, I went back downstairs and said, 'Excuse me. Where do I get something to eat?'

'Dinner,' he said, 'is served from 1700 hours to midnight. Just show your key in the dining room. It is all paid for!'

And that was it – a beautiful meal with wine and brandy. A hell of a change from the stodge at Cambridge Barracks!

Afterwards, I thought I'd better go back to my room and wait for this Atkins guy. By eleven o'clock I was knackered. I got into bed and turned off the light. About half an hour later a drunk fell into the room.

He was called, believe it or not, Tommy Atkins – the name by which all British private soldiers were once known. He'd only got a fortnight to do before he was demobbed and he didn't care a monkey's.

'What time do you get up in the morning?' I asked.

'When you feel like it. Why d'you ask?'

'I said I'd have breakfast at eight.'

'You bloody idiot! Nobody gets up here before ten! Go down and tell 'em to make it quarter to ten.'

I did as I was told.

The next morning, Atkins had a throbbing hangover, but at half past ten he took me off to SHAPE. The Americans were running the duties at the time and I was sent in to see one of their officers.

The guy had the Confederate flag draped on the wall behind his desk. 'Hi, Tony. How are you? How you doing?' he drawled. 'I'm Colonel Jackson.'

'Stonewall, of course,' I said.

'Aha, Tony. You're a guy who knows your history. What a great General. We don't have guys like that nowadays. Sit down. Tell me all about yourself. Where you from?'

'From Liverpool.'

'North or south?'

'The north, of course.'

'Who do you support – the north or the south?'

'The north, of course.'

'Get out of here!' he shouted. 'I won't have any of you Goddamn Yankies in this place. Get out!'

'But I'm from the north of England,' I protested.

'I don't care a shit. Get out of here!'

'But what do I do?'

'Find out!'

I walked out and shut the door. The guy outside said, 'What was that all about?'

'I told him I was from the north.'

'How could you be that dumb? Couldn't you tell he was a southerner? Nobody tells him they're from the north. Well, what's he put you on?'

'I don't know.'

'He must have told you something.'

'Yes, he said, "Find out!"'

'Oh, I see.'

'So what do I do?'

'Find out!'

'Come on, guys. What do you mean?'

'I mean it's lunchtime. Come back later.'

When I returned to the office, I was told that the British soldiers were under a sergeant major, but he was away on leave for a month. Nobody had any idea what I was supposed to do. I was told to go back to the hotel and report in once a week. They gave me ten quid and then sent me to see the Medical Officer.

When I arrived, the MO looked at my papers and said, 'I have to tell you that we have the highest rate of venereal disease for any station in the British Combined Services. I don't want you coming in here and saying you've caught VD off a lavatory seat. No woman I've ever met wears a lavatory seat around her fanny! So piss off and I don't want to see you in here again.'

That was it.

I went straight back to the hotel, where Atkins was lying on his bed.

'What do you do here?' I asked him.

'I haven't done anything in six months. I just spend my time getting pissed.'

That seemed like a good idea. The next day, I set off to look round Paris. I was young and I had money in my pocket. In those days, if you'd ten quid you were doing all right.

One day, when I was leaning over the balcony on the first floor of the Eiffel Tower, a group of American girls came out and stood behind me discussing where they should go next. One of them suggested Sacré Coeur, but none of them knew the way. I offered them directions and got invited along to show them the way.

We went for lunch – they paid. I took them around the sights and in the evening we went to a nightclub – they paid. Then they all gave me a tip and I got laid. The next morning, they introduced me to another group of women tourists and I did the same again.

For a month, I was a tour guide for American women in Paris. I was making good money and getting laid! On Fridays I used to

35

go into SHAPE, pick up my pay and then piss off. I was having a great time!

On the fifth Friday, I went in and the orderly said, 'Booth! Are you the Booth who used to play rugby for the Signals?'

'Yes.'

'Where've you been? There's an order here for you. You've got to report to Fontainebleau tomorrow morning. The Combined Services team is here on tour and they've had lots of injuries. You've got to join them for the rest of their European tour.'

I hadn't done any training for weeks. I'd been swanning around Paris – drinking, eating mountains of food, and getting laid. But I had to go.

The next morning, I joined the Combined Services rugby team at a hotel outside Fontainebleau and was told I was going to play centre.

'Who're we playing?' I asked.

'The French Combined Services!'

'You bloody what! Are you crackers?' I said. 'There's been a terrible mistake. I'm not up to that!'

'You bloody well are. A crowd of fifty thousand will be turning up and you're playing!'

They gave me the kit that had belonged to the centre who'd been injured. He must have been no more than five foot five. The shirt barely touched me and the shorts were no more than a little pair of knickers.

Watching the match was a vast crowd, full of bigwigs, including Montgomery, who was our Commander-in-Chief.

The first half was great and it was three points each at half-time, when they brought on a bucket of tea. I dipped a cup in it, had a sip and went, 'Bloody hell!' It was hot brandy with just a couple of tea-leaves thrown in. While we were knocking it back, an officer came up to us and said, 'Monty says you're playing a marvellous game. He's really proud of you. If you win, you can all have the weekend in Paris!'

At the end of half-time, the bucket was empty and we went back for the second half legless. Within minutes, the whole atmosphere of the game had changed. The French side was kicking and punching. Our full-back was taken off with a broken leg and the captain put me in his place. I was kicked to hell. My nose was smashed in, my goolies were forced into my throat, and I had a black eye. We were all in a hell of a state. They made monkeys of us. We were totally humiliated.

Afterwards, there was a dinner for the two sides. I said to a

French kid sitting next to me, 'It was a good, clean game in the first half. What the hell happened?'

He said, 'We saw an officer come to speak to you during half-time. What did he say to you?'

'He just said if we won we'd have a weekend in Paris.'

'And if you lost?'

'Nothing.'

'Well our Commander sent his aide to us at half-time and he said, "If you win, you will each get a month's leave. If you lose, you all go to Indo-China."'

'Why didn't you tell us?' I said. 'We'd have been all right. We'd have understood. There was no need to kill us.'

He just shrugged and said, 'We had to be sure.'

I was so badly injured in the game, that the team left me behind with a couple of the other guys. When I returned to SHAPE the following Monday, I was told that the British sergeant major had been really put out after the order arrived for me to play rugby. He didn't even know I was in France – we'd never clapped eyes on each other. He was so pissed off that he'd posted me away from the fleshpots of Paris to the ancillary SHAPE headquarters in the château at Fontainebleau.

So I went back to Fontainebleau. Once again, I was put in a hotel, although this time I had my own room. It was terrific! To this day I don't know how many of our guys were there. I knew only about half a dozen – vaguely.

When I reported for work, I was told that I had to keep fit, because I'd been picked to play rugby in the European Games. The Commanding Officer said I had to report in every day, just in case something had turned up for me to do.

Twice a week, I used to go to the French barracks, meet up with their football team and we'd go to a playing-field for a game and some training.

After one of these sessions, I was walking back to my hotel, covered in mud. Walking towards me was a girl who was really beautiful. I thought, 'I can't miss an opportunity like this.' So I asked her if she could tell me the way to the French barracks.

She said, 'Tha must be English. I speak English.' And she did – with a broad Yorkshire accent. We chatted for a while and then she said, 'Why's tha talking to me?'

'Because you're beautiful.'

She said, 'Does tha want to take me courting then?'

I went, 'Tha's got it!'

She said she came from a respectable family and that if I wanted to take her out that evening I had first to go round and ask her mother, who was the local doctor. I took her address and went round at about six that evening.

The girl, who was called Monique, introduced me to her mother – a highly attractive woman in her mid-thirties, who looked like a young Simone Signoret. She was very correct, even stern, and clearly looked with some disapproval on her daughter being picked up in the street by a passing British soldier.

I pretended I didn't speak any French and the mother claimed she didn't speak English. So I sat there and listened while Monique insisted that she knew I wasn't the kind of man who was only after one thing. At last, the mother agreed that I could take her daughter to the cinema, but only if we were accompanied by her younger brother.

The three of us went to see an American picture – Humphrey Bogart and Gloria Graham in *A Lonely Place*. They seemed to have had trouble with the dubbing, because Humphrey Bogart spoke in a high squeaky voice and Gloria Graham sounded like Paul Robeson!

When we arrived back, the mother invited me to have lunch with them the next day after church. Men being what they are, I instantly said, 'I too am a Catholic, madame,' even though I hadn't voluntarily been inside a church since I joined the Army. So I went with them to eleven o'clock mass and then had a most pleasant Sunday lunch. I took Monique for a walk, once again accompanied by her brother. We arranged to meet next on Wednesday evening.

This time, when we went to the cinema, she told me that she had another boyfriend, a Dutch soldier, who was very serious and wanted to marry her. I wasn't ready for that kind of thing, but I kept on seeing her three or four times a week for a fortnight or so. Then she said that there was going to be a big dance the following Saturday to which the whole town would be going. Her mother would have a table and both the Dutchman and I were invited. This was the decision time. If I was prepared to ask her to marry me, she would happily agree; if not, she would become engaged at the dance to the Dutchman.

We went to the dance, and Monique spent most of the time waltzing around with the Dutchman. I sat and talked to Nicole, her mother, who asked me why I was looking so sad. I explained that it was because her daughter obviously preferred my rival. The fact was, however, that I'd very much enjoyed being part of their family life and I didn't want to see it all come to an end.

At ten-thirty, Nicole announced that she was going home and would leave the young ones together at the dance. I could see no point in staying. Having spent several hours in her company, I knew what an attractive and charming woman she was. So I said I'd walk home with her.

When we reached her house, we had a couple of drinks, sat together on the sofa and then kissed. Nicole took me up to the bedroom and locked the door.

About one in the morning, Monique returned and, while her mother and I were lying together in bed, started hammering on the door, shouting, 'I want to talk to you.'

'Go away,' Nicole said, 'I'll talk to you in the morning!'

'I know he's in there,' Monique shouted. 'And I know what you're doing!' Then she stormed off.

Her mother and I spent what was to be the first of many nights together.

Soon, I'd fallen head over heels in love with Nicole. She was a highly articulate, intelligent and sensitive lady who showed me a completely different way of French life than I'd been used to as a soldier. She encouraged me to take an interest in art and French literature and she also taught me much about love. In Paris, I'd been to the Folies Bergère and casinos, but she took me to the theatre and afterwards we went backstage to meet such great performers as Yves Montand and Edith Piaf. She had been one of the few doctors in the Resistance and so was well known throughout much of France. She'd saved the lives of many Allied pilots who'd baled out over France, been injured and were brought in secret to her. That was why her daughter spoke English with a Yorkshire accent – she'd spent several summer holidays staying in Wakefield with the daughters of a RAF pilot whom her mother had saved.

Nicole's husband was the Chief Customs Officer on the Swiss border – a position he'd held during the war, so the Germans presumed they were a safe family. Yet he too worked for the Resistance. But at that time, six years or so after the war, he had a mistress with whom he lived and only returned to Fontainebleau at holiday time to see his children. So there was no question of my breaking up the marriage.

I virtually moved in with Nicole. The only time I went to work was to collect my pay.

One day, I was coming out of the headquarters, wearing my cords and a sweater, when a car pulled up and a fellow said, 'D'you speak English?'

There was no difficulty in recognizing him – it was Humphrey Bogart. He was with Lauren Bacall and their kid, who funnily enough was dressed just like him in an identikit outfit. I showed them round the château, had lunch with them, and he gave me twenty dollars as a tip. I always liked Bogart – a hell of a nice guy!

Time passed most pleasantly. Just before Christmas, Nicole told me I must go to confession so I'd be in a state of grace for the festival.

'How hypocritical that's going to be,' I said. 'I'll confess to committing adultery and the priest will ask me if I intend doing it again. I'll have to say that I don't, knowing very well we'll be doing it again before lunch.'

She said that if I didn't go to confession, we certainly wouldn't be doing it before lunch. So I went along to the church at Fontaine-bleau to make my confession – in French.

Nicole then announced that her husband would be coming home for the holidays.

'Then what's going to happen?' I asked.

'Oh, we'll carry on sleeping together. Don't worry about that. I've known about his mistress for years. He's got his own life and I've got mine. He just comes home at Christmas to see the kids.'

So I had the strange experience of sitting at the dinner table with Nicole, her husband and their son and daughter. Afterwards, she and I went off to bed together, and after a couple of days her husband went back to the Swiss border.

Occasionally I went back to the hotel to see if there was any mail. I was at the desk there one day in February, when a British guy came up to me and said, 'Are you Booth?'

'Yes,' I said. 'Why?'

'I'm really glad to meet you. I haven't been here long, but everybody talks about you. Your name is on the lists but nobody knows what you do. Is it secret or something?'

'Oh, yes. It's very dodgy.'

'Yes, that's what I thought. Must be great being into that. But it must all be nearly finished. You get demobbed soon.'

'Oh, Christ!' I said. I'd forgotten all about it. I was having such a great time. My two years were just about up. What the hell was going to happen?

It was a Friday and so I went straight off to collect my pay. I asked the clerk if she had any instructions for me. She was sure I had to go back to Chester to be demobbed, but said, 'You'd better come back on Monday afternoon.'

Then I had to tell Nicole.

'Stay,' she said.

'I'd love to, but first I've got to get out of the Army. I have to be demobbed in England. If I don't go back home, I'll be a deserter.'

She told me I should go back to Chester and then return. She'd get me a place at the Sorbonne and I could study French history.

We had a lovely weekend. We were sad, but it wasn't serious. I was only going home for a while. After I'd sorted everything out with my parents, I'd be back.

Oh Monday afternoon, I returned to the office. I was wearing cords, a French sweater, a natty jacket; I'd got long hair and a classy married French lover; I was awash with Gallic *joie de vivre*. And there waiting for me was the sergeant major who'd been looking for me in Paris and who'd posted me to Fontainebleau.

'Who the fuck are you?' he said.

'Zero four hundred Booth.'

'You're fucking Booth! I thought I'd never get to see you. You're the fucking invisible man. Where have you been? Well you're on a fucking charge for starters. That's it. You're fucking done, you are, Booth.'

'Why? What have I done?'

'I've had reports of you going into Communist bars. They've all had their eye on you. The Yanks know all about you shacking up with a Communist bird.'

'She was in the Resistance,' I said.

'Oh, yes! Well she didn't resist you much, did she? What secrets did she get out of you, eh? Well that's it. You're never going home. You're going to prison, that's where you're going, Booth.'

'Hang on. I'm demobbed in two days' time.'

'That's what you think. You're still in the Army now. And what are you doing dressed up like some French ponce? Look at your hair. Right, stay there and don't move from that spot. I'm going to see the CO.'

And off he marched. I could hear him barking, 'Sir. We have apprehended Booth at long last.'

Back he came and tried to march me in – except I'd just about forgotten how to do it.

The officer behind the desk looked up and said, 'Hello, Tony.'

I gazed at him and said, 'Oh, hi. You were the scrum half, weren't you?'

'Yes. How are you? I see you've recovered from that awful game.

41

Well take a seat. That'll be all for now, sergeant major.' The poor bugger tried to say something, but he was waved out.

I couldn't believe my luck. He and I were two of the survivors from the Combined Services match and afterwards we'd spent the weekend getting drunk together in Paris. He'd been the CO there for six months and I didn't even know.

We told each other what we'd been up to since last we'd met. Then he asked, 'Well, what do you want me to do?'

'I'd like to get demobbed in France and carry on living here.'

He promised he'd do what he could for me and told me to report back the next morning. Gleefully, I walked out past the sergeant major, who was looking none too pleased.

When I saw the CO on Tuesday morning, he told me that not only had I to return to England but that I had to do so straight-away. So I packed my stuff, caught the train and arrived in London in the early hours of Wednesday morning.

It was late afternoon when I arrived at Blacon Camp in Chester. Everybody was packing up. I was the last to be demobbed that day. My uniform was mouldy – I hadn't worn it for over ten months.

5

All at Sea

After my demob, I went back home to Liverpool. As I'd never needed to take any leave, a grateful country gave me a month's pay in lieu.

When I told my parents that I wanted to go back to France, they said, 'No way can you do that until you're twenty-one!' They expected me to continue helping to support the family. All the time I'd been in the Army, I'd been sending money home. I was the only earner in the household, apart from the little my mother picked up cleaning. My father still wasn't fit enough to work. After a long action fought against the shipping line, he'd been awarded only five hundred quid.

Till the end of the first week, I had an easy time. Then at eight o'clock on Monday morning, my mother woke me up and said, 'You've got to go down the Labour Exchange and get a job.'

I didn't know what I wanted to do. All I knew was that everything I'd done up to then wasn't it. But I had to get some work to tide me over till I was twenty-one. Then I intended to go back to France and study at the Sorbonne.

As I was catching the train into the centre of Liverpool, I bumped into a little old guy who I'd travelled in with sometimes when I was working at the Consulate. I'd felt sorry for him and so I'd always ask him how he was. He was pleased to see me back and asked what I was going to do. I told him I'd no idea.

'Well,' he said. 'Why don't you come and work for Cunard? I'll get you a job in the accounts department. I'm the chief accountant there.'

I'd had no idea what he did, but I accepted his offer – even though I'd always been hopeless at maths. So there I was – stuck in the accounts department. It was bloody ridiculous. There was no chance of success.

I'd been working there for a couple of months and it was obvious that it wasn't going to work out, in spite of my knowing the chief accountant. One of the guys said to me, 'Unless you pull yourself together, you're going to be out on your earhole.'

'What can I do?' I asked.

'Do you play golf?'

'No.'

'Do you act?'

'Why?'

'Well that's what the old man does. He runs this amateur group. If you join it and you're any good, then don't worry about it. You'll be OK until he retires. He can't get many young fellows to join, 'cause it's a poof's game, isn't it?'

To save my job, I went along for an audition. I was given the lead in the play. And that was it for me. The first performance was a magical experience. I walked from the wings into the light and then I was born. For the first time, I really knew what I wanted to do.

A little while later, a bloke in the group, who was absolutely hopeless, said to me, 'I've got a job at Southport Rep.'

'What's that?' I said. I'd no idea what a rep was.

He told me it was a professional group of actors. Until then it had never occurred to me that working-class lads like us could actually be paid for going on stage.

'How much are you going to get?' I asked.

'Twelve quid a week!' he said.

That was a bloody fortune. So I asked him how he'd got in. He told me he'd just written off and had then been given an audition. It all sounded easy and so I decided, 'That's it. I'm going to be an actor.' With that, I threw out of the window my plans to return to France and study history.

Nicole and I had kept up a regular correspondence and so I wrote to tell her of my new-found love for the theatre. She was great. She came over to see me for a few days and we parted with

44

sadness as the closest of friends. If ever I changed my mind, Nicole told me, I'd always be welcome at Fontainebleau.

It had been impressed on me deeply at home that after I was twenty-one I could suit myself, but until then I had to help support my family. I reckoned that before taking a gamble on becoming an actor I'd first got to get a stake. The only way I could do that was either by robbery or by going to sea for a couple of trips. After that, I could throw in my hand. I'd then be twenty-one. There'd be a good chance my dad would be back at his job and my parents would be able to cope without my help.

I worked in the accounts department on land and that was closely related to the purser's office. 'Right,' I thought. 'A purser – that'll do me. Earn a few bob, ponce around the ship dressed in a nice little outfit, and get well fed.'

I went to see the chief accountant and told him about my plans to go to sea after my twenty-first birthday in October. He said he'd arrange things but, before I could be a purser, I'd first have to do a trip at sea as a member of the heavy gang, which, as the name suggests, does all the hard lifting and carrying jobs on the ship.

It was arranged that I'd do one trip to the States in the heavy gang, come back, spend Christmas at home, and then in the New Year go off to the States as the purser on a cruise.

Having come back from France where, as you might say, I'd been getting it regular, I'd got used to home comforts. So, like any other guy, I looked around. I'd had numerous quick liaisons with girls around my age. But they'd all been highly unsatisfactory – I'd been living with a sophisticated woman in her mid-thirties who'd done much to mature me as a lover.

In the summer, a friend of mine told me he was trying to make it with a woman, but she would only agree to go out with him if she could bring along her friend, who was unhappily married. So he asked me to go with him. When I arrived on this blind date, I saw that Lynda, the married woman, was extraordinarily beautiful. I was putty in her hands.

We went out on several of these double dates. My mate was getting nowhere fast, but I was getting nearer and nearer. Eventually Lynda and I went out on our own and she told me the sad story of her life, about how she'd got pregnant and had to get married, and how she hated her husband who'd been away at sea for over six months.

Our affair blossomed and everything was going sweetly. There was no question of us getting married – she knew that I intended to go to sea and then become an actor. But she decided that when I left Liverpool she'd leave her husband and go to live in Scotland with her kid.

We were ultra discreet. Not even my friend knew what was going on. Then one day in September, as I was walking down our street on the way home from work, who should I see but Lynda, pushing her baby in the pram. She nodded to me and pointed towards the entrance to the park. I walked to the shop and bought some cigarettes. Then I went round the back of the park and in through the other entrance.

I sat down beside her on a bench and said, 'What's the matter?'

'Somebody has written to my husband,' she said, 'and told him I'm having an affair. As soon as the ship reaches Singapore, they're going to give him compassionate leave and fly him home. I know he's going to try and get it out of me. His five brothers have already been round, threatening to beat me up if I don't tell them who it is. If any of them find out it's you, they'll kill you. If you can, go to sea now. If not, go to London, go anywhere, but go now. My husband'll be home in a week's time.'

I got into a panic. I knew the family and they were heavy, heavy guys. The whole family was notorious in Liverpool. If you looked the wrong way at any of them, they'd break your leg. What the hell would they do to me for having it off with 'our Jimmy's wife'?

I went straight round to the chief accountant's house, which wasn't far from us and told him I had to go to sea at once. As luck would have it, the ship I was due to join in mid-October was about to sail and one of the heavy gang had gone ill. So there was a vacancy. On the day Lynda's husband landed in London, we sailed from Liverpool.

The ship was the *Britannic*, which was taking to the States the last of the GI brides – the women who'd married American servicemen while they were in Britain. Before we were out of the Mersey, the GI brides and the crew were at it. It didn't stop till eight days later when we arrived at New York. The ship just kept on rocking from bow to stern. It was unbelievable.

There were six of us in the heavy gang. I was twelve and a half stone, over six foot and fit. But I was the lightweight jockey in the group. The others were all giants, weighing eighteen stone of muscle and bone. They needed to be. They did things like humping barrels of booze from the hold right up to the bars at the top of the ship – they couldn't use the lifts in case they were seen by one of the passengers. It was like being cellarmen for the penthouse pub in a skyscraper.

On the first night, I flopped into my bottom bunk, but there was no way I could sleep. We were right next to the engine – it was like being in hell. There was a blue light on, in case anybody was taken short. In this half light, I saw the guy in the bottom bunk opposite get out and come padding over towards me. 'Oh, no,' I thought. 'It's not one of these jobs, is it?'

But no, it wasn't me he was after. It was the guy in the top bunk. Then I heard a chomping and a slurping. I thought, 'I don't believe it.' I knew both blokes. They were captains of the ugly team – both really tough and hard. The guy in the top bunk let out a moan, the noise stopped, and the other guy grunted, 'Don't look or I'll go away!'

It was an hysterical start to my career at sea. From thereon in, nothing surprised me. The crew were in and out of the cabins of the GI brides all night long – it was like a French farce. It was the women's last fling before they arrived in the States. Even as we were docking and they were waving to their husbands on the quay, members of the crew were giving them a last farewell grope.

I survived my first trip and on the second we had diabolical weather in the Atlantic. Normally, we did about 400 nautical miles in a day, but at the height of the storm we did twenty-three in twenty-four hours.

After New Year, I was bumped up to be a writer in the purser's office and joined the ship for my third trip, which was a cruise from New York round the Mediterranean. Then it was much easier.

I moved from being a dogsbody to having someone to look after me, who was called the purser's tiger. He was a Liverpool-Irish Catholic and whatever went wrong he'd blame on the Protestants. So, it'd be, 'Did you see that bloody Protestant dinner we had today?' The broom-head would come off and he'd say, 'Bloody Protestant brushes!'

When he was working, he always used to sing the same lament:

> How would you like to be me,
> Alone in the Caribbean Sea,
> Sitting on a rock
> With a sunburnt cock
> And a mermaid on my knee?

Previously he'd been on the Queen Mary as a deck-steward – a super job – but he'd joined the ship to do this cruise, taking a heavy drop in salary. This intrigued me, so I asked him why.

'Well, we spend a week in Venice,' he said. 'I'll take any job on a ship that's going to Venice.'

'But why?'

'I've got a woman in Venice.'

I left it at that. When we docked somewhere, he never went ashore. He was saving up for Venice. In time we got very friendly, and so I said to him, 'You're putting all your money away. Is that to buy her something?'

'No,' he said. 'It's to pay her.'

'What d'you mean?'

'She's a whore!'

'Bloody hell! You give up a good job and all the tips, just so you can go and visit a whore in Venice! Why?'

He said, 'It's what she does!'

The mind boggled!

One night I got him drunk and said, 'Come on. Tell us what it's all about. What does she do?'

'Well,' he said, 'you see, she goes down on me.'

'That's all?'

'Yes, but it's beautiful. I love it. God, I love it. It's like a week in heaven. It's the greatest thing that's ever happened to me in my life. It costs me a fortune, but I don't care.'

'But you're married, aren't you?' I said.

'I am. Yes.'

'Well, if that's what you really like, why don't you tell your wife?'

'What! And have her do that to me!'

I said, 'Yes.'

'How dare you?' he said. 'My wife's not a Protestant whore!'

'So this woman in Venice is a Protestant?'

'Yes, she is. I had to search high and low to find a Protestant whore in Italy!'

Sure as anything she was a Catholic and was just having him on. But he wasn't bothered – it satisfied his conscience.

During the cruise, I'd also become very friendly with the ship's pianist. At the end of the trip, both of us intended leaving the sea, or 'swallowing the anchor' as it's called – he to play in London clubs and me to become an actor.

When the ship arrived in Venice, we both went off to a night club, looking for girls. There was no chance. All the women in the club were only looking for a paying job. Being artists, we only did it for love! But there was a beautiful Italian girl singing in the club, and so we stayed on.

At two o'clock in the morning, we decided we might as well call it a night and go back to the ship. We asked for the bill. When it arrived, it was two pages of foolscap and would have repaid the Italian national debt. We were well and truly being ripped off and there was no way we could pay the bill.

When we told the waiters this, they turned a bit leery. I tried to communicate in my schoolboy Latin cum Italian. Eventually the manager came over and I said, 'No way did we have all that stuff. I am an actor. My friend is a musician. We are artists. We do not expect to be treated like this.'

'He plays piano?' the guy asked.

'Yes.'

'Let's hear him play.'

To get us out of a jam, he went over to the piano and the guy was brilliant. The girl singer came back on and he played for her. She sang a couple of numbers and then came over to the table. The manager brought a bottle of champagne. I was chatting to her, while my mate had to keep on playing the piano.

At three-thirty in the morning, she said, 'I'm finished here now.'

I said, 'Well, can I take you home?'

'Of course,' she replied. The manager ripped up the bill, we went back to her place, and my mate kept on playing the piano.

He was well pissed off with me, but they asked him to go back the next night. For the rest of the time the ship was in Venice, he had an engagement.

So had I. I spent the week in Venice with the beautiful singer. As soon as I'd finished my duties, I'd go over to her place and we'd make love. Then I'd go with her to the club, where I'd eat and drink on the house.

It came to the last night in Venice. The ship was sailing at six o'clock the next morning. She finished early and we hurried back to her place. When I woke up, I said, 'What time is it? Holy Christ, it's five-thirty!'

I ended up running down the quayside to see the arse-end of the ship just sailing out. A lot of the crew were standing on the stern, shouting, 'See you then! See you! What you going to do now, sailor?'

I went back to her place. She suggested I should stay in Italy, but eventually I contacted the Cunard representative and they sent me by train to pick up the ship in Sicily. As soon as I arrived, I was logged, called to the bridge and told that my career at sea was finished. Until we got back to Liverpool, I had to stay on board. So when all the rest of the crew got off at Palermo to look round Sicily, I still had to do duties.

Now on the cruise there was a number of very heavy American fellows who the crew always treated with the utmost courtesy.

On the third day in Palermo, the ship was almost deserted and so I thought, 'Sod it! I'm going in for lunch.' Although I'd typed out all the orders, I'd forgotten that the dining room I used had been taken over for a private function. I walked in to find all these heavy guys fêting someone I immediately recognized. It was Lucky Luciano, the exiled Mafia boss.

'I'm sorry,' I said. 'I didn't realize.'

'That's all right. Come in.'

One of the guys said to Luciano, 'This is the one who missed the ship. We saw him running down the quay, shouting, "Hey, wait for me! Wait for me!" He's OK.'

Lucky Luciano shook my hand and I got out sharpish.

My career at sea didn't get any better when the ship went on to Naples. I was still confined to ship and so when everybody else buggered off, I was the duty officer. One night, after dinner, I went for a stroll round the deck. The quayside was deserted, and I went to look over the dockside. As I turned the corner, I could see that the door of the bonded store was open and a group of policemen and customs officers were being handed boxes of booze by a couple of crew members. The stuff was then passed down the side of the boat into a customs tender.

'Here! What's going on?' I said.

'Nothing you need bother yourself about, Tony,' one of the crew said. 'Just walk the other way. Say nothing. You'll be taken care of.'

I began to protest: 'But, but what . . . '

'Just bugger off!'

I looked at the customs officers waving machine-guns and said, 'Right! Whatever you say.'

I walked off and went to bed.

The next morning, I was summoned to the captain. The bond had been broken into and most of the booze had been stolen. I was the officer in charge of the watch and so I was asked to explain what had happened. The members of the crew that had been on the watch were all assembled there. They were the guys who'd been passing the gear over the side of the ship.

I didn't say anything. It turned out that every ship entering Naples at that time had the bond broken into. But I was blamed and logged again. I'm still waiting to this day for those guys to see me all right!

My catalogue of disasters continued. While we were still in Naples, the crew asked me to get permission from the captain for them to hold a St Patrick's Day parade through the street. I did. They got pissed and ended up throwing each other into the sea. The Italian newspapers reported that there had been riots on a British ship, so I was on the carpet again.

When we docked at Alexandria, I was asked to produce a concert. All the guys appearing in it told me they'd work out their own sketches and there was no need for me to do anything. It was a hell of a show – very blue – and the audience loved it. But it just made the skipper blue in the face. Once again, I got the blame.

That was about it for me. It confirmed my view that the theatre needed me more than the sea. So, when we got back, I did the decent thing and swallowed the anchor.

6

A Strolling Player

When I returned home from sea, I'd managed to save a hundred pounds. I was rich – really rich!

As I was then twenty-one, I told my parents that I was going to try my luck in the theatre. It was just like saying I was going on the streets. My father said to me, 'If you walk out of that door, you'll never walk back again. We don't want anything to do with the theatre. The last time a Booth was in the theatre was a disaster as far as our family was concerned!'

My great-great-grandfather's brother was the father of the actor John Wilkes Booth, who assassinated President Lincoln!

I thought my father would have been on my side. When he was a kid, he'd won a scholarship to the Royal College of Music, but his parents wouldn't let him go. They thought that men didn't earn their living from playing the piano. When I reminded my father of this, he said, 'If I couldn't do what I wanted, why should you?'

My mother just looked at me and said, 'Who on earth would want to pay good money to watch you on stage?'

But I was determined to go ahead. I knew it was the one thing I wanted to do. For me, acting was the nearest thing to heaven. It was a great way of communicating with people and you got to kiss a lot of girls!

I went down to London and found some digs. I didn't have much of a clue what to do. The only thing I knew was that there was a newspaper called the *Stage*. Then somebody told me it was sold at the railway stations early on Wednesday evenings. I went along and bought a copy. There were two suitable vacancies in it and I applied for both. On Saturday morning, I received two offers of a job. One from Richmond Theatre not only wanted me to work for nothing but also asked me to put fifty quid down to become a student actor. The other was from a touring rep offering me two pounds a week.

Being broke, I plumped for the paid employment and set off on my career as a strolling player with the Earl Armstrong Touring Repertory Players.

I arrived on the Wednesday only to be told that I was going on the next evening in a play. That gave me a day to learn and rehearse my part as the son in *Black Chiffon*. On Thursday evening, I made my professional debut in the village hall of Hutton Rugby – a place so small it's hardly on the map. The play was changed three times a week and so I had to learn a new part every couple of days.

After touring Yorkshire, we moved to Wales for a summer season. We did three plays – *The Marquis* by Noël Coward and two by Emlyn Williams, *Night Must Fall* and *The Corn is Green*, in both of which I played the lead. To create interest and boost the box office, local amateurs played the minor roles in each place we visited.

When we arrived at Dolgellau, a guy was waiting for us at the hall. 'I'm Jones, the grocer,' he said to me.

'Yes,' I said.

'Is this the repertory company?'

'Yes.'

'Well, I'm playing the Abbé in *The Marquis*.'

'Great! Well, we've got to set up first before we can rehearse.'

'I just wanted to tell you I'm here whenever you need me.'

'Great! But we're not doing the play for a couple of days,' I said. 'Though if you need any help, I'll take you over the lines.'

'No, no, no, boy! Don't you worry about me. I was a professional, you know.'

'No kidding!'

'Yes. I toured Mesopotamia in *Chu Chin Chow*! So I know all about it. I've got my own make-up still and I'm a leading light in the local players in Dolgellau.'

'Great. Well, if you want to give us a hand with the set . . . '

'No, that's all right, boy. I'll be getting back to my shop now.'

Like every touring company, we had to carry around our own scenery. We used reversible flats that could be turned round to make the sets for the different plays we presented on stages of varying sizes. We also had to use small rostra. That meant for the major staircase in *The Marquis*, down which the couple descended before their marriage, we had just a few steps up to the rostrum. In Dolgellau, the stage was so small that there was only a narrow gap left between the back wall and this staircase.

On the night we were performing *The Marquis*, Jones arrived hours before anybody else.

'Do you want to go over the lines?' I asked.

'No, no, no. I know them.'

'Well, look. You have to carry a Bible. We've stuck the Abbé's lines in it, just in case you go wrong.'

'I won't need that, boy. I'm an ex-professional.'

'Fine. But it's there if you need it.'

Jones the Grocer changed into the Abbé's costume, which fitted where it touched.

The main parts in *The Marquis* were played by Earl Armstrong and his wife, Kit. Towards the end of the first act, I was sent to bring the Abbé from upstairs so he could marry the couple. I went up the stairs and off-stage to where Jones was waiting.

'Now?' he whispered.

'Yes, now.'

I helped him on to the rostrum. Our cue came up. I walked ahead of him and said, 'I've brought the Abbé.'

Jones the Grocer then stepped, for the first time, into the full view of the audience. As he stood at the top of the staircase, the whole house burst into rounds of applause. He was what he'd said he was – the leading light of Dolgellau's amateur drama! I looked up at him as he stood there. He waved to the crowd, bowed, bowed again even deeper and stepped back.

'Look out!' I hissed.

Jones stepped off the back of the rostrum and straight down the gap. He was five foot ten and weighed fifteen stone. So it was a spectacular-fall! Pandemonium broke out among the audience. It was the funniest event in Dolgellau this century!

I dashed up the stairs. Jones's head appeared over the top of the rostrum. The audience burst into hysterical laughter – the toupée nobody knew he wore was hanging over his left ear!

The leading lady was shouting at me, 'Get him out. For Christ's sake, get him out!'

There was no way I could pull him up. So I ran round the stairs and started a tug of war trying to free Jones. The audience was cheering and applauding. It was unbelievable! Noël Coward never thought of writing it that way.

Then, with a loud 'plop!', Jones was free. His toupée had disappeared and there were shouts from the audience of 'Baldie! Baldie!' He decided to go back for his hairpiece.

'Forget the wig!' I hissed.

By that time Earl Armstrong and his wife were furious. I dragged Jones downstage and he was practically having heart failure. The audience gave him a round of applause and he managed to pull himself together.

The delighted beam on his face suddenly disappeared and he said, 'Oh, my God!'

'What is it?' I whispered.

'The Bible! I've lost the Bible!'

'Don't worry about it. Get on with it!'

'But the lines are in the Bible!'

'So? You know your part.'

'I don't! The lines are in the Bible!'

'What!'

We all gawped at him – a demented actor who'd lost his wig and forgotten his lines!

'Get the bloody Bible!' Kit Armstrong hissed at me.

'No way,' I replied. 'I'm not groping behind the bloody stairs.'

While all this was going on, the audience was in hysterics.

Jones had totally gone to pieces. 'Oh, I'm so sorry,' he burbled. 'It's never happened to me before.'

'Just declare them man and wife,' Kit Armstrong snarled at him.

'All right. All right. I'm sorry,' he whined. Then he said, 'I declare you man and wife.'

'Now, in the name of God go!' said Kit Armstrong.

Jones walked up to the double doors at the back of the set. They opened out on to the stage, but if they were pushed the opposite way they jammed. Jones pushed them the wrong way, locking us all on stage!

He turned and exclaimed, 'I can't get out!'

Kit Armstrong snapped. Shouting, 'I'll kill him! I'll kill him!' she chased Jones up the stairs and off the stage.

I ran after them and pulled down the curtain. It was one of our funniest performances!

That sort of thing happened wherever we went. So we had a lot of good fun. But I'd never worked so hard in all my life for so little pay. We started at nine in the morning and kept going till eleven at night. I learnt how to paint scenery, set lights, build sets, put them up and strike them, stitch costumes, apply make-up, sell tickets at the box office, and play a variety of parts – the whole shooting match. It was a fantastic grounding. Later, nobody could bullshit you – you'd done it all and knew the problems.

At the end of the season, I left the Earl Armstrong Touring Repertory Company and went into a weekly rep. Then I was taken on by an agent, who at one time or another represented every young actor in the country. He was terrific and kept me in work nearly all the time. He wasn't interested in films or the West End – it was reps, reps, reps. I did a lot of work in the provinces and eventually joined the Players for a season at the Liverpool Playhouse.

By this time, my parents had accepted that I was an actor, although they still thought it was just a phase I was going through and that I'd soon come to my senses and get a proper job. As I was in Liverpool, my mother said I should stay at home rather than go into digs. Her generosity may have been partially due to the fact that I was stupid enough to tell her how much I was earning at the theatre. 'That'll do nicely, Tony,' she said and claimed two-thirds of my money.

To conserve what cash I had left, I cycled from home each day to the theatre. That was rather frowned upon by the management. They thought it lowered the tone to have a leading player cycle in, wearing jeans and covered in sweat, while everybody else turned up looking as though they were going to the office.

In those days, Liverpool Playhouse was a snob's paradise. It was full of what were called 'collar-and-tie actors'. Most had been to public school and had private incomes. They had all been to drama school. I hadn't and, more than that, I was a local guy, coming from outside to play the lead in *Desperate Hours*, my first professional part in Liverpool.

At that time, none of my family had seen me act. So my mother, my father, my grandmother and my sister all wanted to come to the first night. I was only in my early twenties and I couldn't take the embarrassment of introducing the collar-and-tie merchants to my family, especially my Irish grannie. I knew she would have had a few and would start going on about, 'I remember him when. . . '

'All right,' I said. 'I'll make all the arrangements. I'll get the tickets. Come to the theatre. Go straight in. Don't talk to anybody. See the play and then go home. Please, don't come backstage!'

The director at Liverpool Playhouse was Willard Stoker, whose rich family put a lot of money into the theatre. He was a sweet guy, whose ambition had faded, but he was very middle class about the whole thing. On first nights he used to stand out front in evening dress to welcome the playgoers.

The first two acts went well. I hadn't even looked at the tickets I'd given my family and so I didn't know where they were sitting. I was back in the dressing-room during the second interval, when Bill Stoker came in and said, 'My dear, you're doing wonderfully well.'

'Thanks, Bill,' I said.

'Your mother, your father and that delightful lady, your grandmother, are really enjoying it! I took them for a drink at the interval and they met Maud!'

Now Maud Carpenter ran Liverpool Playhouse like her fief. She was the biggest snob I've ever met in my life and she did not like me at all. At the thought of Maud Carpenter meeting my grandma and having a drink with her, I went, 'Oh, God, no!'

It nearly destroyed me before the third act, but I managed to pull myself together. Afterwards, I could only think, 'How the hell did Willard Stoker find out my mum, my dad, my sister and my grandma were coming to the theatre? They must have identified themselves! I'll kill 'em! I'll kill 'em!'

The play was a huge success and the cast all went for a drink afterwards. While everybody was saying how good the play was, I was thinking, 'I don't care a shit. I'm going to kill my mother and father. And what the hell has my grandmother said to Willard Stoker?' All I wanted to do was to leave the company, get home and chew arse.

When I arrived, I banged on the front door. My sister opened it. I barged straight past her and shouted, 'What the hell went on? What were you doing? I told you just to go to the theatre, do nothing and talk to nobody.'

My mother told me what had happened. My father had arrived home from the docks and they'd got ready to go to the theatre. They'd caught the bus into the centre of Liverpool, walked down to Williamson Square where the Playhouse was, went through the doors, ignoring everybody, and arrived at the entrance to the circle.

The girl asked for the tickets. My father had put his hand into the jacket of his best suit and discovered he'd left the tickets in his other suit. The girl called the assistant manager who asked what the problem was. My mother then blurted out the whole story. Willard Stoker was brought over. Gushing with friendliness, he'd shown them to their seats and at the interval had taken them for a drink and up to Maud Carpenter's office. They had met everybody!

I was terrified because of what they might have said, but it turned out my grandmother had played the whole thing up and had been charming. She'd talked about Galway and asked why Liverpool Playhouse didn't do more plays about the Irish problems. Everybody at the theatre was charmed by them. They were terrific.

Not that it helped me with Maud Carpenter. A little while later, I was leaving my bike by the stage door when I heard Maud saying to Willard Stoker, 'But it's terrible. He totally lowers the tone of the company. Fancy coming in here on a cycle, wearing jeans and a sweater. I've never seen him in a suit. I doubt if he's even got one.'

I knew I'd lost with her. However, I did get on well with all the actors – they were a decent bunch, even though it was such a middle-class company.

I stayed on a little longer at Liverpool Playhouse and during that time struck up a friendship with another young actor in the company. We used to go crumpeteering together. At that stage, the Royal Court in Liverpool was the number one touring date and so all the big names turned up there. On Wednesdays, we used to go to the matinees there and on Thursdays they came to our matinees.

We got to know the doorman well at the Royal Court and for a beer he'd mark our card as to the likely ladies in the company: 'Tell you what. The understudy is a right goer!' – that kind of thing. Then after the show, we'd go backstage, chat up the ladies concerned, invite them to have dinner and hope that Nature would take its course. On the whole, we did reasonably well. It was a nice little arrangement.

Then one week there was a ballet company at the Royal Court. Before the show, we went to the stage door and I said, 'Well, Ernie, what's the score?'

'No chance, Tony,' he said. 'No chance at all.'

'Why?'

'This corps de ballet. They work hard, you know. They're that knackered doing the barre all day, that when they've finished their performance they're shattered. They haven't got time for any of that.'

As we had the free tickets, we thought we'd see the show anyway and chance our arms. Going in to the theatre, I said, 'I'll tell you what. Let's get some binoculars and we'll sit there and have a bit of fun looking up the tutus!'

We sat at the front of the stalls in a not very full theatre. When the corps de ballet came on, we examined each one in turn with our binoculars, nudging each other and comparing notes. Then we'd follow one girl all around the stage until she got into a terrible tizz. We had a whale of a time!

Afterwards, we went back to the Playhouse and did our performance. At that time, we were doing *The Merchant of Venice* and I was playing Gratiano. Still being a trifle short of funds, I only had one jockstrap. That night, I washed it, stuck it on the radiator and went off home – forgetting there was a matinee the next day.

Fortunately, on Thursday, I arrived in time for the matinee, but when I got to the dressing-room I discovered that my jockstrap was still soaking. So I decided to take a flyer and wear nothing under my tights. In those days, the tights were cotton and weren't elasticated. I pulled them on and to keep them up tied a piece of string round my waist.

My friend was playing Bassanio and we entered together during the first scene. As we walked on stage, I felt a strange whoosh from the audience and thought, 'My God, what's that?' I turned and looked out. In the first two rows of the stalls was the entire corps de ballet from the Royal Court. Every one of them was peering through binoculars and they'd got us! They followed our every movement. With fifty pairs of eyes staring at me I was all too aware that I wasn't wearing a jockstrap!

When we came offstage after the opening scene, we had a big laugh about it. We liked their style – it showed a great sense of humour. That made the score one all – great! But we were determined they weren't going to put us off. We were going to show them how good we were.

Things went well until the trial scene. My character, Gratiano, enters at the beginning, but says nothing for several pages. So for quite a time I was sitting on a three-legged stool towards the front of the stage. All the time, I was aware of being closely observed through the corps de ballet's binoculars.

Then it came to the point where I jumped up and said, 'A second Daniel, a Daniel, Jew!' As I did so, I threw my arms out and heard a terrible rip. I turned my back on the audience, folded my arms and started to feel the seams of my shirt. I couldn't find anything amiss. I turned to my friend and whispered, 'Is my shirt all right?'

He looked and said, 'Yes.'

'Did you hear a rip?'

'Yes.'

'Sure it's OK?'

'Yes.'

The scene was carrying on. I returned to my seat and sat down. Within thirty seconds, there was pandemonium among the corps de ballet. All the glasses were pointing at me – straight at my tights. I was sitting there, looking out front, thinking, 'I'm not going to fall for that one! How long do you think I've been at this game?'

By now there was uproar among them and I was the focus of attention. 'There's no way,' I said to myself, 'that they're going to get my hand edging very slowly up my leg to see if I've ripped my. . . my. . . tights. Oh, God, I haven't, have I? I'll tell you what though – there's a hell of a draught.'

Very slowly and casually, I moved up my hand. All the ballet dancers started giggling. Then I put my hand in front of myself and found the gaping hole in my tights. Without knowing it, I'd been giving the first ever full-frontal, exposed performance on the stage of the Liverpool Playhouse!

The corps de ballet gave me a round of applause. I had to do the rest of the scene with my back to the audience, holding myself into the remains of my tights.

That, I reckoned, made the final score Ballet Company twelve, Liverpool Players one. It was a rout.

The incident was just about the climax of my career at the Liverpool Playhouse. I left at the end of the season and returned to London. My agent continued to find me work, and I spent most of the next couple of years in reps and on tours up and down the country.

At the time, I was still officially in the Army Reserve and in 1955, when I was appearing in *Macbeth* at the Manchester Library Theatre, I was recalled to do my two-week reserve training. I'd dodged it for several years, but this time they sent a policeman to the theatre to tell me that if I didn't turn up I'd be arrested. Everybody was supposed to turn up on the Saturday, but I was given special permission to go on the Monday.

Because of the part I was playing, I had a beard and long hair. I wasn't about to shave it off for the Army. My uniform was at my mother's in an outside shed. When I went to pick it up, it was green with mould.

I arrived at Blacon Camp after the pubs closed on Monday afternoon. When I walked into the guardroom, wearing jeans and with my long hair, they were not pleased. According to them, I was absent without leave and so I was nicked. I was confined to barracks and told to put on my uniform. I refused because of the condition it was in, so they also charged me with disobeying an order and not looking after my kit. Eventually, the list of charges was a mile long.

The next morning, I was up in front of the Commanding Officer, still wearing my civvies. They tried to march me in, but no way – I just strolled. I knew I was only there for a fortnight and they could stick me inside for the whole of it if they liked.

The colonel looked up, stared at me and said, 'Macduff!'

I said, 'Yes.'

'Oh, hello. I saw you in *Macbeth* at the Manchester Theatre. It was fantastic. A great production.'

We had a long chat and then he gave me a chit to say I was excused all duties and didn't have to wear a uniform. I spent the fortnight at Chester having a great time – getting up when I wanted to, going to the races and nipping back to Liverpool. Just before I left, I was told that I'd been promoted from Operator Grade Three to Operator Grade One!

I returned again to London and, shortly afterwards, my agent rang me up and said, 'I've got this part for you in Manchester. It's playing the vicar in the play *Rain*. You know, the one where you reform Sadie Thompson?'

'Great,' I said. 'It's a terrific part.'

I borrowed the money from him and caught the train to Manchester. At one of the stops, somebody got off and left behind a copy of the *Daily Mirror*. I started to read it and when I got to page four went, 'Wow! Who is that? She is beautiful. She is something else.'

Underneath the photograph of the gorgeous girl stretched out on a rug, it said, 'Pat Dean is to star as Sadie Thompson in a new production of *Rain*.' I read it again and then said to myself, 'No kidding! This is going to be a very interesting play! I can't wait to meet her!'

When I arrived in Manchester, I discovered that the play wasn't *Rain*. It was a modern version, *A Girl Called Sadie*. Still, I was the leading man, playing opposite Pat Dean, the incredibly beautiful woman whose photo I'd seen in the *Daily Mirror*. She was even more ravishing in the flesh – a stunning blonde, with a sensuous mouth, luminous eyes the colour of gooseberries, a taut uplifted bosom that might have been drawn by a sexist cartoonist, a minute waist and the most beautiful pair of long legs that reached to eternity. And I was being paid to work with her – and kiss her!

She'd recently separated from her husband, and she made it clear she didn't want to have anything to do with any other man. But I pursued her. I bought her drinks, invited her out to lunch – and got nowhere.

But I was determined. In the second part of the play, she had to shock the other characters in the scene. She pulled off her dress and stood centre-stage with her back to a fireplace, her legs apart and her hands on her hips. She was wearing black high heels, black stockings, black suspender belt, black knickers, and a black basque.

I wasn't involved in the scene and so I used to go behind the fireplace, sit on the floor out of sight and say things to make her laugh. I didn't succeed. So I hit on a way really to distract her. I filled a squeezy bottle with water and put it in the fridge for an hour. When she was playing her sexy scene, I lay on the floor behind the stage fireplace and shot a stream of ice-cold water on to her beautiful rounded bottom. She gave a muffled cry and staggered forward, rubbing her thighs together trying to get rid of the dribbling water. That night I had to hide when she came offstage!

Eventually, I gave up chasing her. It was then that she asked me out for a drink and our love affair started.

Later, she told me that at first she couldn't stand me. 'I thought you were a big-headed bastard,' she said. 'You just walked into the first rehearsal and said, "Hello. I'm Tony Booth. You're lovely. What you doing tonight? I've nowhere to stay – I'll stay with you."'

'I bloody well didn't say that to you!'

'All bloody but!'

Fortunately, she revised her original opinion of me.

As we travelled around the country, we fell more deeply and more passionately in love. I was completely captivated by her. Not only did she have the most perfect figure, but she was vivacious, compassionate, intelligent and had the most infectious laugh. She was also, without doubt, one of the best actors I'd ever worked with. A little while later, she changed her stage name and soon became known to millions as Pat Phoenix.

7

In and Out of the West End

Pat and I had a great deal in common – we were young, passionate, smitten with the theatre, homeless, broke and very much in love. We were also part of the new wave of working-class actors and actresses breaking into the theatre during the mid-fifties.

At the same time, television was becoming really popular and, as people stayed at home more, provincial theatres were closing. It was clear that if I wanted to be successful I had to find work either in television or in the West End. So I decided to leave the touring company. 'That's it,' I said to myself. 'I'm never going to do any more of this travelling crap again. I'm going to London and I'll try to get something in the West End.'

Pat decided to keep on touring with *A Girl Called Sadie*. For a time our love affair continued but, as we went our separate ways, we grew further and further apart. Eventually we stopped seeing each other.

I gave up my agent, determined to find my own work. The first job I went for in the West End I managed to get. It was in *No Time for Sergeants*. I'd made it to the big time at last! But my dreams of finding instant fame and fortune were soon shattered. There were thirty characters in the play and I had only a few lines. Nobody was going to spot me there – that was something that happened only in Hollywood movies.

I learnt a hell of a lot from an American actor called Barry Nelson, who was in the play both on Broadway and in London. He reinforced my belief that every performance is different. There are different audiences, the actors feel differently – somebody may have a cold one night and so on. When I first started acting, I used to get into a lot of trouble, accused of being inconsistent. But I knew I wasn't – I was reacting to what was happening around me. Even if the roof fell in, some actors would ignore it and just carry on. But Barry didn't. In the play, he had lots of speeches to the audience. Although he always stuck to the script, every night seemed different. It was beautiful to watch and I became a great fan of his.

I was in *No Time for Sergeants* during the Suez Crisis. On the radio it said that all reservists had to report immediately to the nearest military camp. I totally ignored it and went off on protest marches and demonstrations in Trafalgar Square. This time, the police didn't arrive to arrest me!

After I'd been in the play for about nine months, the Asian flu epidemic struck and immediately hit the company. I had been playing two parts, covering about five others as first understudy and about ten more as second understudy. There were about twenty actors for the thirty speaking parts. By the end of the first week of Asian flu, the cast was reduced by half and I was playing five parts. We were hit even harder in the second week. Barry Nelson and five other actors were playing all the parts – it was ridiculous.

There was one black actor in the play. At that stage in the fifties, there was no possibility of having a black understudy. So when he went ill, a white actor had to black up. It was such a hell of a job to put on all the make-up that, even when there were only five of us playing all thirty parts, he couldn't play any other character.

In one performance, I remember having to play the orderly, opening the door and saying, 'Stockdale, the psychiatrist will see you now. Go in and wait for him.' As he walked in, I ran round backstage, put on a white jacket, walked on stage and said, 'Ah, Stockdale, sit down.' There wasn't even time to stick on a false moustache. The audience must have wondered what the hell was happening!

One night, I played ten parts. Understudies who hadn't set foot on stage before were coming on and playing four parts. It was chaos, but we carried on. At the end of the first week when we collected our wages, the management gave us each a one pound bonus! A meeting was called and we all said this was unacceptable. We were then given an extra pound per night.

At the time, I had a bedsit in Stoke Newington. Every day, I caught the 73 bus from the Green to the West End. Towards the end of the epidemic, I knew I was coming down with Asian flu. But, as the show was so badly up the creek, I set off for the theatre. I struggled down the street and was twenty yards from the bus stop when the bus moved off. I tried to run for it and, for the first time, I knew what Cockneys meant when they said, 'He couldn't raise a gallop.' I was zapped. I missed the bus, turned round and crawled to the nearest phone box. I rang the theatre and croaked, 'I can't make it.' I missed four performances out of eight that week and the management docked half my pay!

A few weeks after the flu epidemic, I came offstage one night at the first interval and the stage-doorman said, 'Tony, a young lady called Sue wants to see you. I've stuck her up in your dressing-room. She says she's a friend of yours.'

It was a girl I'd met briefly eighteen months before when I'd been in a summer show at Llandudno. For a couple of weeks she'd worked as an ASM, but she'd been sacked because she was useless.

She said, 'Tony, I've nowhere to go. I'm feeling really ill. I saw your name on the bill outside and wondered if I could come and sit in your dressing-room for a while.'

'What's the matter?'

'I just need to sit down. I knew you would help me. You will help me, won't you?'

'Of course I will.'

'Do you mind if I stay here?'

'Of course not. I've got to go on and do the rest of the show, but you're welcome to stay.'

At the second interval, I returned to the dressing-room and asked her how she was.

'Oh, I feel a lot better,' she said.

'That's great. What are you doing later?'

'Nothing.'

'Well, let's go for a drink.'

After the show, in the pub, she said, 'Can I come home with you?'

'Of course you can,' I said, 'if you want to. Sure.'

We set off for my bedsit. On the way, she said, 'I still feel quite ill.'

'That's terrible,' I said. 'Have you got the flu or something?'

'No. I'll tell you when we get to your place.'

When we arrived, I said to her, 'Well, what's the matter?'

'I've had an abortion,' she announced, 'and it hasn't worked.'

'Oh, my God, how terrible!'

'I don't know what to do. I don't know where to go and I've got nobody to turn to. Will you look after me?'

'Of course,' I said. 'It's terrible.'

And it was. In those days abortions were illegal.

I sat her on the bed and said, 'Shall I get a doctor?'

'No, no. Please don't get a doctor. If you do, I'll be in real trouble.'

'So what can I do?'

'Please just get a bucket and then leave me.'

I didn't have a bucket and so I had to knock up a woman in another of the rooms. When I took it back, Sue told me to wait outside. It was midnight and I was standing in the corridor outside my own bedsit!

Then I heard a terrible thud. I rushed back in. Sue had fallen on the floor, she was breathing strangely and she looked terrible. There was blood all over the place.

'This is ridiculous,' I thought. 'There's only one thing I can do.' So I dashed down the street and phoned for an ambulance.

When I got back, Sue was still in bad shape. She was just about to miscarry. I didn't know what the hell to do.

Fortunately, the ambulance soon arrived. As the blokes came in, she was saying to me, 'Don't leave me. Don't leave me.' I held her by the hand and went with her in the ambulance to the hospital.

I was told to wait in a room. Half an hour later, the door opened. A doctor walked in and said to me, 'You're the one!'

'What do you mean?'

'The girl.'

'Yes?'

'Bastards like you should be shot!'

'What?'

'We've only just saved her life. You know that?'

'But that's great.'

'Not for you. I'm reporting you to the police for performing an illegal abortion.'

My jaw dropped and, as he turned on his heels, I shouted, 'Just a minute! Just a minute! It wasn't me, honest!'

'They all say that,' he said. 'The ambulancemen told me there was a bucket of blood in your room. Luckily for you, they got her here in the nick of time. But if anything goes wrong and she dies, you'll go to prison.'

'Hold on, please! I don't really know the girl. I don't even know the girl's surname.' Then I told him the story and convinced him.

'Oh, my God,' he said. 'I'm sorry. Forget whatever I said. How do we get in touch with her parents?'

'I haven't a clue. I think she's come up to London just for the operation. I seem to be the only person she knows.'

Fortunately, the girl survived. She never told her parents, as far as I know. After she came out of hospital, she stayed at my place for a few days and then I saw her off – 'Thanks a bundle, kid!' Appearing in the West End wasn't all beer and skittles, mother!

While I was in *No Time for Sergeants*, an actor in the company brought round a chap he'd met at drama school. It was the actor, Tom Bell. We were introduced, went for a drink and got on like a house on fire. We became close friends.

In all, *No Time for Sergeants* ran for a year. Tom and I had intended to buy a flat together, but, as always, I was sailing so close to the wind that, when the show ended, I had only one week's wages. The lease on my bedsit had come to an end and so Tom and I went to sleep on the floor of another actor's room. It was above a greengrocer's in Ladbroke Grove – a right dosshouse.

We both signed on with the same agent, insisting that we were interested only in films, television and the West End. Not surprisingly, very little work came our way. The only regular income we had was the dole. One day, when we were both broke, we went along to see Ron, our agent. He said, 'I'll tell you what I'll do. I've bought this block of flats in Hampstead and you can clear it up and do the painting. I'll pay you two quid a day. I'm sleeping there at nights to keep an eye on the place. Be there at eight in the morning so I can go to the office. Then you can work there till I get back.'

Ron never turned up until eight in the evening and so we were working there twelve hours a day. When he eventually arrived back, he'd give us the two quid – or he did for the first few days. Then it was, 'I haven't got it at the moment. Hang on.'

At the end of the week, we were owed for three days. So Tom Bell said, 'You're the hard one. Ask him for the money.'

I did and he handed over ten quid. 'This isn't enough,' I said. 'You owe us two quid each for three days. That's twelve quid.'

'No, no, no,' Ron said. 'I've had to take a quid off each of you for my commission! After all, who got you the job?'

That was Ron – a successful agent, always looking after number one! Shortly afterwards, both Tom and I decided we'd be better off without an agent and set about finding our own work.

We knew it wouldn't be easy. So we were extremely interested when we heard about a place called 'The Soup Kitchen'. It was a cheap eating-place, next to the Express building off Fleet Street, where actors could eke out their dole by doing a little moonlighting. We both went along and got taken on for a quid a night, plus an extra quid for the taxi fare home. We were told there'd also be tips.

We had to work from six in the evening till one in the morning. As Tom hadn't done any waiting and I'd picked up the rules of the game while at sea, I did the winging while Tom stood behind the bar handing out the stuff. Most of the customers were printers from Fleet Street who came in for a good, cheap meal. But they never, ever tipped. The place was often packed and most of the time we were run off our feet.

To save our sanity, we devised a system where each evening we played a different part. One night I'd play Brando and Tom would play Steiger in *On the Waterfront*. The next night I'd do Humphrey Bogart and he'd be Cary Grant. The punters loved it, because they never knew who'd be serving at their table.

After we'd been working there a couple of weeks, Tom and I had a stroke of luck and managed to get a flat in Pembridge Mews at the back of Notting Hill. As it was six quid a week, we needed the money earned at the Soup Kitchen and so we worked there every night.

One evening, during a bit of a lull, a guy walked in and straight-away I could see he had presence. He was the kind of guy you didn't muck about with. He sat down at a table and I went over. I cut out all the acting bit and just asked him what he wanted. He ordered starters, soup, steak, pancakes, and coffee.

He sat there, minding his own business, and ate his way through the entire menu. Then he called for the bill. It came to just under a fiver – which was a lot of money then. He put his hand in his inside pocket, went through his other pockets and said, 'Oh, hell! I've got my car keys and half a crown. That's all. I was meeting a journalist, I changed my suit and I've left my wallet behind.' Now I'm an actor and I knew this guy wasn't acting. He obviously wasn't trying it on – he'd genuinely forgotten his wallet. 'I'll tell you what,' he said, 'I'll bring it in tomorrow.'

'Look,' I said. 'It's not down to me. I just work here. I'll have to ask the manager.'

The manager was sitting behind the till, and I said, 'See that guy over there? He hasn't got any money. He can't pay and he says he'll bring it in tomorrow.'

'No, he won't,' the manager said. 'Get it off him!'

'How am I going to do that?'

'Search him.'

'You're kidding!'

'Well, somebody's got to pay.'

'He will. He says he'll bring it in tomorrow.'

'You don't believe that, do you?'

'Yes, I do.'

'Well, I'll tell you what. If you don't get the money off him, I'll stop it out of your wages.'

'Oh, come on!'

'Starting tonight – two quid.'

'How am I going to get home?'

'Catch a bus.'

'Oh, that's really sweet. Thanks a lot.'

I went back to the table and the guy said, 'What's the matter?'

'OK. I'll put it to you straight,' I said, and sat down at his table. 'I'm an actor and I'm just working here 'cause I need the money. Now I believe you, but the manager says if I don't get the money off you, he's going to stop it out of my wages.'

'I'll have a word with 'im,' he said.

'No, please don't. This is between you and me. If you don't bring the money in tomorrow, I'll be working three nights here for nothing just to pay it back.'

He looked at me and said, 'Give me your name, kid.'

'Tony Booth.'

He wrote it on the back of the bill. Then he passed it over to me and said, 'Put your address on.'

'Why?'

'I'll send you something.'

'There's no need. Just come in and pay tomorrow.'

'I will pay, but I also want your address. I'm very grateful to you. OK?'

I wrote my address, we shook hands, and he left.

That night I got no pay. Tom and I walked to Victoria and caught the 52 bus home to Notting Hill.

The next evening, I walked into the Soup Kitchen and the manager said, 'Your friend hasn't been in.'

'That's all right,' I replied. 'He'll be here.'

Seven, eight, nine went by. Then at about half-past nine, when the place was crowded, this guy came in. He said to me, 'You did me a favour, Tony. I'll never forget it.' He walked up to the manager and gave him a ten pound note. When he was given the change, he handed the fiver to me.

'No, you don't have to give me that,' I said.

'No, no. You did me a favour.' Then he turned round and addressed the crowded restaurant: ''Ere, listen to me.' Everybody froze and the place was as still as a morgue. He put his hand on my shoulder. 'This guy is Tony Booth,' he said. 'I wants you all to know he done me a great favour. So, he's all right, see!'

Then off he went. At the first table I went to, there were two journalists. One of them said to me, 'How long have you been in with the Richardsons then?'

I said, 'What!'

'Don't you know who that is?' he said. 'That's Charlie Richardson, the gangster.'

'You're having me on!'

'Didn't you notice how he shut everybody up? When he walked through here, it was like parting the Red Sea,' he said, obviously impressed. 'So, you've been doing him favours, eh? We'll have to keep an eye on you. You ain't a guy to mess about with!'

Afterwards, most of the people who came into the Soup Kitchen seemed to have heard about the young, out-of-work actor who was in with the Richardsons. It did my standing no harm at all!

About ten days later, early in the morning, I was in bed when there was a bang, bang, bang on the door of the mews. I staggered over to the window, opened it and looked out. There was a fellow with a van outside and he called, 'Tony Booth?'

'Yes,' I replied.

'Come on, down 'ere, quick.'

'What is it?'

'I've got something for you. 'Ave you got anybody what can give an 'and?'

I got Tom out of bed. We went downstairs and opened the door. The guy unlocked the back of the van and said, ''Ere, cop 'old of that.' And he pointed to a cardboard packing-case full of Marlboro cigarettes. God only knows how many were in it.

'What's this?' I said.

'A present from the Richardsons,' he said, hauling it out. 'Come on. Get it inside quick. I've got to be off.'

'What's the problem?' I said, as we dragged it inside.

'Well, it fell off the back of a lorry, didn't it?'

So there we were with thousands of knocked-off fags. We were terrified. Tom and I chainsmoked them, gave them away, lit the fire with them until they'd all gone. I've never smoked a Marlboro since!

Life at the Soup Kitchen continued to be adventurous. One night, Tom had gone off early and after work I set off on my own to catch the bus at Victoria. The night was balmy and moonlit. I was wearing a donkey jacket, jeans and desert boots.

It was one-thirty in the morning and, apart from the odd taxi, there was nobody around as I walked down Pall Mall. Then I saw a guy coming towards me with his coat slung across his shoulders, carrying an umbrella. 'Oh hell! Here we go!' I thought. 'It's Hello-Sailor time and I'm the sailor!'

I was a few feet away, when the guy said, 'Excuse me. Have you got a light?'

Just on the offchance that he was straight, I handed him my lighter. As I did so, he touched my hand. I just wanted to get the hell out of there. Then as he lit his cigarette, I saw his face and instantly recognized him.

I was speechless, but he said, 'I've got a nice place above Admiralty Arch. Would you like to come back with me for a drink?'

'Are you crazy?' I said. 'Are you totally out of your mind? Importuning at this time of night in Pall Mall! I could be anybody. Your whole career could be up the creek. I could be a Russian spy for all you know. Go home, man! Go home to bed!'

'How dare you?' he said. 'What do you think I was talking about?'

'Forgive me. I've taken it wrong.'

'That's all right,' he said. 'How about coming back for a drink? I've got a beautiful flat.'

'Look. You've been drinking. Forget it. Go home and just be thankful you haven't met somebody who'd blackmail you.'

'You know who I am. I'm flattered.'

'Of course I know who you are. You're Selwyn Lloyd, the Foreign Secretary.'

'And you still don't want to come back with me?'

'No, I bloody well don't. Go home.'

'Please yourself,' he said and walked off.

8

The Big Break

As I didn't have an agent, I discovered that the only way to get to see anybody was to write a snotty letter, accusing them of nepotism, corruption or worse. Occasionally, I was successful and the odd spell of work took me briefly away from the charms and delights of the Soup Kitchen.

During one of my letter splurges, I wrote to the casting director of ABPC, because I knew the company was making a film about the Army. Not receiving a reply, I wrote to Stuart Lyons, the assistant casting director, and accused him of never seeing any new actors and always using the same old clique. Much to my surprise, I received a reply, asking me to go and see him because he was appalled by the letter I'd written.

Stuart and I hit it off and after ten minutes he told me he'd been instructed to give me short shrift because of the way I'd written to the company. But, he told me, he thought there might be something in the film for me. He stuck his neck out and obtained for me the smallest speaking part in *Ice Cold in Alex*. I played the military policeman, who at the end of the film came on with an officer, played by Basil Henson, to arrest Anthony Quayle and take him off.

The director was Jimmy Lee-Thompson, an intense, short man with dark hair, who'd just given up smoking and drinking. As a result, he was somewhat strung out and spent a surprisingly large amount of his time tearing up paper into small pieces.

Although the film was made in those halcyon days when money was no object, the director had run into difficulties. A long time had been spent on location and the film was running over. John Mills, the film's star, had a penalty clause in his contract which meant that he was being paid an additional daily rate. That, for an actor, is a rare and precious situation, and so John Mills, not unnaturally, was not fretting about the delay.

I was called to the ABPC studios at Borehamwood for my first ever day's filming. *Ice Cold in Alex* was being shot in page order.

We shot the first scene and then I had to sit around for four days until I was called back in to deliver my solitary line to John Mills. I was very nervous. John Mills was totally relaxed. For the close-up, he sat at a coffee table on a small rostrum. So instead of looking down at John Mills, I was eyeball to eyeball with him. Such are the strange and wondrous ways of making films!

By this stage poor Jimmy Lee-Thompson was getting more and more neurotic. Everywhere he walked, he was constantly strewing torn-up pieces of paper which the script girl busily retrieved. He was not in the best of humour.

We started the scene and it was my big moment. I had the line: 'Sir, I've come to collect the prisoner.' John Mills then delivered his speech. We rehearsed it and then Lee-Thompson said, 'Let's shoot it. We're wasting time!'

I said my line and John Mills started speaking when from somewhere came the sound of rapid heavy breathing.

The sound man shouted, 'Cut! Cut! There's something wrong.'

Lee-Thompson, in despair, said, 'Oh my God! Let's do it again.'

We started for the second time and as John Mills was talking I could still hear the heavy breathing.

Once more, the sound man shouted, 'Cut!'

Lee-Thompson jumped up and down and said, 'We can't waste time on this! Let's get on with it.'

We did it again and again. After sixteen takes, the director was nearly out of his mind. The pressure was all on me, because there was no way Lee-Thompson could take it out on John Mills. So he said to me, 'What are you doing? Are you making that noise? What's going on?'

I could only shrug.

When we came to the seventeenth take, the tension on the set was unbearable. I said, 'Sir, I've come to collect the prisoner.'

73

John Mills opened his mouth and yet again there was the sound of heavy breathing.

Lee-Thompson threw a tantrum. He marched up to me and demanded, 'You! Are you breathing?'

'Yes,' I replied.

'Well, they're picking it up on the sound. Don't you know anything about filming? It's your breathing that's causing us this delay. I'm going to tell you this for the first and last time – I won't have any breathing actors on my set!'

I was totally stunned. For the eighteenth take, I said my line and then pinched my nostrils, pressed my mouth closed and held my breath. John Mills started and yet again there was the distinct sound of heavy breathing.

Lee-Thompson shouted, 'Cut!' He looked at me and I was purple in the face.

'It's not me,' I gasped.

'Well, it's somebody,' he said. 'Somebody is breathing on my set. Who is it?'

At that moment, John Mills's spaniel came panting out from under the table!

'Oh, look,' Lee-Thompson cooed. 'It's the doggie. He wants a drink of water!'

When *Ice Cold in Alex* was shown, the whole scene, including my solitary line, had been cut!

Shortly afterwards, I heard that auditions were being held at the Theatre Royal, Stratford. At that stage, Joan Littlewood's Theatre Workshop seemed to be a spiritual home for my type of actor – or so I thought. I wrote off, heard nothing and so sent them one of my snotty letters. I received a snotty letter back, inviting me for an audition.

The minute I walked into the theatre at Stratford-atte-Bow, Gerry Raffles, who was then the money man behind the enterprise, made it clear that he didn't like me at all. As far as he was concerned, I was trying to force my way into a company that he believed should select its own actors.

With Joan Littlewood sitting in the stalls, I did my set piece and then was asked to improvise. That held no fear for me – I'd been doing it since the earliest days of my acting career. The difficulty for them was stopping me! But at the Theatre Royal I knew I was going down like a cup of cold soup. So I stopped.

'That's very good,' Joan Littlewood said, 'but what I really want from you is something different.'

'What's that?' I asked.

'A private moment. I want you to give me your most private moment.'

I was so pissed off that I thought, 'Have you got the balls to sit down on stage and wank?' I decided I hadn't. So I settled for walking to the back of the stage and pissing on the wall!

They went bananas! I was kicked out and told never to darken the doors of the Theatre Royal again.

As I was leaving the theatre, a guy stopped me and in an American accent said, 'That was the greatest thing I've seen in the theatre! First I saw your improvisation and then you go and piss on the back wall! It was something else. Now I know why they say the British theatre's come alive!'

'Glad you liked it,' I said, thinking he was some kind of nut.

'I want you to take the lead in my next play.'

'Oh, yes. Where?'

'Here.'

'Fat chance! They've just thrown me out of the place!'

'It doesn't matter. I'm the writer and the director. I cast my own play.'

'Who are you then?'

'My name's William Saroyan.'

I'd got nothing to lose. So I gave him my address. A few days later I received a letter from him asking me to have lunch with him at the Savoy. Afterwards, I went back to his room for a drink. On his desk was a typewriter on which there was a plaque, saying, 'Presented by the Remington Rand Company to William Saroyan, the great American writer.'

'Wow!' I said. 'Fancy them putting that on your typewriter!'

'Yes. They asked me what they should put on it and I told them that!'

Saroyan and I hit it off together. Unfortunately his play, which was called *Sam, the Highest Jumper of Them All*, wasn't much good. I had a great time, because I was given an improvised dialogue with the audience. But, at the end of the fortnight's run, the play sank without trace. I left the company and went back to the Soup Kitchen.

Shortly afterwards, I heard that the BBC was doing a North Country play and that the director was Stuart Burge. I wrote to him, saying that I was from the North Country and wanted to be considered for a part. I didn't hear anything. So I wrote again. When once more I didn't receive a reply, I sent him an overnight telegram – it was my favourite way of reaching people. You could get lots of words on it for only a few bob and it always got straight through. Secretaries were far too scared to open a telegram addressed to the boss.

In the telegram I said: 'YOU'RE LOOKING FOR NORTH COUNTRY ACTORS. I AM A NORTH COUNTRY ACTOR. I'VE WRITTEN TO YOU TWICE AND YOU HAVEN'T REPLIED. HOW DOES ANYBODY GET THROUGH TO YOU? DON'T YOU PAY ANY ATTENTION TO ACTORS? I EXPECT TO HEAR FROM YOU BY RETURN. TONY BOOTH.' Then I gave my address.

The next day, which was a Tuesday, I received a telegram back, saying: 'RING STUART BURGE IMMEDIATELY.'

I rang and was put through to his secretary, who said, 'Don't you know it isn't done to send telegrams? Mr Burge was most distressed to receive yours. His mother hasn't been well and so he was extremely worried. He wants to have a word with you. He'll see you at twelve o'clock today.'

When I got to the BBC Stuart Burge started to give me a hard time – 'How dare you send a telegram? How dare you impugn my integrity?' I just let him rant on until he asked, 'What do you know about this play?'

'Nothing,' I said. Figuring I'd nothing to lose, I went on, 'That's the way it is with people like me. Do you know what I did last night? I walked home from the restaurant where I work so I'd save the quid taxi fare. I've acted in the West End, at Liverpool Playhouse, at Manchester Library – but I can't get to see you guys. The actors you use for North Country plays are a disgrace. It's all "Ee, by gum", and that kind of junk. It's terrible.'

Then he asked me about my attitude to trade unions and that led us on to talking about politics. He was a fascinating and able man and we were getting on well together. Suddenly he asked, 'Are you sure you don't know what this play is about?'

'I haven't a clue. How should I know? I just met a guy in a pub who said you were doing a North Country play. That's all I know.'

'All right. I'll tell you what I'll do,' he said, handing me a script. 'Here's the play. Take it home and read it. Come back and see me at ten o'clock tomorrow. Then I want you to read the part of John – the big speech on page thirty-six.'

As soon as I got out of the place, I started reading the play. It was a ninety-minute *Play for Today* and John was on every page. Everything I'd been saying to Stuart Burge, John said in the play. Every attitude John adopted was mine. It was just as though the play had been written for me. By the time I'd got back to Notting Hill, I'd finished it. I loved it, but thought, 'Will the BBC ever give the leading part in such a play to an unknown actor?' Part-time waiter becomes star! That kind of thing just doesn't happen. I hadn't even got an agent – I was muddling along, not seeming to know my arse from my elbow.

But I worked on the speech and on Wednesday morning went back to the BBC. As I walked in, Stuart Burge said, 'Well?'

'Well, it's me, isn't it?' I said.

'Yes. I think it is.'

'It is. It's everything I believe. It's the way I am.'

'OK. Read the big speech.'

I did. He asked me to read some more – and then some more. I ended up nearly reading the whole play.

Then Stuart Burge said, 'This is terrible.'

'Oh, yes,' I said, waiting for the put-down. 'I know. . . '

'No, believe me. The situation is that the play is on offer. It's on offer to Patrick McGoohan. Now I'm going to be totally honest with you. It's now twelve-thirty. I've given his agent till three o'clock this afternoon to accept it or reject it. The point is he's asking for so much money that the BBC can't afford it. We've gone to our limit. If he turns it down, you've got the part and you start rehearsing on Monday. If Patrick McGoohan accepts, then I'm sorry – that's it.'

'Well if he settles, is there anything else?'

'No. I'm sorry – it's an all or nothing. I only see you as John. I don't see you playing anything else. There's nothing more I can do till three o'clock. Give me your phone number.'

Tom and I didn't have a phone at our place in Pembridge Mews. So I had to give him the number of the public telephone box on the corner.

'I'll ring you before four o'clock,' he said, 'to let you know one way or the other.'

'It'll definitely be before four? 'Cause I've got things to do,' I said, even though the only thing I had to do that night was work in the Soup Kitchen. But I wanted to be outside the phone box when he called.

'Definitely,' he said. 'Before four, I promise!'

As I walked out of his office, I felt sick with anxiety.

Back at Notting Hill Gate, I began pacing up and down outside the call box at two o'clock. I waited and I waited and I waited. Three o'clock arrived, three-thirty, four, four-thirty, five – nothing! I had to fight to keep people out – 'You can't go in there! It's out of order. A dog's just been sick on the floor!' I was having a hell of a time – it was the only phone box on a busy street.

At five o'clock, I knew I'd blown it.

I went to the Soup Kitchen, worked half a shift, they gave me a quid, I went off, met a friend of mine, and I got legless. About eleven o'clock at night, I met a young actress I knew, told her the whole story. She took pity on me, very kindly invited me back to her place, and consoled me. I stayed with her that night and all Thursday, until it was time for me to start work at the Soup Kitchen. It was two o'clock on Friday morning before I arrived back again at the mews.

At ten o'clock, there was a loud bang on the door. I staggered downstairs and was handed a telegram: 'RING STUART BURGE IMMEDIATELY.'

'What to tell me?' I thought. 'That I haven't got the part?' I'd got a hangover and so I decided to go back to bed and ring him at lunchtime.

A couple of hours later, I went to the call box and got through to Stuart Burge's secretary. She was almost hysterical: 'It's you! Don't go! Stay where you are! I'm putting you straight through!'

'Tony Booth?' Stuart Burge said.

'Yes,' I said. 'And before you say anything, I understand. I wish you luck. I'd really liked to have worked with you.'

'No, no, no. Don't hang up!'

'What's the matter?'

'Patrick McGoohan turned it down! You've got the part! I've been trying to get you for two days. What sort of house do you live in? You've got some very odd people answering your phone!'

'It's a large house and a lot of people . . . ' I said, and then, 'What do you mean, I've got the part?'

'I can't pay you much!'

'Don't worry! I'll take it!'

I went straight round to see him and was told that I'd be paid one hundred guineas for playing the lead.

In those days, actors didn't receive their money until the programme was finished. That meant I would have to spend three weeks rehearsing the lead in a play without any cash in my pocket. I couldn't afford to do that and so I used to arrive at rehearsals at ten in the morning and work until Stuart Burge let us finish – which wasn't usually until six or seven in the evening. Then I'd go straight on the bus to the Soup Kitchen, where I'd do a stint on the tables until two in the morning. I'd get up bog-eyed and set off for the next rehearsal at ten.

At lunchtimes, I could never afford to buy a round and so everybody thought I was a tight-wad. But all the cash I had was the quid I'd earned from the previous night's work. There was no way I could buy the rest of the cast the large gins and Martinis they were downing.

But the rehearsals went well and the play was terrific. Written by Roddy Barry, the son of Bertrand Russell, it was called *Pay Day* and was based on his experiences as a Bevan Boy down the mines during the war. In his last week at work, there was the first accident there'd been in that pit for fifty years. It left him paralysed from the waist down.

The play was recorded all in one piece. At the end, John – the character I played – leaves the pit and goes to London. In the last scene, John burns his pit boots in the station waiting-room. I did my speech, put the boots on the fire – but they didn't burn. We tried five or six times – still the boots didn't burn. Then we ran out of time.

I was the only actor involved and so they decided the only thing they could do was to book a studio on another day for fifteen minutes to film the scene again. That meant being given a double fee! I went along to the studio and once again the boots wouldn't burn. For fifteen minutes they tried, but when the time was up there was nothing for it but to go away and book the studio for another try. The third time, you should have seen the boots burn! They had to call the studio fire brigade to control the blaze! But I was given another fee. That meant I actually received three hundred guineas for playing the part!

In the week before the play was transmitted, I wrote to the six biggest theatrical agents, asking them to watch it. Four of them answered saying they would.

The play went out at nine o'clock on a Sunday evening. I set off in good time to see it on a friend's television. As I was crossing London, everybody was going out! 'What are you doing?' I wanted to ask them. 'Why are you going out? There's a great play on television. Go back home!'

When I returned home the next morning, telegrams had arrived from all four of the agents – all asking me to do nothing until I'd spoken to them. I went to see the four of them and it was at that time I learnt a most important lesson for an actor or actress – never take an agent just because you like the person; always accept the agent who's keenest to represent you. The best agent I ever had was one who couldn't stand me – we barely spoke to each other.

This time I made the mistake of accepting the agent who flattered me and bought me a few drinks. I signed a contract with him on Friday. When I went to his office the following Monday, I discovered he'd left and had flown off to Hollywood. I was thrown with somebody else who didn't want me. I was with him for nine months, during which he found me barely any work, even though *Pay Day* was runner-up in the *Prix d'Italia* and I was nominated for actor of the year.

Fortunately, the day after *Pay Day* was transmitted, I was offered and accepted a part in *The Life of the Party*. I was to be given a hundred pounds a week – which was big money. If I'd had a pound less, I'd have also been paid for rehearsals. I didn't know that and so I accepted the hundred – another lesson!

The rehearsals went on for a month. During that time, I spent the days working like hell on the play at the Lyric Theatre, Hammersmith. Then each evening I did a stint in the Soup Kitchen to earn enough money for the fares and my keep.

Alan Badel played the other lead. As an actor, I like eye contact, but Alan never looked me in the eye. At the time, he was the big star and I was the kid who'd just done one television play – so I didn't really know how to deal with this. I spoke about it to the director, who promised to have a word with Alan. But in rehearsals he continued to look at my hairline, at my chest, or over my shoulder – anywhere but into my eyes.

During the rehearsal period, I was losing weight rapidly and not getting much sleep. Not only was I working in the theatre and waiting on tables, but I was conducting an active love life. With far more lust than good sense, I had three regular girlfriends. What free time I had was spent with them – separately, of course. So most of the time I was knackered. It was perhaps because of this that Alan's behaviour really phased me.

One lunchtime, I asked him if we could have lunch together. I said to him, 'Look, Alan. I've got to level with you. Why don't you ever look me in the eye?'

'I can't,' he replied.

'Why?'

'Because the last person I looked in the eye was on my twenty-first birthday and his head was in my hands.'

'What d'you mean?'

'I was a Commando during the war and on my twenty-first birthday I was on a raid. I went to strangle a young German guard. As I pulled on the wire, his head spun round and when he died this young kid was staring into my eyes. Now I can't look anybody else in the eye. All I'd see is that young German guard.'

Can you imagine how I felt? Poor Alan! What a terrible experience.

We continued rehearsing with Alan avoiding any eye contact.

On the Friday, ten days before we were due to open, I was feeling very hungry. 'Sod it,' I thought, 'I'm going to have fish and chips for lunch!' I wolfed them down and got a fish bone lodged in my throat. When I went back to the theatre in the afternoon, I was gagging all the time. The director, a man called Frith Banbury, wouldn't stop for an earthquake. His line was, 'So you've got a fish bone caught in your throat. Well, carry on!'

So I carried on. At the end of the rehearsal, I rang the Soup Kitchen to say that I wouldn't be going into work. I went straight to the Eye, Nose and Throat Hospital in Golden Square where a doctor examined my throat. He told me that I needed an operation.

'Is it going to be a long job?' I asked.

'No,' he said. 'We'll do it tomorrow morning and you'll be out in the afternoon.'

That suited me fine. For the first time, there were to be no rehearsals that Saturday, because Alan had to be somewhere else. But we were going into the theatre on Sunday. So I stayed in the hospital that night. It was great – I slept between clean sheets, had a bath and a good meal.

The next morning, I had the operation and I came round from the anaesthetic late Saturday afternoon. I opened my eyes and tried to speak – but there was nothing. Not a sound! As I was gesticulating wildly, a nurse came along and said, 'Oh, you've lost your voice, haven't you? It often happens. But you'll be all right. The surgeon didn't find anything in your throat.'

She then passed me a pad and I wrote, 'How long before I can speak?'

'Four or five days,' she announced.

I wrote again: 'I'm opening in a play in nine days' time.'

'Fat chance,' she said. 'Now go back to sleep.'

Then I passed out. Later that evening, I asked the nurse to phone Frith Banbury to tell him what had happened. I only knew the number of the theatre so she couldn't ring him till the following morning, when I should have been at rehearsal.

At lunchtime on Sunday, Frith arrived at the hospital. I still couldn't utter a sound. I went blue in the face trying to make a single squeak.

Frith barked at me, 'What are you doing here? You should be at the theatre. Get out of that bed!'

Desperately I mimed that I'd lost my voice.

'Don't be so ridiculous,' he said. 'Get out of bed!'

The nurse assured him that my voice had gone and that I'd be out of action for at least five days.

'All right,' Frith said to me. 'I'll put on the understudy, but you be back as soon as you can.'

At that stage in the rehearsals, I hadn't been all that brilliant, but the understudy must have been disastrous, because, at nine o'clock on Tuesday morning, Frith arrived at the hospital and said, 'Get dressed. I'm taking you to a specialist in Harley Street.'

Off we went to see the theatrical throat doctor, who had beautiful waved hair, the most elegant of manners and a wry sense of humour. The first thing he said to me was, 'Been down on a wrong 'un, have you?'

Then he peered down my throat. 'Jesus Christ!' he exclaimed. 'What butcher have you allowed to operate in here? Whoever it was has massacred your throat!'

I couldn't do anything but shrug my shoulders.

'When do you open?' he asked.

'A week today,' I croaked.

'A month today – maybe! I'll do what I can, but I'm afraid this butchery is not a very good advertisement for the National Health!'

He proceeded to put what seemed to be a flaming torch down my throat. That gave me breath that would stop a dragon at a thousand paces.

'How are you now?' he asked.

I squeaked a reply.

'Ah, you made a noise!' he said. 'Get to rehearsal.'

It was half-past eleven when I arrived by taxi. Everybody was standing around waiting for me. We started with the first scene, but it was all utterly ridiculous. I could barely make a croak. But the director insisted on going through the whole thing. We didn't finish till six o'clock. There was no way I could go in to work at the Soup Kitchen. All I could do was to catch the tube back to my place and crash out.

I went every day to see the doctor in Harley Street and bit by bit my voice got a little better. By the time it came to the dress rehearsal on Sunday, I could manage a loud whisper. It was farcical. It was an Australian play and I was supposed to drink cans of Foster's lager. But, because of my throat, it made me feel sick. They had to place buckets at every exit so that when I'd taken a drink I could rush off and throw up.

On the first night, Alan Badel was superb and his notices were

82

brilliant. But I was inaudible, I frequently had to dash off the stage and, at each interval, the throat doctor was spraying my throat with a blowlamp. It was, therefore, my fault that the play wasn't a success and we closed after a fortnight.

9

Escapes and Escapades

A few weeks later, Tom Bell landed a part in a film and left the mews. For a while I hung on to the place by the skin of my teeth, but eventually I had to give it up and I moved to a flat in Notting Hill Gate. My agent continued to avoid finding me a part and so after a further six months I found myself another agent. Almost immediately I was offered a part in *Coronation Street*, which had only just started.

In those days, actors received their expenses only after they'd travelled. Now Manchester is Manchester and there was no way I had enough money for the fare from London. I went to see my agent and asked to borrow ten pounds. He sat me down and gave me a long lecture about why it was the policy of the agency never to lend any money to an actor. Apparently, Robert Donat had been given an advance of twenty-five thousand pounds for a film he was going to make, but he died before shooting commenced and the agency never recovered any of their money.

I didn't know anybody who could lend me the money. I did my stint at the Soup Kitchen on a Saturday night, left at two o'clock in the morning, and started hitching to Manchester. There was hardly any traffic about, it was peeing down with rain and I had to walk at least fifty miles. I arrived there at seven o'clock on Monday morning like a drowned rat.

I was just in time for the start of rehearsals and, of course, one of the first people I met was Pat Phoenix. Things were a bit strained between us. I thought she was a bit snooty and she told me later that I seemed distant. She was involved with someone else and it was clear that there was no possibility of our relationship being rekindled. We didn't say much to each other. But I did tell her what had happened and she took me to see the production assistant so I could ask for an advance.

'Yes, of course,' he said. 'How much do you want? Will fifty be all right?'

For a moment I thought he meant fifty shillings, but he gave me fifty pounds, for which I was extremely grateful.

I did four episodes, which in those days went out live. A fortnight later, on a Friday, I returned to London on the train with Arthur Lowe. His mother had packed his case and a picnic box for him. He opened up the case to show me. It had everything in it – long johns, pyjamas and clean shirts. 'Do you know how old I am?' he said. 'And she still treats me like a bloody schoolboy!' But I was very grateful to Arthur Lowe's mother for the wonderful supper she'd prepared for her son and which I ate on the way back to London.

Two days later, on the Monday, the actors' strike began. Apart from those who were already under contract, all actors and actresses – including me – were out of work for the next nine months. During that time, I did what I could to keep body and soul together – working on building sites and other casual work. There were also times when I just played the familiar role of unemployed actor.

My first floor flat at Notting Hill Gate had a balcony on which I often used to sit, catching the sun. One afternoon, towards the end of October, during one of those mellow Indian summers, I was lounging out there when the French windows of the flat next but one to mine opened. Out on to the balcony walked a vision of a girl. I thought, 'My God. She lives so close and I've never clapped eyes on her before. What the hell have I been doing all this time?'

I waved and smiled. She smiled and waved back.

After a while she went in and shortly afterwards I saw her leave the building. So I dressed and rushed downstairs. I managed to catch her up, we got talking and arranged to meet for dinner that night.

It was a most enjoyable evening, especially as we ended up in bed together. She said that she'd like to see me again, but she wasn't a free agent. She was being kept by a well-known actor, whose name she couldn't possibly tell me. It was all very embarrassing, she told me, but she had to be on call in case he rang. However, any night he wasn't coming to see her, she'd be delighted if I'd call round. Well that suited me down to the ground, because I'd a couple of other girlfriends I needed time to visit.

Our casual love affair continued as a heavy winter set in.

One night I'm in bed when the phone rings and she says, 'I've just had a call and he's not coming round tonight. Why don't you come over? It's freezing and I badly need warming!'

'I'm cold too,' I tell her. 'I'll be there in two minutes!'

I scamper over to her place and we make love. Afterwards, we're lying in bed when the front door opens, then slams, and I hear the unmistakable voice of Peter Finch singing. It's only going to be moments before he's in the room and there's going to be a confrontation – and I'm naked, which is no way to be when trying to give an irate actor whom you admire an acceptable reason why you're in bed with his mistress!

She panics, jumps out of bed, and hisses, 'Get out on the balcony. I'll take him into the kitchen. Then you can come back in, pick up your clothes and get out!' With that, she shoves me straight on to the balcony and closes the French windows. It's just in time, because at that moment Finch comes through the bedroom door.

'Darling!' he rumbles, opens his arms and advances towards her. She's standing with her back to the French windows. I'm on the balcony – at two-thirty in the morning, ankle-deep in snow, freezing cold and stark naked. I'm all too aware that this isn't a good move on my part.

As I skulk out of view, hidden by the curtains, Finch grabs hold of her and says, 'You look so lovely standing there with the moonlight behind you!'

'Come on, Finchie,' I think, as my teeth begin to chatter, 'you can do better than that!'

She tries to drag him off to have a drink in the kitchen, but he'll have none of it. 'No, no, no,' he insists. 'Let's go to bed.'

'Oh, no,' I think, rigid with cold. 'Get him out of there so I can do my Tom-and-Jerry tiptoe off through the bedroom.'

But Finch has his way and they tumble on to the bed. By this time, I know that he's been drinking heavily and that there's no way he's going to have an orgasm for at least a day and a half.

I'm blue with cold, desperately holding on to the rapidly shrivelling remains of my manhood.

Looking across the next balcony, I could see that I'd left a fanlight open in my flat. There's only one thing I can do. I have to climb across the balconies and shin up the pipe through the window and get into bed, otherwise I'm going to be found dead, frozen into a solid block of ice.

But it was easier said than done. Because it was Notting Hill Gate, in order to discourage burglars, the railings were topped with spikes and above these was barbed wire.

It would have been hard enough at the best of times, but I had to set off in the dark, with snow on the ground, freezing cold, stark bollock-naked, trying desperately not to catch it on the barbed wire. Eventually, after a great deal of effort, I make it on to the next-door balcony. I'm gasping for breath like a beached walrus, my hands and my legs are scraped and dripping with blood – I'm in a hell of a state.

As I tiptoe past the French windows, I glance in and there on the bed is a fellow making love to a lady. At the same moment as I see her, she spies me strolling starkers past her window. She lets out a scream. Like a demented mountain goat, I leap over the spikes and the barbed wire on to the balcony of my flat and press myself against the wall, making myself as inconspicuous as possible.

The French windows of the neighbouring flat are flung open and on to the balcony I'd just left walks another naked man. 'You're out of your fucking mind,' he announces. 'What are you talking about – a naked man on the balcony? What are you – crackers?'

'But he's out there,' I hear this woman's voice say inside the flat. 'He was standing there looking at us. I saw him.'

He then turns round and says to her accusingly, 'Why did you have your eyes open? If you'd been enjoying it, they'd have been closed, wouldn't they?'

With this, he walks back inside and slams the doors. I'm still standing there, frozen in fear. I have to wait until I hear the bed rocking again before I try to shin up the drainpipe. Believe me, stark naked it ain't an easy task!

After a good ten minutes – and I was young and fit then – I manage to climb through the pivoted fanlight and I fall flat onto the parquet floor, almost killing myself. I lie there for about five minutes before I drag myself to the kitchen, drink the remains of a bottle of brandy, put on pyjamas, socks, jeans, two sweaters and a pair of gloves. Then I clamber into bed, because I'm still shaking all over with cold and my teeth are chattering.

I've just settled down, when the front-door buzzer goes. I think, 'Oh, hell, no! It's Finch. She's told him and so it's going to be pistols at dawn!'

Reluctantly, I get out of bed and turn on the intercom.

A voice whispers, 'Is that Tony Booth?'

'Yes.'

Another whisper: 'This is the police here.'

'Yes?'

'We don't want to frighten you, but there's a burglar in your flat.'

'You're kidding!'

'No, we're not. And not only that – he's stark naked! Are you alone?'

'I bloody hope so!'

'Well you'd better let us in and we'll search the flat.'

So I press the button to unlock the front door and rip off my socks, jeans, sweaters and gloves. Then I put on an old dressing-gown and open the door to my flat.

These two guys are standing there. 'Don't turn the lights on,' one says.

'OK.'

They switch on torches and start peering around. 'He's in here somewhere.'

But it's only a one-bedroom flat and so it doesn't take them long to search the place, although they look everywhere, even under the bed.

'He's not here,' they say at last. 'It's all right. He obviously scarpered because he knew you were a fellow. Must have been looking for a woman. That means we'll have to search all the other flats – just in case.'

I walk with them to the door. 'Who told you about this alleged naked robber?' I ask.

'An old lady opposite – in her seventies, she is,' one of the coppers says confidentially, 'got up to go to the toilet, glanced out of her window and reckoned she saw a naked man climbing into your flat. Not only that. She claims there was not just one, but two naked men. Apparently, she saw another one on your neighbour's balcony!'

'Must be out of her tiny mind,' I assure them as they leave. 'Even brass monkeys wouldn't be seen dead wandering around starkers on a night like this!'

That was the last night I spent with Peter Finch's mistress!

Shortly afterwards, the actors' strike was settled. That very day, my agent rang me up and said, 'They want you to go back on *Coronation Street.*'

Before the strike, working on *Coronation Street* I'd earned a hundred pounds a show – so for the two shows in the week I was paid two hundred pounds. At the time, the permanent cast were only on fifty quid a week. So I was well paid. We were told that the post-strike deal meant that actors would receive four times the fee they'd previously been earning.

'That's fantastic,' I said to my agent. 'Nine months out of work and now I'm going to be paid eight hundred pounds a week!' It was a fortune.

'I'll find out,' he said. A short while later he rang me back and said, 'The fee's fifty pounds.'

'So that's fifty pounds for each show?' I asked.

'No – fifty a week, for both shows.'

'Hang on a minute,' I said. 'According to the new agreement I get four times the fee. So it's fifty quid times four – two hundred quid a week. That's exactly what I was earning before the strike. Tell them seventy-five quid times four and it's a deal.'

He said he'd get in touch with them again. But five minutes later, he rang me back. 'You've got it all wrong,' he said. 'The fee they're offering is fifty quid – not times four or anything like that. It's a straight fifty quid a week.'

'So after a nine-month strike, they're offering me a quarter of the fee I was paid before?'

'That's it,' he said. 'And they say you can take it or leave it.'

'Tell them to stuff it,' I said, thinking they'd come back. They didn't. It was twenty-six years later before I next appeared on *Coronation Street*!

However, in the aftermath of the actors' strike my television career began to take off. My agent kept me solidly in work. I became the rent-a-villain. One week I'd be in *Z Cars*, the next week in *No Hiding Place*, and the following week in *The Saint* – that kind of thing. It was – for me – unbelievably regular work. For the first time in my life I began earning real bread.

There was also film work. During the early sixties, the studios loved testing actors and actresses for film parts. In my opinion this was due to their sadism – they had no intention of using any of them. They'd already made up their minds who was being given the part. But they could satisfy Equity and the public that they'd searched high and low for exactly the right man or woman.

I went along to one of these tests and afterwards the director said to me, 'Next week, we're testing actresses. It's a bedroom scene. Would you like to come and play the man in the scene? We'll pay you a hundred pounds a day for the week.'

'How many actresses are there?' I inquired.

'We're doing one an hour, six hours a day. That means there'll be thirty.'

'You mean you're going to pay me five hundred quid to go to bed with thirty girls?'

'Yes.'

'You've got it,' I said. This was more like it!

I had a thoroughly enjoyable week. At the end of it, I was asked if I wanted more. I did! For about a year, whenever there were tests, I was employed by the studio, just as the tease is for the stallion in a stud. I did the trials – the stars did the performance! But I went to bed with a lot of actresses – all in the name of art.

Once, through working as a tease, I did land a part in the film, *Mix Me a Person*. It starred the American actress, Anne Baxter, whose many films included *All About Eve*, for which she'd been nominated for an Oscar. But in this film she was supposed to play a Cockney psychiatrist – such is the mystery of film casting! Although she spoke about her childhood in the East End, her attempts to speak with a Cockney accent were soon knocked on the head. Donald Sinden was her husband and the young lead was played by Adam Faith, who was then a successful pop singer. The director was Leslie Norman, the father of – and not many people know this! – Barry Norman, the film buff. I was cast as a young heavy, with the memorable name of Gravy Browning, who in one scene in the film had to force his attentions on a young woman.

When we came to play that particular scene, the girl suddenly became very shy about having me tear her clothes off and throw her into bed. So the director ordered a closed set – which means that only essential crew are allowed to be present. But there's an enigma in films – they're called *standby* electricians, *standby* painters, *standby* carpenters. Nobody ever sees them until it's a closed set and then they appear, knowing that the actors are up to no good!

On a closed set, there is total silence. The actress was obviously extremely embarrassed by the fate worse than death which was about to befall her in the shape of me having my filthy way with her. After I'd taken off her clothes and pulled her into bed, the cameras were stopped, a dressing-gown was held open for her, she got out of bed, put on a pair of jeans, climbed back into bed and we recommenced filming.

In between my chewing her ear, fondling her shoulder and the other things that men do at moments like that, she had her lines. As she spoke, I heard really heavy breathing.

'Stop,' they said. 'We must do it again.'

This time I knew there wasn't a dog under the bed! I thought, 'No wonder she's getting more and more upset. Some dirty bastard is enjoying this far more than he should be.' It really was unacceptable. The guy was practically having an orgasm.

We did the scene several times and during every take there was heavy breathing. Eventually, Leslie Norman decided to cut and print.

The dresser appeared with a voluminous dressing-gown. The actress pulled it on and fled. I wasn't allowed that privilege. Not the entire crew, but the greater majority stood round the bed where I was lying face downwards.

'You can get out now, Tony!' they said.

'I'm all right,' I said. 'I'll leave it a while.'

'No, no. You can get out now!'

'It's all right. I'm exhausted.'

The bedclothes were dragged off and I desperately tried to cover the hard evidence that I'd entered so thoroughly into the scene.

In self defence I said, 'What about that dirty bugger who was doing the heavy breathing! Which one of you was that?'

'No, Tony. It wasn't us,' they all protested.

Leslie Norman said, 'Well I could hear it. I don't know who it was, but it was disgusting. But don't worry. We'll overlay it with music.'

Someone at last brought me a dressing-gown and away I went.

The next day, I went to see the rushes of the bedroom scene. As soon as the actress and I were in bed, the heavy breathing was clearly audible. I was just about to turn to Leslie Norman and say, 'Hear that!' when I realized who was doing the heavy breathing. It was me! I was doing the heavy breathing. I was the dirty bugger! No wonder the actress fled!

There was a big opening night for the film in the West End. The bedroom scene was in the picture and even I shifted uncomfortably in my seat. Everybody to this day is convinced that I was actually making love, but I know the actress was wearing jeans and there is no way that I was doing it. But it certainly sounded and looked as though I was!

Later that week, when the reviews came out, Alexander Walker commented on the highly erotic scene that had obviously been added to the film. On the Sunday, Dilys Powell attacked me personally. On Monday they cut the scene out of the picture!

During this period, I was involved – as I have been most of my life – with several left-wing movements. During a CND demonstration in Trafalgar Square, I was picked up by the police and – purely by chance – slung into the same van as the playwright, John Osborne. We were taken to Bow Street police station.

The duty sergeant looked at us and said to a constable, 'This is John Osborne, writer, and Anthony Booth, actor. Put the bleeding intellectuals into the same cell!'

It pleased me no end, but I think Osborne was slightly offended that he'd been lumped in with me!

They took us down to a cell and slammed the door. Already in there was the writer, John Arden. About ten minutes later, we were talking away when the cell door opened and in was ushered Bertrand Russell. A hush fell!

'Oh, hello there, Bertrand. Can we help you?'

'Not at all,' he said in his precise little voice. 'I'm quite all right, thank you. Don't worry.'

The three of us immediately agreed that Bertrand Russell, the revered old man, should have the one bed in the cell.

When it was offered to him, he said, 'Thank you. But do you mind if I do something first?'

'Not at all,' we said. It was a marvellous moment for me. There I was, locked in a cell with these three intellectual giants. What a stimulating evening it was going to be!

Bertrand Russell undid his trousers and dropped them to the floor. Then he pulled down his long johns. He had wrapped around him, dhoti-fashion, a blanket, which he duly took off. 'She told me to wear it,' he said, 'because, you see, sitting on a cold pavement you get terrible piles! There's also a risk that you will be arrested, and they don't give you very clean blankets in these cells. So, this way, I've always got my own blanket!'

He pulled up his long johns and then his trousers. He lay down on the bed, pulled the blanket over him, and promptly went to sleep! The rest of us then kept quiet. That was the end of our intellectual evening!

While I was living at Notting Hill Gate, I also got to know the Hampstead intellectual set who spent Sunday afternoons at each other's houses discussing politics, sex and religion. One Sunday I was invited to the home of Donald Ogden Stewart – the American scriptwriter who received an Oscar for *The Philadelphia Story* and was then blacklisted in Hollywood in the McCarthy anti-Communist witch-hunt. He was living in the Hampstead house that had once belonged to Ramsay MacDonald.

I went because I was interested in the free food, free drink and free love. At such gatherings, the women were always splendid – blue-stocking chic. It was a beautiful summer's day and everybody was doing their bit on the lawn. After downing a few glasses of wine, I wanted a pee and asked where I could find the nearest lavatory. I was directed to one through the study. As I was standing there having a wee, I glanced up and on the wall saw what I took to be copies of two beautiful paintings by Picasso and Pissarro.

When I got back out on to the lawn, I said to a guy there, 'You Hampstead lot really are something! Fancy having a Picasso in the downstairs bog. It might be a reproduction, but it's brilliant!'

This guy looked at me and said, 'It isn't a repro. It's real.'

'Oh, bugger off! What do you take me for?'

'No, seriously. Haven't you had a look round the rest of the house?'

'No.'

'Well go now. Start in the study. You'll find the whole house is full of masterpieces of modern art.'

I went back into the house and began looking carefully at the incredible paintings that covered the walls. As I was walking out of the study, I bumped into Donald Ogden Stewart.

'I was just admiring your paintings,' I said.

'Oh, do you like them? If you're interested, I'll tell you how I got them. Come into the study and have a drink.'

We sat down and then he told me the most remarkable story.

After he was forced to leave America in the early fifties, he received an invitation to spend some time in the USSR. First he and his wife flew to France, where his royalties had been mounting up. Owing to the tight postwar exchange controls, he'd been unable to transfer them out of the country. So he intended to spend the lot during a week in Paris, before flying on to the USSR where he'd also got royalties.

As soon as they arrived, his wife said, 'I've always wanted to buy some French lingerie. Can't I just buy a few things while we're here?'

'Darling, do what you like,' he said. 'We've got a mountain of French francs that have to be spent.'

She went out and bought about five thousand dollars' worth of the best silk lingerie, nightdresses and negligees. These were all parcelled up and taken with them on their flight to the USSR.

When they arrived at Moscow Airport, they were greeted by a reception committee, headed by the Minister of Culture and his wife. They escorted the Ogden Stewarts to their hotel. As the Minister was running through the proposed programme of receptions with Donald, the two women went off into the bedroom. Suddenly there was a scream. Both men jumped up. The bedroom door opened and standing there was the Minister of Culture's wife, rigged out in French knickers, frilly bra, suspender belt and silk stockings – the whole works. She was ecstatic and when she was told that she could have them as a present from the Ogden Stewarts she burst into tears of gratitude. And understandably so – such finery was unknown at that time in the USSR.

Later that evening, at an official reception, Marshall Zukov sidled up to Donald and said that his girlfriend had been shown the exotic underwear being worn by the Minister of Culture's wife.

'Is there any chance,' he asked, 'that I might be given say a pair of knickers for my girlfriend?'

'Sure,' Donald said, knowing they'd got more than enough.

But after a couple of days, the whole thing had become extremely embarrassing. Everywhere they went, somebody or other would be begging for an article from their cache of French lingerie. So Donald had a word with the Minister of Culture. 'This can't go on,' he said. 'It's really getting out of hand. It's very difficult for us to say no to any of these famous people. But soon there won't even be anything left for my wife.'

'I understand,' the Minister of Culture said. 'You have been most generous to my friends. I have a proposal for you. You give everything that remains to me. In exchange, I shall give you for each item a modern Western painting of your choice.'

'How can you do that?' Donald asked incredulously.

'It's simple. Stalin hates modern Western art. He says it is decadent. We have whole storehouses full of such paintings, just locked away. You can help yourself. I shall take you tomorrow so that you can see for yourself.'

The next day, the Minister of Culture arrived and as they were being driven through Moscow he said to Donald, 'There is only one condition. You may select only two paintings by each artist. Apart from that you may take what you wish. How many articles do you have left?'

'About fifty.'

'Then you must select fifty paintings.'

And that is what Donald did. From the USSR, he and his wife flew to London, where they took up residence in Hampstead. The paintings arrived with their baggage and decorated the walls of their house. Whenever they became desperately short of money, they sold one. But, when I last visited their home, most of them were still there – including masterpieces by Picasso, Pissarro, Monet, Matisse, Renoir, and Gauguin.

I know that during the war, American servicemen often got a hell of a lot in exchange for a pair of silk stockings, but there can't have been any who struck a better deal than Donald Ogden Stewart!

10

Film Fun

In 1963, when I was an established rent-a-villain, I received a telephone call from Seven Arts inviting me to call at their offices to meet the famous director Henry Hathaway, whose many films included *How The West Was Won*. He was about to direct a remake of Somerset Maugham's *Of Human Bondage*, with Kim Novak and Laurence Harvey.

I went to see Hathaway. We liked each other immediately and he gave me quite a good part as one of Kim Novak's boyfriends. The film was being shot in Ireland and I was guaranteed three weeks' work over three months. As it wasn't known when I'd be required, I was to be paid from the day shooting started a weekly retainer of two hundred pounds a week. In the mid-sixties that was a considerable sum of money that could buy you a fair stack of salt-beef sandwiches. I would also be paid extra for every day I was filming.

I returned with delight to my flat in Notting Hill and read the script. I'd got a couple of juicy scenes with Kim Novak and so I waited in eager anticipation. Ten days later, a cheque for two hundred pounds, minus my agent's ten per cent commission, landed on my mat – my first week's retainer. Another week passed and the same thing happened again. I'd made three hundred and sixty quid and I hadn't shifted my arse! 'This is the life,' I thought.

During the third week, I was called to fly to Ireland on the Saturday so I could meet Hathaway, discuss my part and start filming the following Monday. At Dublin airport, I was picked up by a car and driven to my hotel. It was a beautiful country house that was up in the hills above Ardmore and approached only by a long, winding road. The views were breathtaking.

I arrived wearing my only suit, which in the mid-sixties was the height of fashion. It had a high velvet collar and a long flowing jacket. Clutching my battered holdall, I walked into the hotel lobby, where I was met by Henry Hathaway.

'That's great,' he said. 'You're wearing the costume! That's perfect.'

'No, no,' I said. 'It's mine.'

'OK. So it's yours. We'll hire it! I'll pay you ten pounds a day for your suit!'

Even though I was somewhat miffed that he thought my clothes were so old-fashioned they'd do for *Of Human Bondage*, I accepted with alacrity.

Later, over dinner, I had an interesting conversation with Henry Hathaway about Hollywood and the Oscar awards which were just about to be made.

'Everybody knows the awards are a carve up,' I said.

Hathaway didn't take kindly to this and said, 'How dare you? I'm a member of the panel and I can tell you they're not.'

'Come on,' I said. 'I bet you voted for a film made by the last studio you worked for, didn't you?'

'Maybe,' he said.

'Well that's how it's carved up. That's why a great actor like Brando hasn't received an Oscar, whereas others get it for playing the game or just reaching a certain age.'

Our animated but amicable discussion about the Oscar awards went on for hours and before we knew where we were it was two in the morning and we had to be on set first thing. So we both retired to get a few hours' sleep before getting up at the crack of dawn for what was to be my first day on the film.

When I arrived at the studio, I discovered that I wasn't needed till ten o'clock. Then we began a scene in which Kim Novak played the part of a Cockney waitress in a tearoom. I was introduced to her, a most pleasant lady. Henry Hathaway greeted me with a growl and told me he'd got a monumental hangover and that I'd disillusioned him about the whole film industry so that when he returned to Hollywood he was going to dig deep for any signs of corruption.

We started rehearsing the scene. Kim was very nervous, because Hathaway was growling like a bear with a sore head. Her Cockney accent left a lot to be desired – so much so that when she said her first line I had to stop myself laughing. She made Dick Van Dyke in *Mary Poppins* sound like Bob Hoskins!

In the scene, Kim Novak was standing by the table at which I was sitting. After four or five lines of dialogue, Hathaway turned to me and said, 'Have you ever heard anything like it in your Goddamn life?'

I said, 'What?'

'The accent! For Christ's sake, she's supposed to be a Cockney!'

Poor Kim just stood there. I felt it best not to say anything.

'If that's Cockney,' Hathaway continued, 'I'd hate to hear what a mess she'd make of any other accent. I've suffered this for three weeks. I can't take any more of it. Where is the dialogue coach? Mind you, she needs more than a dialogue coach. She needs a head coach.'

It was an extraordinary outburst.

Then he said, 'Carry on!'

I delivered my line: 'I'll have crumpets and tea.'

Kim said, 'Anyfing else?'

Then Hathaway exploded: 'Anyfing else? Anyfing else? Anyfing else? Have you ever heard anything like it? Baby, not only can't you do an accent, you can't damn well act.'

I didn't know what was going on. The whole crew were standing there awestruck. Kim went bright red, but didn't move.

Hathaway leant across the table and said to me, 'I didn't want her. I wanted Liz Taylor. But I get this broad. You can see she can't act. So what would you do, Tony?'

I wished I was somewhere else. 'Don't involve me in this, Henry,' I said.

But that was only openers. He then set about demolishing Kim. It was a dreadful, unacceptable thing to do.

After a few minutes, I did pluck up enough courage to interrupt him: 'I think that's enough, Henry. We're just actors and we're only trying to do a job. You're upsetting Miss Novak.'

But there was no stopping him. He went on for another ten minutes and at one point I had to stand up and restrain him because it looked as though he was actually going to hit her.

He only ended his torrent of abuse when Kim burst into tears and ran off the set. Then he sat down next to me and shouted, 'Get me a coffee!' He put his arm around me and said, 'Am I glad I got that off my chest.' He called for the first assistant and told him: 'Get Novak back down here.' Then he embarked on a catalogue of the problems he'd encountered with the film and Kim in particular.

Eventually the message came back that Miss Novak would not leave her dressing-room.

'All right,' Hathaway said. 'We'll just sit here and wait.'

His continuing diatribe about the evils of the Hollywood system was eventually interrupted by the first assistant who said: 'Miss Novak has telephoned the producer and Ray Stark has driven from Dublin and is with her in her dressing-room. He wishes to see you, Mr Hathaway, in a few minutes.'

'Let's see if the little shit has the nerve to show his face on my set,' Hathaway responded.

I was caught in the chair with Hathaway's arm around me. He was going over our discussion about the Oscar awards when the doors opened and in came Ray Stark, a hard, silver-haired Hollywood producer who was wearing dark glasses and a scowl. He oozed power as he walked across the set and pointed to Hathaway. 'You,' he growled. 'You're fired. Get off the set.'

Hathaway stood up and threw the script in the air. 'Ha, ha, ha,' he said. 'You don't sack me. I quit!' He turned to me and said, 'Come on, Tony. Let's go!'

Then Hathaway walked. I stayed where I was.

Stark looked around and said, 'That's it. You can all go home. We'll be in touch when we're ready to start shooting.' Then off he went.

Everybody was stunned. I said to the first assistant, 'Now what happens?'

'You heard the man,' he said. 'Go back to the hotel.'

I went to my dressing-room, had lunch, and was driven back to the hotel, thinking, 'Oh, my God! What am I going to say to Henry Hathaway?'

He wasn't there. I was told that by the time he'd got back to the hotel his luggage had been packed and put on the drive outside. A taxi was waiting and had whisked him off to the airport.

In the evening, the first assistant arrived with my air ticket and the next day I flew back to London.

Weeks passed and every Tuesday a cheque for one hundred and eighty pounds arrived from Seven Arts.

One day, some ten weeks later, the phone rang. It was Jenia Riesser, the casting director for the film. 'Hello, Tony,' she said. 'What are you doing?'

'I've been waiting for you to call.'

She laughed and said, 'Well, I've got a part for you.'

'What's that?' I asked.

'In *Of Human Bondage*.'

'But I'm already in the film.'

'What do you mean?'

'Well I flew over to Dublin and that terrible thing happened with Hathaway.'

'Oh!' she said, 'there've been two directors since then! So do you still want to play the part?'

'I'd love to.'

'Great! Well, I'll get on to your agent and we'll talk about money.'

'But I'm already under contract!' Then, like a fool, I said, 'I receive a cheque every Tuesday.'

'Oh, my God! I'll ring you back.'

Half an hour later she phoned and said, 'That contract's cancelled!' If only I hadn't opened my big mouth, Seven Arts might still have been paying me a weekly cheque to this day!

However, the next contract gave me even more money than the first! I returned to Dublin to restart work on the film. When we met again, Kim Novak hailed me as her hero. She told everybody that not only had I been the only one who'd stood up for her when Hathaway had gone berserk but that I'd actually hit him!

The new director of the film was Ken Hughes, who with Bryan Forbes had totally rewritten the script. Ken was another Scouse and we got on well. The only problem for me was that, though he loved Kim, he hated Laurence Harvey. Every night at the hotel, he bent my ear about how impossible it was working with Harvey. 'Oh, no,' I thought. 'It's like being with Hathaway all over again!'

In the new script I had a fight scene with Laurence Harvey and Ken Hughes told me how much he was looking forward to it. 'I'll give you twice your daily rate,' he said, 'if you punch him in the gob!'

Everybody who went on the set was buttonholed by either Laurence or Ken and told how useless the other one was. No wonder it was such an unhappy picture. The final result is there for everybody to see. The film was a mess. It didn't make any money – and it didn't deserve to.

When I had my fight scene with Laurence Harvey, the tension on the set was unbelievable and I was piggy-in-the-middle. Half the crew and Ken were urging me to sock Laurence and the other half wanted me to punch Ken. When it came to the actual take where I was to hit him, Larry, instead of moving away from the punch, ducked into it and so, by accident, I did actually hit him. He went smack on his behind into a stack of dustbins. The crew cheered and burst into applause.

But Laurence Harvey was magnanimous in defeat – or at least I thought he was. We got on reasonably well. One day, he and I were talking and he said to me, 'How do you feel about clothes?'

'What do you mean?'

'Do you have many clothes?'

'Me? No. I'm not into that kind of thing.'

He said, 'Oh, I am. I love shoes.'

'Do you?'

'Yes. I've got hundreds of pairs. Last summer I was making a film in Spain and I had some fantastic shoes handmade there. They look wonderful. The only trouble is that they were sent on after I'd left and they don't fit. Can you believe it? They made a special last and I've got fifty pairs of shoes all different sizes. Only about a dozen fit me. How are you off for shoes?'

'Well, I've got the pair I'm wearing and another pair at the hotel and that's it.'

'I'll tell you what,' he said. 'Go to my dressing-room, tell my dresser I sent you and pick out whatever you like. Go on. It's OK.'

'Wow! Thanks, Larry. Do you really mean it?'

'Course I do. Go and help yourself. They're beautiful shoes.'

Off I went to his dressing-room. I quickly tried on half a dozen pairs. Laurence Harvey's feet were bigger than mine, but I figured I could stuff Kleenex in the toes and they'd be all right for wearing at interviews and funerals.

I was sitting there debating this when Larry came in. 'Stand up,' he said, 'and let's have a look.' I did as he asked and he said, 'They look great, don't they?'

'Yes. But they're a little big.'

'Don't worry about that. Do you want them?'

'Yes, please.'

'That's great. You can have them.'

'Well thanks, Larry.'

'How many pairs do you want?'

'Well, just those four there.'

'Great. They're yours. Fifty quid a pair!'

'What?'

'That's what they cost me.'

'You're kidding! I thought you were giving them away.'

'OK. I'll tell you what. We're both actors. You can have them for thirty quid a pair!'

I said, 'Larry, I wouldn't pay thirty quid for any of them. I've never paid thirty quid for a pair of shoes in my life.'

'Oh, well,' he said. 'Take them off then and piss off!'

One evening at the hotel I had a late dinner and I was alone at my table. Sitting close-by was a man, whose name was Alex Dandino. He'd moved from Glasgow to Dublin, where he was a successful businessman. He was an amazing character. In his late forties, he was goodlooking and dressed in a silky Italian suit, Gucci shoes and silk tie. His two female companions were young and beautiful.

He was drinking heavily and it wasn't difficult to overhear his conversation. I was totally fascinated by his accent, an incongruous and inimitable mixture of Italian, Glaswegian and Irish. In the space of a breath, he went from 'Mama Mia', to 'Yer ken what I mean, hen?' and 'Jesus, Mary and Joseph!' I gathered from what he was saying that one of the girls was his mistress and that the other was her sister, whom Alex desperately wanted to get into his bed. He was of the opinion that she was a virgin and, therefore, a most special prize for his Italian machismo. He told everybody, including each passing waiter, that he'd give anything to deflower this Irish maiden. But she wasn't having any and her sister, Alex's mistress, was more than a little pissed off by the whole thing.

After a while, Alex Dandino glanced over to my table, recognized me and asked if I'd like to join him and the girls for a brandy. I was fascinated by the whole set-up, which bordered on the ludicrous – a straight-laced mistress trying to fend off her lover's clumsy advances on her younger sister, while desperately trying not to antagonize him. So I joined them.

At midnight, as we left the dining room and repaired to the lounge for more drinks, Alex distributed largesse to all and sundry in the form of twenty-pound notes. When Alex weaved his way off to the lavatory, the younger girl said to me, 'Please don't go. As long as you're here he won't try anything on.'

Always easily persuaded by a pretty face, I stayed. Just after one o'clock in the morning, Alex fell into a drunken stupor on the settee. The younger girl said she was feeling tired. She asked if I'd mind taking her up to my room so she could rest. Then when Alex came to, her sister would call for her and they'd all drive back to Dublin. It was an offer I couldn't refuse!

I spent a couple of pleasurable hours in her company. I don't know where Alex got the idea from, but I can only say that the young lady was not a virgin! At three o'clock, her sister knocked on the door to say that Alex had recovered and was inquiring about the whereabouts of her sister.

I went with the hotel manager to see the three of them off. Outside the entrance was a large gravel courtyard, at the far side of which stood a solitary car – a brand new, white Rolls-Royce that was Alex's pride and joy. Beyond the courtyard, there was a sheer thirty-foot drop to a huge lawn which a week of almost continuous rain had turned into what, in the moonlight, could be seen to be a shimmering bog.

'Are you sure you're in a fit state to drive?' the manager asked Alex.

He insisted that he was.

'At least let me reverse the car back to the entrance,' I said.

Alex would have none of it. 'Nobody else is going to drive my car,' he said.

The girls got nervously into the back and Alex stumbled into the driving seat. He started the engine, lowered his window and waved goodbye. He threw the car into gear, took his foot off the brake, accelerated and the car shot off into the night, heading straight for the moon. For what seemed like an eternity, it hung in mid-air and then fell the thirty feet flat on to the lawn. Waves of spray cascaded into the air and the engine stalled.

The manager and I looked at each other in horror. 'Did you see that?' he said to me.

We slithered down the escarpment and squelched the sixty or so feet to where the car had sunk up to its axles, smack in the middle of the muddy lawn. By the best of good fortune, nobody was injured. The two girls were crying in the back and Alex Dandino was slumped over the wheel being sick. We dragged the three of them out and had the devil's own job getting them back up to the hotel.

I repaired with the two girls to my room so they could both have a bath, while Alex laid out on a settee and demanded a medicinal bottle of brandy, which he proceeded to drink. A taxi was called. When it arrived, Alex gave a wad of notes to the manager as compensation for the trouble he'd caused. Then he and the two girls, clad only in the hotel's bathrobes, were driven off to Dublin.

It was another three weeks before I finished work on the film. Every time I went off to the studio, I was driven round the lawn and the driver said, 'Doesn't that white Rolls-Royce look fine standing there? It's just like a monument. It's a modern Sphinx. That's what it is.'

God only knows how they ever dragged it out! But in my mind it stands there still – a constant reminder of a bizarre but most entertaining night!

11

Till Death. . .

During the campaign for the 1964 General Election, the Labour Party staged a vast rally at Wembley. I was invited to go along and do my little bit, reading telegrams and that sort of thing. When George Brown was speaking, he announced that he'd managed to secure a seat for his brother, Ron. At this, I shouted, 'Nepotism!' People around me on the platform hissed at me to be quiet, but I shouted, 'This Party is against nepotism!' And many in the audience took up the cry, 'Nepotism! Nepotism!'

Afterwards, I was having a drink backstage in the artists' bar, when in walked a guy called Johnny Speight. He said that he loved what I'd done to George Brown and that it was great he'd actually been heckled from the platform. Then he told me he'd liked my work on television and that he'd been asked by the BBC to write a script for a *Comedy Playhouse* series of twelve different programmes. The idea was that the viewers would be asked to select the three they liked best and that each of these would be made into a series.

Over a drink, he told me he'd completed the first draft of the script. It involved an East End working-class family, consisting of a bigoted father, his long-suffering wife, their daughter and her left-wing husband. The part of the son-in-law had been intended for Michael Caine, who was a friend of Johnny Speight's, but

105

Michael Caine had become too big a star for the part and so Johnny said he'd like me to play it.

Later, he showed me the script. As soon as I read it, I knew it was going to be a hit. There wasn't anything like it on television at that time. It dealt with politics, sex and religion – subjects which were not then considered suitable for television comedy. I was sure it would romp home the winner in the competition. At that time *Comedy Playhouse* was usually nothing more than a vehicle for established comedians, but *Till Death* was to be played by four straight actors and actresses.

However, because of Michael Caine, Johnny Speight had made the son-in-law a Cockney. So I said to him, 'Why has every witty working-class bloke got to be a Cockney? In any case, there are a lot of Cockney actors. If you want me to play it, why can't I be a Scouse? Then there can be a conflict between the north and the south. He can support West Ham and I can support Liverpool. Then they can really detest each other. I think it'll create far more tension and make it much more interesting.'

'What a great idea,' he said. 'I'll change it.'

Of course, I was inordinately flattered that somebody was prepared to change a script for me. Also I'd never before played comedy on television and I wanted to know what it was like. So conceit and flattery dropped me in the shit – and deservedly so!

For about a month, I met Johnny practically every day and we talked about the script. Because I was already cast, I was in on the ground floor. So I went with him to meet the producer, a man called Denis Main Wilson, whom we used to call 'Brain-drain' Wilson – a nice man, but a bit of a prat. When I was introduced to him, he shook hands and said, 'I used to be a nutter, but I'm cured now!'

It was obvious from things that were said that the powers-that-be in the BBC's Light Entertainment Department were less than enthusiastic about the script Johnny Speight had submitted. But it had been commissioned and, albeit reluctantly, they let it go ahead. The other characters were then cast. My wife was to be Una Stubbs, her mother was to be Gretchen Franklin, and the bigoted old man was to be played by Leo McKern.

There were endless discussions at the BBC about the name of the Leo McKern character. Originally he was called Alf Ramsey, because Johnny Speight loathed and detested Alf Ramsey, who was then England's football manager. Main Wilson insisted that the name had to be changed. On Wednesday, the week before we were due to start the rehearsals, he, Johnny Speight and I were driving around, looking for a location that could be filmed for the credits.

'What name are we going to use?' Main Wilson suddenly asked in his posh, clipped Peckham accent. 'Alf Ramsey just will not do.'

'Call him what you like,' Johnny said.

'No, no,' Main Wilson replied. 'You're the author. You must choose. We cannot have a name you do not like.'

'Oh, hell,' Johnny said. 'I don't know. Where the hell are we? What's the name of this street? That'll do for the name.'

We looked and it was Garnett Street. That's how Alf Garnett acquired his name.

The following night, Thursday, I went out for a drink with Johnny and then crashed out at his place. We were woken up at ten o'clock the next morning by Denis Main Wilson phoning to say: 'Terrible news! I've just received a radiogram from Leo McKern. I shall read it to you. "BECALMED OFF THE AZORES. UNABLE TO BE AT THE REHEARSALS ON MONDAY. GOOD LUCK FOR THE SHOW. LEO." '

It was catastrophic. There were only two days before the rehearsals started.

Brain-drain Wilson started ringing around to find a replacement. Everybody, but everybody who was rung was either working or turned the part down. It wasn't till late in the afternoon that we were told the part had been sent to Warren Mitchell.

The first readthrough of the script was scheduled for ten-thirty on Monday morning in a small, windowless room in the basement of Broadcasting House. I'd stayed the weekend at Johnny's and we arrived in good time, full of optimism and enthusiasm. At half-past ten, everybody was there – apart from Warren Mitchell.

We sat around and drank coffee. Quarter to eleven came and went – still no Warren Mitchell. We began to think he'd changed his mind and that we didn't have anybody to play the part. Could we get a plane to fly Leo McKern back from the Azores?

At eleven o'clock, the door was flung open and in came Warren. We were all sitting around a big table. It was the first time any of us had met the guy. Denis Main Wilson introduced us all. Then Warren threw the script along the whole length of the table towards Johnny Speight and said, 'That's the biggest load of crap I've read in my life!'

It was a great opening line after being half an hour late! Nothing about the car breaking down or about trying to save a young girl who was being assaulted on the tube. No, he was straight on to the attack.

107

This is great, I thought. Johnny and I grinned at each other. I like his style, I thought. He's ideal for the part!

Warren then went into a ten-minute tirade about the script. As he went on, it began to dawn on me that he meant every word. He wasn't being the Alf Garnett character. By the Wednesday, Warren and I weren't on speaking terms. We were totally different and could not agree about anything. I was in despair, wondering what I'd let myself in for. It was like a madhouse. If this was *Comedy Playhouse*, they could stick it!

The situation was only redeemed for me by Una Stubbs. I got on with her straightaway and established a genuine rapport. She is one of the greatest human beings I have ever met. That girl is something else! She is totally prepared to see the other person's point of view. She is gentle, kind and understanding, with constant good humour. She's the kind of person about whom you think, 'There must be a snag somewhere.' But believe me – there isn't.

On Thursday, there was a technical rehearsal. During this, Johnny gave us a new scene to do. Afterwards, as we walked off the set, Warren tapped me on the shoulder. I turned round and he said, 'When are you going to learn your lines?'

For me, being an actor is a great expression of joy. It's not about dreading having to go into rehearsals because of constant bitching and recriminations. I was furious.

'Was I dead-letter perfect or was I not?' I asked the script-girl.

She was terrified. 'You were,' she whimpered.

'Every word was as per the script?'

'Yes.'

Then I turned to Warren and said, 'Now apologize.'

'No, I won't,' he said. 'You didn't know your lines!'

I swung round and walked out. I had a few drinks, went home, took the phone off the hook and got into bed.

The next morning, I woke up at eight o'clock and thought, 'There's only one thing to do. I'll have to grasp the nettle and go off to the rehearsal.'

As I put the phone back on the hook, it rang. 'Yes,' I said.

'Main Wilson. BBC.'

'Oh, Christ,' I thought. 'This is it!'

'Are you coming in?' Brain-drain went on.

'Of course.'

'Well, I have to tell you this. Warren was absolutely out of order. He apologized to everybody last night and he will apologize to you today.'

'Good,' I said. 'I look forward to that.'

I expected Warren to knock on my dressing-room door and just say he was sorry. I then wanted to say that was great, but we couldn't go on with this stupidity. A major problem seemed to be that I was convinced *Till Death* was going to be a great success, but I knew Warren thought it would die the death of all times. We were recording the programme that day in front of a live audience. Whatever we thought, we had to bind together – otherwise it was certain to be a flop.

But there was no knock on the door. We were called to the set. I walked on and Warren was standing there. When he saw me, he said, 'Everybody stop! Stop the banging! I have an announcement to make.' Then in front of everybody he gave his apology. 'I am sorry. Those who were there will know why I am making this apology to Tony. My director rightly insists that I apologize to my fellow actor. It was totally wrong of me to make the baseless accusation I did.'

That was terrific! Not one word was directed to me. His apology was given as a big production number to the whole company. Now we really had a perfect working relationship! On the day we were to record the first *Till Death Us Do Part*, Warren and I were still not speaking to each other.

We did the final rehearsal with all the crew present and there wasn't a single laugh. Then the cast had a meeting with the director and Johnny Speight. It was reaffirmed that we should play the parts absolutely straight, as we'd done at rehearsal, and make no attempt to play to the gallery for cheap laughs.

After the audience had arrived, the cast was introduced to them. I didn't know this happened and I felt such a prat. Then we started. We played the first fifteen minutes of the best comic script Johnny Speight had ever written to stony silence. Nobody in the audience understood what was happening. My bravado was starting to disintegrate. It would have been nice if there'd even been a titter every now and then. Warren had smoke coming out of his ears. All his worst suspicions had been confirmed. But all the time, he was playing Alf Garnett straight down the middle. And he was brilliant.

Suddenly he said a line and the audience got the joke. Then he went totally berserk, threw his character out of the window and became a caricature of 'a bleeding lunatic'. We overran by nearly twenty minutes. But you've never heard laughter like it. Once the audience had started laughing, there was no stopping them. They laughed and laughed. At the end, they stamped and cheered. We all knew that, whatever happened to the other programmes in the *Comedy Playhouse* series, we'd won.

When the show was transmitted, it started with the first five or six lines of the original show and then it cut straight to the last twenty-seven minutes when the audience had become hysterical.

In the bar afterwards, the whole cast were jubilant. Even Warren and I felt we were comrades-in-arms. The drinkers amongst us slammed down as many drinks as we could and in no time at all Brain-drain, Johnny and I were with a fine wet sail, heading for trouble. We found it in the shape of Tom Sloane, the Head of Light Entertainment.

Johnny, whose stutter got worse when he'd been drinking, said to me, 'You know w-w-what this f-f-fucking idiot reckons? W-W-We've got n-n-no chance!'

I said to him, 'Oh come on! You've got to be out of your mind! *Till Death* has got to be a winner!'

Tom Sloane then said, 'There is no chance of it ever being a series.'

'You've got to be wrong,' I said. 'It's going to be a series and a smash hit at that.'

'No, it's not,' Sloane said.

'Look. The *Radio Times* is printing voting papers. I bet you at the end of this *Comedy Playhouse* run, we will beat everything out of sight and finish first by a mile.'

'No it won't,' he said.

'What d'you mean?'

'We've already selected the first three that are going to be made into a series.'

'Do you mean it's a fix, a proper little carve up?'

'All that I said was that we've already decided.'

I was totally disgusted. I believed it actually was a competition to allow the public to decide what programmes they wanted, but this guy had already made up his mind. He hated *Till Death*. As far as he was concerned, it was about working-class slobs who swore and revealed appalling attitudes to God, the Church and the Royal Family.

'Well I bet you,' I said, 'that you get so many votes that you'll have to bring us back.'

Tom Sloane said, 'Over my dead body!'

'Look, Tom,' I said. 'I bet you twenty pounds that you're wrong.'

'You've lost!'

I never received the twenty pounds. But *Till Death Us Do Part* did get the largest number of votes and reluctantly the BBC had to bring it back as a series. However, it took over a year.

By the time we came to start rehearsals for the series, Gretchen Franklin was in *Spring and Port Wine* in the West End and couldn't play the mother. She told her best friend, who happened to be Dandy Nichols, a superb actress, and she took over the part. So in the first series, one actress played Alf's wife in the opening episode, while another actress played the part in the remaining six episodes. Nothing was ever said and few people seemed to notice!

The cast worked with Johnny Speight very much as an ensemble and ideas were constantly being developed at rehearsals. It was Warren who first came up with the idea of calling me 'Scouse git' and that stuck. On another occasion, Johnny had written a line where Alf called his wife, 'a silly old cow'. Main Wilson said, 'You can't say that word. The BBC will never allow that!'

There followed a discussion that went on for an age. While the rest of us were having our say, Una Stubbs, as usual during such arguments, sat there silently doing her embroidery. After about half an hour, Warren said, 'I just can't see what all the fuss is about. This is absurd.'

Una looked up and said, 'Yes, it is. All that you're talking about is a moo-cow.'

The rest of us together went: 'She's got it. Silly old moo!' And that's how the famous catch phrase was born – straight out of Una's embroidery!

The first series was put out at seven-thirty on a Monday evening, at the same time as ITV's number one television show, *Coronation Street*. There were seven episodes in the first series. Within three weeks, we'd knocked *Coronation Street* out of the top ten. At the end of the series, the whole lot was repeated again on Saturday evenings. We went straight in at number one. Yet that is the only time the BBC has repeated any series of *Till Death*!

All the time, we were treated as though we were the lepers of the BBC. We were shunted out to rehearse in church halls and scout huts in the most out-of-the-way places. The bosses of the Light Entertainment Department informed us that the success of the series didn't guarantee another. But eventually a second series was commissioned.

This time the programmes went out on Wednesdays and were recorded two days before, on the Monday. Johnny Speight was so slow in delivering the scripts that they were submitted to the BBC only on Monday the week before. We'd have Tuesday off and start rehearsals on Wednesday.

There was always a lot of argument about whether certain swear words could be used. One script started with my saying to Warren Mitchell, 'You don't half talk a load of crap, you do!'

He then said, '*I* talk a load of crap? *You* talk a load of crap!'

The whole exchange went on like that up to the punch line.

We did this at rehearsals, but on Monday morning there was a big attack on *Till Death* in the papers by Mary Whitehouse, because we were going to use this terrible four-letter word 'crap'. She was asking for the Prime Minister to intervene and stop the show!

On Mondays, the final camera rehearsal always took place in front of an audience. For the first few shows, there had been only a couple of people there. But, by this time, there were six hundred or so people. It was as large an audience as there was for the recording. People working at the BBC used to come, so they could go home and tell their friends what was happening in that week's show. There were queues for the camera rehearsals – the commissionaires, secretaries, telephone girls, actors from other shows, everybody.

This particular Monday, Dennis Main Wilson called the cast together and announced that there would be a closed set for the camera rehearsal. He then gabbled on: 'The DG, the ADG, the AADG, the HoB 1, HoB 2, HoLE, AHoLE and other heads of department are coming here. The show is in grave danger of being called off because of the obscene language being used. We've given the matter a lot of thought and we've decided to make changes. Tony, you will no longer say, "You don't half talk a load of crap, you do!" Instead you will say, "You don't half talk a load of nonsense, you do!" Then Warren will reply, "*I* talk nonsense? *You* talk nonsense!" And so on. Then we'll take out all the "bloodies" and the "bleedings" and replace them with "blimies".'

At this, Warren went berserk: 'This is disgusting. This is called censorship.' And he gave it the whole bit, until it built up into a confrontation between him and the producer.

Brain-drain finally said, 'I am ordering you to do as you're told.' With that, he sent us off to our dressing-rooms to wait until we were called – after the arrival of the DG, the ADG and so on.

At twenty-past four, as I was standing beside the set waiting to go on, Johnny Speight sidled up to me and said, 'I-I-I've 'ad a talk with Warren a-a-and this is fucking c-c-censorship of the worst possible kind. It's an infringement of liberty. Ar-ar-ar-artistic integrity is at s-s-stake 'ere. We should not do this. I-I-I and Warren 'ave decided wh-wh-what your first line should be is, "You don't 'alf talk a load of fuckin' bollocks, you do!" Then he will reply in kind. S-S-So I-I-I want you, Tone, to go on there and give it your all.'

Now I may have green eyes, but I wasn't born yesterday. I realized that I'd be the fall guy, because I had to deliver the first line. So I said, 'Look, Johnny. I'm prepared to say anything, 'cause I feel the same as you. It's all a load of crap. But I shall want it in writing – whatever you want me to say.'

'Oh, no,' he said. 'Just take my word for it.'

'No, not me. Here's my script. You write on it exactly what you want me to say and sign it. Then I'll do it.'

'Come on, Tone,' he said. 'What's the matter wiv you?'

'For once in my life, I'm trying to use my head!'

He wrote it all down and signed the script.

Eventually, Hugh Carleton Greene, the Director General, arrived with his small entourage. They sat alone in the centre of the vast studio. The DG, or 'Carlton Towers' as everybody called him, was head and shoulders above everybody else, looking as though he was standing while the rest were sitting down.

Just before we went on, Warren told me that the girls – Una and Dandy – didn't know what we were going to do. It was just between him and me.

Everything was ready and even the cameramen were on their best behaviour. Because the DG was there, nobody was coughing, they'd all combed their hair and were wearing collars and ties.

'Standby, studio.' They rolled the captions and the music started.

They cued me and I said, 'You don't half talk a load of fuckin' bollocks, you do!'

Warren replied, '*I* talk a load of fuckin' bollocks? What about the load of fuckin' bollocks *you* talk?'

At this, the boom operator nearly fell off the platform, the cameras started shuddering up and down, and the floor manager groaned, clapped his head and walked away. Dandy and Una looked as though we'd gone completely insane. Afterwards we discovered that up in the control box Brain-drain had passed out and his personal assistant had taken over.

So nobody stopped the show and I continued: 'No more fuckin' bollocks than you talk!'

'All right then. What fuckin' bollocks do I talk?'

'What about you saying Stalin was a fuckin' American spy?'

By this time, Warren had got the bit between his teeth. He'd decided this was great. He couldn't say a line without some four-letter word. It became contagious between the two of us. We were saying, 'Bollocks! Up yours!' and so on, just as proper Eastenders would speak with a Scouse thrown in among them.

While all this was happening, the cameras were banging into each other and the studio was filling up rapidly with engineers, make-up girls and wardrobe assistants, all desperate to see and hear what was happening.

After five minutes, Dandy turned round and said, 'Bollocks to the pair of you!' Well, we were genuinely shocked!

Warren wasn't going to leave it at that and so he said, 'You wash your fuckin' mouth out! I'm not 'avin' a wife of mine fuckin' talking to me like that!'

And so it went on. The only person who hadn't used a four-letter word was Una. The rest of us – me, Warren and Dandy – were swearing away non-stop. Just before the end of the show, Warren and I got up to go to the pub. As we reached the door, I had to ask Una for some money. She gave me a quid and then said, 'Stick it up your fuckin' arse!' It was astonishing!

After that, we walked off and the girls had about thirty seconds of dialogue before the final credits. They then left the set and joined the two of us in the hallway. We all hugged, kissed each other and said, 'Well, that's the end of all our careers. We'll never work again for the BBC!'

Then the floor manager's voice of doom crackled over the intercom: 'Please will the cast come on set. The DG would like to have a word with them.'

We walked sheepishly through the door and stood there. Carleton Greene came on to the set and solemnly shook hands with the four of us. He stepped back and looked us up and down. Then he said, 'Great! Don't change a fucking word!'

As he walked off, the four of us applauded him all the way to the door. What a governor!

After that, there was nobody at the BBC who was going to object to the word 'crap!' The episode was recorded and transmitted just as Johnny Speight had originally written it.

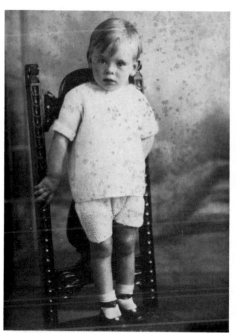

Above left: Butter wouldn't . . . 1935

Above right: Usual position – back to the wall 1958

Below: You get to eat as well. *The Country Wife,* as Horner. 1969/70

Above: The joke's on page 3. c. 1968

Below: A night out with the in-laws. From the film of *Till Death Us Do Part.* (BBC)

Left: As the Inspector in *Spider's Web.* "Baffled of the Yard". 1985 (*Laurence Burns*)

Below: Hello Sailor. With Pat in Yugoslavia. 1984 (*B. Thomas/ News of the World*)

Above: As Howard in *The Man*. 1984 *(G. Ivan Barnett)*

Below: As Carl in *The Verdict* by Agatha Christie. 1984

Above: Brutus in *Julius Caesar,*
with Steven Yardley

Mine Host, *Albion Market*. 1986 (Granada TV)

With Pat. Around 1983 (*News of the World*)

Above: Always the bridesmaid. Best Man at Bet Lynch's wedding, with other members of the of *Coronation Street.* 1987

Below: With my Apocalyptic Head On! 1987 *(Steve Yarnell)*

12

Rôle Play

For me, the art of acting is to capture the soul of the character. To do that is to achieve a certain immortality. So I've always tried to capture the essence of a character. I don't start from the outside and work in – I don't first decide, for example, to wear glasses and have a limp. I always work from the inside to the outside – and find that I'm wearing glasses and have a limp.

The biggest challenge I ever had as an actor was when I was cast as the White Rabbit in *Alice in Wonderland* at the Royal Shakespeare Theatre, Stratford-on-Avon. How do you capture the soul of a rabbit? All I know is I spent six weeks chasing a white rabbit around the stage trying to catch up with it and only at one point did we ever fuse as one.

I was working on a series of *Till Death Us Do Part* when I got offered the part of the White Rabbit in the Christmas production. I accepted readily. It was a great part. But the rehearsals clashed with those for *Till Death*. I was told not to worry about it. The rest of the cast would have five weeks' rehearsal; I'd have to manage with two.

We were so busy and so far behind that I didn't have time even to look at the *Alice* script. We recorded the last episode of the series on a Monday. The next day, I went to my first rehearsal of *Alice* and as I sat on the tube I started to read the part of the White

Rabbit for the first time. I turned over a page and a stage direction said, 'White Rabbit sings'. Nobody had told me that I was supposed to sing! Another direction said, 'Ballet. White Rabbit and Alice.' Nobody had mentioned a word about ballet! That was doubly unfortunate, because I can't sing and I can't dance.

I'd been called early to rehearsal so they could plot me into the show. I went straight to the director and said, 'Look. Someone's made a terrible mistake. You've obviously been rehearsing with an understudy. If he sings and dances, for God's sake be sensible and use him. There's no way I can sing and dance. A ballet? Are you mad? You're totally out of your minds! Have you seen me move? I'm elephantine! It's ridiculous.'

'Don't worry, Tony,' the director said. 'You can handle it. Don't worry. You're backed by an orchestra and a chorus. Rex Harrison made his name mouthing "Why Can't the English Teach Their Children How to Speak?" Why can't you do the same?'

To cut a long story short, they talked me into it. 'All right,' I said. 'But the ballet's out of the question.'

'No problem, Tony. All you do is stand there and let Alice dance around you.'

And that's what happened. I'd only one thing to do. At the end of the ballet, Alice did a solo dance, turned round and ran up to the White Rabbit who lifted her up, put her on his shoulder and danced off.

After a fortnight, we went off to Stratford. At the dress rehearsal, I got caught up in Alice's dress and managed to lift her up only as far as my chest.

'Don't worry about it, Tony. You'll be all right on opening night.'

On the first night, I started my song, expecting the chorus to join in. But the whole lot of them dried – they forgot their lines. I was stuck there alone, speaking the song with a mute chorus. At the end of the first act, Sally Smith, who was playing Alice, did her dance and turned to face me. Suddenly the White Rabbit and I became as one and in that magic moment I was the White Rabbit. As Alice hurtled towards me, I was petrified and my little rabbit heart was in my throat. But I grabbed her round the waist and to gales of laughter from the audience I lumbered off with her into the wings.

At the matinée the next day, I was determined to pull myself together. The song went well and it came to the end of the ballet. As Alice came towards me, I knew I could do it. I grabbed her by the waist and threw her up into the air and she practically disappeared. As she came down, I grabbed her by the ankle. She collapsed down my back and I staggered offstage, carrying Alice – who was upside down with her skirt over her face – like a sack of potatoes.

It wasn't the high point of my theatrical career, but at least it gave me some idea why actors are warned not to perform with animals, especially white rabbits!

The ever-increasing popularity of *Till Death* had many effects on the cast. None of us could walk down the street without being recognized. Everywhere I went, people would bellow, 'That Scouse git!' It also meant that, by the time the second series had started, my face had become so well known that I virtually couldn't get any other work, particularly in television.

Only having seven weeks work in a year, I soon became desperately short of money. When I lost my flat, I couldn't afford to rent another. One day I was in the YMCA having a swim, when a young New Zealander called Matthew came up to me and told me he worked for Theo Cowan, an important PR representative for people in the theatre. 'Funnily enough,' he said, 'a magazine rang up the office today and asked if we handled you, because they wanted to do an interview with you. But I couldn't do anything. I didn't know how to get in touch with you. If you like, you can give me your address and I'll fix it up.'

'As a matter of fact,' I said, 'at the moment I'm sleeping on a friend's floor.'

'Are you really?' he said, obviously somewhat bemused.

'Yes, I am.'

'Well,' he said. 'I've got a shed I've converted in the back yard of Cowan's office. It's on a short lease. I was living there, but I'm just moving out. You can have it for fifteen shillings a week, if you'd like.'

I went with him to have a look at the place, which was in Clarges Street. Sure enough it was a shed where they'd used to do the baking for the house. He'd done it up beautifully – all the walls were whitewashed and the old ovens were made into cupboards. It was furnished and there was a phone. The only drawback was that there was no hot water – but for fifteen bob a week who could complain?

I moved in. It was a hot summer and the place was cool and airy. Everything was great. But when winter came the place was freezing.

While I was living there, a glossy magazine contacted me to say

117

they were doing a series on 'The Bathrooms of the Stars' and asked if they could do one on me. 'Sure,' I said.

The only way I could have a shower was to fix a shower attachment to a wash basin in an office on the first floor of the main building and stick it through the window. Then I'd dash down into the courtyard and have a shower. So this was what they photographed. But, because the sun was shining and there was ivy growing up the outside wall, it looked magnificent! Everybody else had sunken baths and wall-to-wall carpets, but it looked as though with my backyard shower I was living in more luxurious circumstances than any of them.

I had a terrific time at Clarges Street. The place was always full of mates and girlfriends. We had incredible parties. At one of these, there was a guy from the *News of the World* who then wrote a detailed description of my lifestyle. Somebody in my mother's street, took her the report. She rang me up and played hell with me. I hadn't even seen it, but apparently the journalist had described everything that happened in my backyard shed. In his article, he claimed he'd made his excuses and left, but I can tell you he didn't!

Peter Sellers, who was one of Cowan's clients, came down to see my hut, because he'd heard tales of the goings-on there. 'It's a funny business,' he said to me. 'When I first started, I paid Theo Cowan fifty quid a week to get my name in the papers. Now I'm paying him five hundred a week to keep it out!'

One night, Tom Bell came round to Clarges Street and said, 'Come on. I want you to meet an incredible woman. She's married to a peer, but they're now separated and he gives her five hundred quid a week to stay away from the family home.'

'So what's wrong with her?' I asked.

'Nothing. She really wants to meet you. She gives fantastic parties and has her own terrific flat.'

He then went on to describe her and, though a man of iron, I gave in easily! We went round to her place and Fay was everything Tom had said. She was one of the most beautiful women I've ever seen in my life. Her hair was strawberry blonde, she had the figure of a Greek goddess with legs that went all the way to her armpits, and her deep brown eyes were extraordinary. The left one was a lazy eye, which strangely made her seem even more attractive. We struck up what can best be called a healthy relationship. Having spent some time living in the shed at Clarges Street, I was easily persuaded to stay the night in her luxurious penthouse flat.

Fay was a fascinating woman. When she was sixteen, she'd

become the first English stripper in Paris to receive a thousand pounds a week. At twenty, she'd met and married her English lord and when she was twenty-four they'd separated. When we met, she was in her late twenties and stunning. Everywhere she went, she literally stopped traffic. She also had an awfully attractive voice, because she spoke slowly, deliberately and erotically to mask the Cockney accent she sometimes lapsed into when we were alone together.

We got on so well that I stayed on in her flat. At the time, I was about to start work on an episode of *The Saint*. At the end of the first day's filming, I went back and said to her, 'Fay, I've got a lot of work to do on this script for tomorrow and I've got to be up by six in the morning.'

She said, 'I'll tell you what. First I'll make you a cup of coffee. Get undressed and climb into bed and I'll bring it to you. Then you can study while I make dinner. Afterwards we can make love and go to sleep.'

'Terrific,' I said.

She brought in the coffee, I swigged it back and forgot all about the script. We started making love and about five o'clock in the morning I said, 'This is ridiculous. I've got to look at the script.'

'That's all right,' she said. 'I'll make you another cup of coffee.'

I studied from five to six, rushed to the studio and worked all day, dashing around like a blue-arsed fly. I came back and the same thing happened again – making love till five, learning the script and off to the studio. This went on for three days and I couldn't believe that I was doing without sleep. Although I returned to her flat totally exhausted, after a few minutes there I was suddenly full of energy. She certainly seemed to be having a magical effect on me!

On the fourth night, when I arrived back, I said, 'Fay, I'm so exhausted I've got to go back to my place for a rest.'

'No, no,' she said. 'Just lie down and I'll make you a coffee.'

I collapsed on the bed while she went off to the kitchen. Suddenly I remembered that I wanted to tell her about something that had happened that day on the set. I jumped up and went into the kitchen to find her with a phial putting drops of colourless liquid into my coffee.

'What are you doing?' I asked.

'I'm giving you medicine.'

'What is it?'

'It's harmless. Everything in this house has got some in – the

119

whisky, the gin and even the lemonade. You've been having it ever since we met.'

'But what is it?'

'Liquid methadine. I've taken it for years. Don't worry about it. It's good for you. Why do you think you're screwing like a bunny rabbit? You're on speed!'

I was horrified, threw a fit and left. I'd had no idea what had been happening. All over the weekend, I suffered from total exhaustion.

After I'd finished filming, she contacted me and said, 'I'm sorry about what happened. I know I shouldn't have done it and I promise I'll never do it again. Please come round to see me.'

I couldn't resist. So I went back.

We stayed in the flat for three days and nights on the trot. Then in the middle of the fourth night, she got up to go to the bathroom. When she came back, she stood naked in the doorway and said, 'Boofie, Boofie, I'm so bored. All we've done for four days is to stay in the flat. I want to go out.'

It was a cold December night and outside it was peeing down. I just wanted to sleep, but to humour her I said, 'Of course, Fay. I'll take you anywhere you want. Tomorrow, eh?'

'No, now.'

'But it's two o'clock in the morning. Where the hell can we go to now?'

'Anywhere,' she said. 'But take me somewhere.'

Ad libbing rapidly, I said, 'All right, Fay. You've been every-where and seen it all. But have you ever been fucked on Hampstead Heath on a wet December night?'

'No, never,' she said.

'OK. Get yourself ready and I'll take you up to Hampstead Heath, where I shall do the most indescribable things to you and your screams will not be heard.'

'Oh, my God, yes!' she said. 'Don't move. I'll be back!'

She went off again to the bathroom and I assumed she'd be in there for another half hour, forget all about it and come back to bed.

Much to my chagrin, at about a quarter to three, she turned up in the doorway. She was wearing full make-up, high heels and a beautiful silk negligee. 'I'm ready,' she cooed.

'You're kidding,' I said. 'It's nearly three o'clock. Are you sure you want to go?'

'Don't worry. The rain's stopped and the moon's out. Let's go!'

'Come on, Fay. Tomorrow, eh?'

'No, no, no. You promised me you'd take me on Hampstead Heath and my screams would not be heard.'

'OK,' I said. 'All right then. You win. Just let me put my jeans and sweater on. And what about you? Are you really going out like that?'

'Of course.'

'Don't be stupid. It's December. You'll catch your death of cold.'

'All right. I'll put something else on.'

She went away and I got dressed. Fay returned, wearing a mink coat over her negligee.

'I'm ready,' she said.

'OK,' I said.

She threw me the keys to her white Mercedes and we went down to the underground car park. We drove from her flat in Lancaster Gate up to Hampstead Heath. During the entire journey, she was listing all the naughty things she expected me to do to her when we arrived.

The moonlight was so bright that it was almost day and, although it had stopped raining, everywhere was soaking wet. I drove to Jack Straw's Castle and into the car park at the back. There was a car already there. I don't know why, but I pulled up next to it.

As soon as we'd stopped, Fay slung her mink into the back of the car, jumped out and rushed across the car park. She stood, legs akimbo, with the moon behind her, delineating her body, and the wind billowing her beautiful blonde hair. At the top of her voice she yelled, 'Boofie, Boofie, come on. I want you to fuck me on Hampstead Heath. Boofie, Boofie, you promised to do indescribable things to me. What are you doing, Boofie? I want you. I want you.'

'Just coming,' I said, getting out of the car which, I decided, had to be locked because of the mink coat lying on the back seat. After I'd checked all the doors, and while Fay was still urging me to hurry, I glanced at the other car and looked straight through an open window into the eyes of a police sergeant. There were two other policemen in the car and, in the bright moonlit night, Fay was screaming at the top of her voice, 'Boofie, Boofie. Fuck me, Boofie.'

The sergeant said, 'Well, Boofie, what are you waiting for? The lady says she wants to be fucked!'

'Ah, ah, ah,' I burbled nervously. 'Don't worry. She's been drinking. I'll get her back.'

I started to run across the car park, shouting, 'Fay, Fay. Quiet, Fay. It's a police car. Fay.'

She turned and took off across the Heath like a gazelle. I stumbled after her, slipping and sliding on the wet grass. Eventually I managed to catch her and said, 'Fay, there's three policemen back there.'

'I don't care about that,' she said. 'You promised that you'd do indescribable things. So come on.'

Much as I fought her, she overcame me. We ended up, churning about in the mud of Hampstead Heath. By the time we'd finished, her negligee was in tatters and we were both mud-besmattered.

Eventually, much bedraggled, we returned. Fay had lost her high-heels and was leaning on my shoulder. We entered the car park to a round of applause from the three policemen, who were leaning on their car. As we approached, the sergeant said, 'Well, Boofie, I'll tell you what – I've seen you on television, but never a performance like that!'

Years later, I was in a pub in Hampstead and John Hurt said to me, 'Is it true that, despite having three policemen in hot pursuit, you still insisted on having your way with a blonde on Hampstead Heath?' Stories sure change in the retelling!

A few weeks after the episode on Hampstead Heath, Fay and I were lying naked on her bed drinking champagne, when the front door opened as far as the chain would allow it.

A pucker, upper-class voice, created by nine hundred years of oppressing the peasants, bellowed, 'Let me in, you whore.'

'My God,' Fay says. 'It's my husband!'

She jumps out of bed and runs to the door, trying to shut it. I'd just managed to leap out and stand with my naked back against the wall, when the door is kicked in – a feat that mightily impressed me. I've tried to do it several times and have only managed to crunch my foot or put my knee out of joint. Fay screams as in bursts this gigantic, ex-Guards officer.

'You've got a man in there,' he shouts.

Fay cries out, 'What are you doing here?'

He sees me and says to her, 'I'll deal with you later.' Then he punches her so viciously that she lands on the floor in a crumpled heap. 'First,' he says to me, 'I'm going to kill you.'

'Just a second,' I say. 'It's not what you think!' That was the best excuse I could come up with!

'Isn't it?'

'No, no. And why should you care? You're divorcing your wife.'

'Who told you that?'

122

'She did.'

'She's a lying whore!'

'Look. Just leave her alone. I'll get dressed and go.'

'Oh, no. I'm going to kill you.'

'Come on,' I say feebly. 'Can't we talk about this?'

He strides over and smashes me in the face, knocking me clean across the bed. Then he strides round after me, saying, 'Now I'm going to tear your balls off and stick them down your throat!'

This concentrated my mind on my vital organs, because cowering there naked I was not in the same position to fend off the attacks of an enraged husband as I would have been if fully clothed.

He grabs me and starts banging my head against the wall. I am not coming out of this well! Suddenly, I feel as though I'm covered all over in what I took to be sweat, but as Fay jumps on his back and he pulls my head away I see on the wall a splattered patch of blood. 'My God,' I think. 'This guy's trying to brain me!'

I'm allergic to blood – especially my own – and I've tried to avoid spilling it all my life. So I'm none too pleased about this. As he throws his wife off, he lets go of me. As I slide down the wall, my hand finds the champagne bottle that had been left beside the bed. Now I'd played lots of heavy guys who'd threatened people with bottles, so I knew how it was done.

I spring up, clutching the bottle and assuming the well-known fighting position I'd used in films and on television. 'All right,' I say. 'That's it over and done with. Settle down and talk about it with your wife while I get dressed.'

'Oh yes,' he says. 'I knew you'd be the kind of bastard who'd fight with a bottle.'

'You're bloody right, I am. I'll brain you if you come near me again.'

He moves towards me. I lift up the bottle – and champagne pours out all over me! He hits me and still clutching the bottle I thud into the wall.

He steps towards me again. 'I'm warning you,' I say. 'One more step and I'm going to give it to you.'

'Oh, really,' he says and comes on.

I bring the champagne bottle down on his head with as much force as I can muster. In films, the bottle always shatters and the person falls to the floor. None of that happens. This guy steps back, looks at me and says, 'Now I'm really going to kill you.'

My knees start to give way and we both hit the deck at the same time. It'd been a delayed reaction and he'd sparked straight out!

Fay comes crawling across the bedroom and starts screaming at me, 'What have you done? You've killed him. You've killed my husband. He gives me five hundred quid a week!' Just then he groans. So we know he isn't dead. 'Get out of here,' she says to me. 'He'll kill you when he comes round. I never want to see you again! Get out!'

While she cradles his head in her lap, I manage to get dressed and at three o'clock in the morning stagger down the stairs into Lancaster Gate. Then I realize that blood is pouring out of the back of my head. Fortunately, an empty taxi passes and I ask him to take me to St Mary's Hospital, Paddington.

'What's happened to you?' the taxi driver asks.

'Oh, somebody mugged me.'

At the hospital, I had twenty stitches put in my head and was found to be suffering from concussion. I heard later that Fay and her erstwhile husband had got back together again and as far as I know are living happily ever after. I was left with the scars!

13

The Swinging Sixties

Till Death Us Do Part had a lot of things to answer for. One of them was that ours was the first television comedy series to be filmed. We opened the floodgates to the garbage that followed.

The filming took place at Shepperton. In charge of the studios was John Boulting, although the producer of the film was a man called Jon Pennington. Because they didn't have that much faith in the project, the director we were given was Norman Cohen, who'd never before made a full-length feature film. He was a gentle, most amiable Irish guy.

As the film progressed, Warren became more demanding in what he took to be his quest for perfection. We were on a low budget and pushed for time. If there were more than three takes, there was a full accountants' enquiry!

The infamous day arrived when we turned up for the pub scene. On television, quite a bit of the action took place in a pub. We used a set that fitted into a small corner. At eight-thirty in the morning in a studio at Shepperton, we walked into a Victorian gin palace that must have covered an acre. Sitting around was a comic-book collection of lovable Cockney characters, including a couple of pearly queens.

Warren took one look and hit the roof. He called over Norman Cohen and the set designer. In no uncertain terms, he told them they were out of their tiny minds and that there was no way the set could be used for the pub in *Till Death Us Do Part*. And he was right – the set was ridiculous.

Norman Cohen said, 'I'm sorry, Warren. We're pushed for time and this is the set. You saw the plans and approved them.'

'Yes,' Warren said. 'But the sketches didn't look anything like this, did they?'

They then produced the plans to show him that the pub had been built exactly as designed. It was approaching nine o'clock and Warren was saying that there was no way he was going to work on that set. Meanwhile, I was reading the *Sporting Life*, Una was doing her embroidery and Dandy was sifting through her pills.

Eventually, it was clear there was an impasse. Norman was nearly in tears and sent for the producer. While we waited for Jon Pennington to arrive, Warren went back to his dressing-room and Dandy, Una and I went off for a cup of tea.

At half-past nine, we all returned. Warren told the director, the producer and the designer that there was no way the set could be used. He wanted the set used on television. It was pointed out that the set-up in the studio had cost a lot of money and that there was no way they could pull it down and build another set. As it was, the film was running late.

'I don't care,' Warren said. 'Get John Boulting down here.'

He was told that Boulting wouldn't be at the studio until ten o'clock.

So fifty or so extras and the rest of us were told to go away and return at ten o'clock. Dandy, Una and I went to Warren and asked him to change his mind, pointing out that it was, after all, only a very small scene. But he was adamant – he would rather not have a film than work on that set.

'This,' I thought, 'should be very interesting!' Having worked for him before, I knew that Boulting was not the kind of man who took kindly to that type of attitude from anybody.

At ten o'clock, the four of us returned to the set. Five minutes later, John Boulting arrived. He looked Warren straight in the eye and said, 'Are you going to do this scene or are you refusing to do this scene?'

'Well, no. I'm not refusing.'

'In that case,' Boulting said, his voice sharp with anger, 'get back to work and don't bother me. I've far more important things to do than listen to you.' He looked at his watch. 'You're now two hours behind schedule. Make sure you make them up today.'

He walked off and that was the end of Warren's rebellion!

126

After I'd been working on the film for three weeks without a break, I arrived home one night totally exhausted. Fortunately, I didn't have to go to the studio the next day, but I was so shattered that I told my girlfriend I'd have to go straight to bed as soon as we'd had dinner. While she was preparing the meal, I lay on the settee, watching television. When the commercials came on, I crashed out. I came to at the end of the break. In that three minutes a lot had happened.

I'd no sooner passed out, when I heard my father crying out, 'Help. Help. Help. Nurse. Nurse. Nurse.'

I found myself standing at the end of a hospital bed where my father was lying. He said to me, 'Oh, thank God you're here. Get the nurse. I can't make a sound. I'm having a heart attack. I'm dying. Get the nurse. I need help.'

I could see that my father was choking on the terrible pain. He was dying. I knew I wasn't able to call out for help and so I said to him, 'Keep calm. Give me the pain. If I take the pain, it'll ease your pain.'

'It won't work,' he gasped.

'It will work. Believe me. Let me take the pain.' Suddenly I began to feel a severe stabbing pain in my chest. 'That's right,' I said. 'Give me your pain.' The steel bands I felt across my chest drew tighter and tighter. I knew that if it continued I was going to die. I knew then that I couldn't do that for my father. 'That's enough. That's enough,' I sobbed. 'I can't take any more.'

'It's all right!' my father shouted and I knew he'd made a sound that would be heard in the ward.

That's when I came to with a cry and sat up on the settee.

My girlfriend rushed in and said, 'What's the matter?'

'My God,' I gasped. 'My father's just had a massive heart attack. He's in hospital in Liverpool. They've got to get to him. He needs help. I've got to phone the hospital.'

'Pull yourself together. What hospital is it?'

'I don't know, do I?'

'Don't be ridiculous. Think about it.'

'I can't remember.'

'Well, who told you?'

'Nobody told me. I had an out-of-body experience. Honest to God, I saw my father in a hospital bed. And the worst of it was I couldn't die for my father. Don't you understand? If he dies, I'm going to be destroyed, because I let him die.'

'Why don't you get through to directory enquiries?'

'Do you know how many hospitals there are in Liverpool?'

'Ring your mother.'

I did. There was no reply. I rang my sister. There was no reply.

By then I'd settled down and my girlfriend said to me, 'Have a brandy. You've been overworking and you're exhausted. Why don't you just go to bed and take a sleeping pill? Tomorrow, you can lie in and you'll feel much better.'

I went to bed and immediately crashed out. When I woke in the morning, I saw that my girlfriend had unplugged the phone by the bed so that I'd have an uninterrupted night's sleep. I plugged it back again and immediately it rang. It was my sister.

'Where have you been?' she said. 'I've been trying to get you all night.'

'It's Dad,' I said. 'He's had a heart attack.'

'How did you know?'

'Is he all right?'

'Yes. He'd been taken into hospital with chest pains. They'd settled him into the bed and the nurses had just left him to sleep when he called out. They rushed back. He'd had a massive heart attack. But they managed to save him.'

My father and I had been barely on speaking terms, but I drove up to Liverpool desperate to know if he'd confirm my out-of-body experience. When I arrived at the hospital with my mother, brother and sister, we walked up to the bed. My father gently brushed them aside and held his arms out to me. It was a thing he'd never done in his life. I leaned over to him. He put his arms round me and kissed me on the lips. Everybody, including me, was astonished.

'It did happen then,' I whispered.

'Yes, but don't say anything now,' he whispered back.

We sat round the bed for a while and talked. When it was time to go, my father, for the first time in his entire relationship with my mother, dismissed her and said, 'I want to talk to Tony alone.'

The others went off, presumably believing that my father was about to tell me, as the eldest son, where he'd hidden the family treasure! There could be no other reason why he'd want to say anything to me – we hadn't had a private conversation for donkey's years.

I sat by the bed. My father took my hand and said, 'You saved my life. I'll never forget that. But please don't tell anyone.'

'Why, dad?'

'Because they'll put me in a mental home. I don't want to die there. I told a nurse that you'd been standing by my bed and she looked at me as though I was soft in the head.'

'Of course I won't say anything, but between you and me it did happen, didn't it? I was here at the end of the bed.'

'Yes. And you took the pain.'

'But I couldn't take it. I couldn't take any more of the pain.'

'It was enough. I was able to cry out. You know, Tony, we've never been that close, but I've always loved you. I want you to know that.'

I was deeply moved. The whole experience had forged the bond between us that for so much of my life had seemed so insubstantial. My father came out of hospital and began to recover, but sadly a few months later he died.

Apart from the odd spurts of work provided by *Till Death*, I was usually unemployed, although I was having a lot of fun. About this time, Matthew, my New Zealand landlord, split from Theo Cohen and set up his own PR firm. As he was short of cash, he said he needed to use the backyard hut in Clarges Street that I rented from him, but that I could sleep in his office which was above Stricklands in Soho's Old Compton Street. I moved there for nearly a year. So at the time when *Till Death* was at the peak of its success, I was kipping on an office couch.

As the people used to arrive for work at nine o'clock, I had to be up by then and be ready to get out until five, when they left. I'd go over to the French shop, have some croissants and coffee, go into a bar and generally loaf around Soho. As I was part of the number one television show, there were a lot of people who didn't mind loafing around in my company. So I had a splendid time and met most of the great characters of Soho at a time before the Street Offences Act when Soho was full of the ladies of the night, petty crooks, writers and artists.

One of the best-known people around Soho was Ringo Charlie. He was a tout who lived by his wits. Right opposite the pub in which we used to drink, there was a dirty bookshop. In the summer, he'd sit by the door looking out for punters. When he thought he'd seen one, he'd dash out, do his spiel, take their money, send them off on a wild goose chase and come back into the pub.

This particular day, we were sitting there when a chap wearing a bowler hat and striped suit began looking into the window of the dirty bookshop.

'Oh, boy,' Charlie said. 'There's a face. I'm away. I'll be back in a few minutes.'

Charlie dashed across the road and stood behind the man in

the bowler hat. 'Don't look round, sir,' Charlie said. 'Don't look round!'

'I beg your pardon.'

'Don't look at me! Don't look at me! Just keep looking in the window. Is there anything I can do to help you?'

'Please go away!'

'No, no. It's quite all right. You're after something and I'm here to help you. There is a lot of dodgy characters here in Soho. Believe me, the place is full of dodgy characters. You can get ripped off something terrible. You know that, sir. Don't look at me! Don't look at me! Keep looking in the window! It's all right! There's a lot of law around. There are plain clothes men all over the place. I'm telling you, this is a very dicey situation we both find ourselves in. But you look like a very respectable gentleman who's got a problem. Now what can I do for you?'

'How do you know I've got a problem?'

'Well it's just the way. . . Don't look, sir! Don't look at me! Just keep looking into the window! You just look the type that's got a problem. Now I understand all about problems. I am a mass of problems. Don't look, sir! Don't look! Keep looking in the window!'

'Have you really? What sort of problems?'

'I have all sorts of problems – sexual problems, mental problems, physical problems. What sort of problem have you got?'

'I. . . I. . . well. . . Who said I've got a problem?'

'I'm sure you've got a problem. We've all got problems.'

'Oh, yes. All right. I have a problem.'

'You have a problem, sir. Well you've come to the right place. Don't look! Don't look, sir! Keep looking in the window! Keep casual! Keep casual! Relax! Relax! That's it. That's great. You're doing well. Now, look. What's your problem?'

'I don't know how to put it.'

'It's all right. Think of me as a priest.'

'A priest?'

'Yes. I was going to be a priest but I'm not now. Don't look! Look in the window! Look in the window! Well, what's your problem?'

'I have a wife.'

'Oh, that's a problem, sir. That's a problem. You want a girl, is that it? You want two girls? What do you want – a live show, animals, schoolgirls, schoolboys?'

'How dare you! Who do you. . . '

'Of course, of course. I'm only telling you that because that's the sort of trap you can fall into when you're in Soho. We're in a

130

very dodgy place here. You're lucky you met me. I mean I could be the police. I could be a con man or worse. I'm not, I assure you! Don't look at me! Keep looking in the window! Keep looking in the window! Now, what's the problem?'

'I don't know how to put it.'

'Put it in your own words, sir.'

'Well the problem is this. . . um. . . My wife. . . oh!. . . my wife is. . . well she's. . . I suppose you'd call her frigid.'

'Frigid? My God, that's a terrible problem. Look in the window! Don't look at me! Don't look at me! That's all right. Don't worry about it, sir. You have come to the right man. I can get you some gear that will have your wife swinging from the chandeliers. Believe me. But it's going to take time.'

'Oh! How much time?'

'How much time have you got?'

'I've got to get back to the. . . to the. . . '

'Office. Yes, sir, the office. Well, how long have you got?'

'Half an hour.'

'Half an hour? That's a terrible problem for me, sir. This stuff is imported. It's dynamite. And it's going to cost me to get it in half an hour.'

'How much will it cost?'

'Twenty pounds.'

'Twenty pounds!'

'Yes, well you. . . Don't look at me, sir! Look in the window! Look in the window! Keep looking at that book! That's it. That's it. Have you got twenty pounds?'

'Yes, but. . . '

'No, I don't want twenty pounds from you now. I'll meet you back here in twenty-five minutes. Be looking into this window. Is that all right, sir?'

The man nodded.

'Be back here in twenty-five minutes. Now you go to the left and I'll go to the right. Don't look at me, sir! I'll see you back here.'

'How will I recognize you?'

'Don't worry about that, sir. I'll know you.'

'All right. Thank you very much.'

'That's all right, sir. That's all right.'

The punter took off and Charlie was straight back into the pub.

'Can anybody lend us ten bob?' he said.

'What d'you want ten bob for, Charlie?'

'I'll tell you when I get back.'

He was given ten bob and off he went. In minutes, he was back with a tube of Pro-Plus, which was a pep pill then on sale in every chemist's. Charlie dipped the tube in his beer and began to scrape off the label.

Twenty minutes later, the punter was back outside the shop. Charlie rushed straight across the road.

'Keep looking in the window, sir!' he said. 'Have I had problems? Have I had problems trying to get this stuff? Now I am telling you this stuff is so hot that it's unbelievable. For God's sake, don't give your wife more than two of these pills at a time. If you are rash enough to give her more than two, she'll go berserk. She'll take on everybody. She'll take on a brigade of guards. This is red-hot stuff I'm giving you. And I'm sorry, but I had to pay a lot more than I thought. It was short notice. So it's thirty pounds.'

'Thirty pounds! You said it'd be twenty!'

'I know I said twenty. Don't look at me, sir! Look in the window! Just look in the window!'

'I haven't got thirty pounds.'

'All right. Make it twenty-five.'

'Twenty-five then.'

'Don't hand me the money now, sir! What we'll do is you pass it with your right hand and I'll take it with my left.'

'You give me the pills first.'

'All right, all right. I'll give you the pills. Put them straight in your pocket. Don't look at me! Don't look at me!'

The exchange took place.

'Good bye, sir, and good luck!' Charlie said and was back in the pub. 'Right, lads,' he said. 'Twenty-five quid, just like that! We'll be able to drink all afternoon!'

About a month later, I was walking down Old Compton Street with Ringo Charlie. Coming towards us on the opposite side of the road was a chap in a bowler hat and striped suit. Suddenly he shouted, 'I say. You!'

Charlie said, 'Keep walking. Keep walking.'

'What is it?' I said.

'Keep walking. Keep walking.'

'Hello, you,' the chap shouted. 'I want to talk to you.'

We started to walk faster.

'What's the matter?' I asked Charlie.

'It's that punter I sold the Pro-Plus to.'

'Oh, Christ!' I said.

'That's all right. Keep walking.'

We were now almost running, but the chap sprinted across the road and grabbed Charlie by the arm.

'Let go of me! Let go of me!' Charlie growled.

'But you're that fellow who sold me. . . '

'I never sell stuff. I've never done anything like that. I don't know who you are. This is my friend, Tony Booth, the famous actor. How dare you do this in front of me! Tony Booth will vouch for me. I'm as straight as a die. What are you talking about?'

'No, no. It's about those pills you sold me.'

'I don't sell pills.'

'No, no. I want more. They were magic! They turned my wife into a nymphomaniac!'

'Oh, you mean those pills? Well, sadly, the price has now gone up to thirty quid. Meet me back here in half an hour.'

The guy came back in half an hour. Every month after that, Charlie sold him a tube of ten-bob pep-pills for thirty quid!

My spell in Soho ended when I took over from Matthew the tenancy of the shed at the back of Clarges Street and returned there. But after a short stay, I was told by dear Theo Cowan that by having a stream of ladies visiting me I was lowering the tone of the building. As I owed him a month's rent, he took the opportunity to give me notice!

At the time, we were recording a series of *Till Death* and there was a part in one of the episodes that seemed ideal for an actor I knew, called Kenneth Fortescue. I recommended him and he was given the part.

I was having a chat with him one day at lunch and mentioned that I had to leave Clarges Street.

'What are you going to do?' he asked.

'I don't know,' I replied. 'Working on this, I haven't got time to look for another place. I don't know what I'm going to do.'

'As a matter of fact,' he said, 'my mother has a flat in Nell Gwyn House. She's had the place since before the war. It's a controlled rent and it's six pounds a week. She's just moved to the country, but all her furniture's still there. I'm paying the rent, but I don't want to live there. Why don't you come back, have a look and if you like it you can move in?'

He took me back to this flat on the sixth floor of Nell Gwyn House in Chelsea. I couldn't believe it. Compared with the shed in Clarges Street, it was paradise. It actually had hot water and a proper kitchen!

I paid a month's rent in advance and stayed the night.

The next night when I came back from rehearsal, I thought to myself, 'I've never before seen so many beautiful girls in my life as there are living in this block.' Then when I told someone in the Queen's Elm in Chelsea that I was living in Nell Gwyn House, he said, 'That's Charvering Heights.'

'What do you mean?'

'Don't be stupid! "Charvering" is a good old Cockney word for screwing. What floor are you on?'

'The sixth.'

'I didn't know you were on the game as well, Tony!'

'What are you on about?'

'The sixth floor of Nell Gwyn House! That's why the whole building's called Charvering Heights, because the sixth floor's the home of the best high-class whores in London!'

It turned out that they lived in every other flat on the sixth floor but mine. They were my neighbours, and so I got to know them well. One, called Tricia, came from Liverpool and when she didn't have a client I often used to go to her place for a drink. She and her friends had a fund of stories, many of which involved some of the most important men in London. It was surprising how often I recognized people getting in and out of the lift! Less surprising is the fact that Nell Gwyn House was owned by the Church of England.

The crowd of us that used to drink in the Queen's Elm included Johnny Speight, Sean Connery, Michael Caine, Peter O'Toole, Ronny Frazer and Richard Harris. We were known as the Wild Bunch. One night, we'd all made an arrangement to stay on in the pub to watch one of Mohammed Ali's title fights. But, at about eleven-thirty, one of the actors had an altercation with the landlord who said, 'That's it! You can all piss off! I'm not going to risk my licence for the likes of you.'

We stood out on the pavement discussing where we should go. My place was the nearest and so we went back there. The arrival of these well-known faces made the doorman jump to attention – as did the girls on the sixth floor. Those that were not otherwise engaged were soon ringing up to say, 'Is it true that Sean Connery is with you?'

'Yes, he is.'

'Oh, I've got some champagne. I'm on my way round. I'd love to meet him.'

It went from there being half a dozen of us in this small flat to a party of about thirty people, half of whom were London's best-paid call girls. Booze was arriving from everywhere. When Ali won, there was lots of singing and general rowdiness. At about four o'clock in the morning, everybody left in a crescendo of noise.

Two days later, I received a letter from the Church Commissioners giving me notice for holding a rowdy party in a respectable building. The girls were all appalled and wrote letters to the Church Commissioners saying how badly I'd been treated. It took me years to live down the disgrace of having been thrown out of Nell Gwyn House, the best-known knocking shop in London!

14

By Invitation

As I had to move from Nell Gwyn House, a musician I knew said I could use his flat in Hanson Street while he was away on tour.

While I was staying there, I was asked to present the prizes for the Injured Jockeys' Fund at their annual dinner, which was held at Newbury Race Course. I've always loved racing. Knowing it was a good cause and thinking that I might pick up a good tip, I happily agreed to go.

It was mid-November and, about five days before the dinner, the old banger I had broke down. I dragged it into a garage and was told it would cost an arm and a leg to fix and that it would take at least a week.

I asked around, but none of my mates could lend me a car. It was going to cost me a fortune to hire a cab to Newbury and back again. Because it was a charity do, I wasn't being paid expenses!

The night before, I went into the pub on the corner of Hanson Street, which was frequented by local Greeks and Irish. I was bemoaning my fate to the landlord, when a guy sitting at the bar said, 'What's the problem?'

I told him and he said, 'That's no problem. You can borrow my car.'

'But I don't even know you.'

'Don't worry. I know you and you live just round the corner.

You fill the car up with petrol. I'm a betting man. If you get a good tip, pass it on.'

'Well, at least let me give you something.'

'No, don't be silly. Just take the car. Here's the keys. You can take it now. It's parked outside. Come on. I'll show you.'

We went outside and he pointed to a white Jaguar.

'That's the car,' he said.

'You're kidding!'

'No, I'm not. I'm lending it to you. It's a pleasure. Have a good time, Tony!'

'But I don't even know your name!'

'That's all right. Just call me Jock.'

'OK, Jock. But how will I get the car back to you?'

'Just drop the keys behind the bar on Saturday evening. I'll pick them up later.'

I bought Jock a couple of drinks and we talked about racing and football – the kind of things guys talk about in pubs.

The next day, I got in the Jaguar and swanned off to rehearsal. We didn't finish till six-thirty. Then I drove back, got my bib and tucker on, picked up a girl I was taking to the dinner, and started off.

By that time, it was a quarter to eight. It was in the days before the M4 had been completed. To reach Newbury, you still had to drive through the centre of towns. It was a terrible drive on a damp November evening.

I was the guest of honour at the dinner, and I arrived in Newbury at nine o'clock. It was Friday night, but the place was a ghost town. There was nobody about. On race days, the place was full of signs to the course, but I was going to a private dinner and so there was nothing. I had no idea of how to get there.

At last I saw a solitary figure walking along. I pulled up and asked the way to Newbury Racecourse.

'Take the first right,' the guy said, pointing left.

'You mean left, don't you?'

'That's right. Go to the end of that street and turn left,' he said, pointing right.

'You mean right, don't you?'

'That's right. When you get to the end, turn right again.' He pointed left. 'Then your first left' – pointing right – 'and you're there.'

Of all the people living in Newbury, I'd got to pick on the village idiot! However, I figured all I'd got to do was to take the opposite

137

direction to the one he'd said. I started off and soon became hopelessly lost.

Ten minutes later, I arrived at a perimeter fence. I drove along it and eventually arrived at an entrance. I'd just pulled up, when floodlights were switched on and over a loudspeaker a voice said, 'Stay where you are. Do not get out of the car. You are on government property.'

A group of guys rushed out and surrounded the car. I clambered out in my evening dress and was immediately recognized.

'What's going on?' I asked.

'That's what we were going to ask you, Tony. What you doing here?'

'I'm on the way to the racecourse.'

'Well this is the Regional Seat of Government!'

They then directed me to the racecourse and I arrived there at about ten-thirty, having missed the dinner and just in time to make my speech. I was well pleased! But they were very hospitable and we stayed carousing there until the second cock.

I'd had so much alcohol that I'd drunk myself sober. They tried to persuade us to stay but, having knocked back a gallon of coffee, I left the racecourse at about three-thirty in the morning.

It was raining. I drove at about sixty over the brow of a hill into a well-lit avenue. About three-quarters of a mile ahead, I saw a police roadblock.

'You know what's going to happen?' I said to the girl. 'They're going to ask me if it's my car, aren't they?'

I put my foot on the brake and came to a halt about six inches from the barrier. Immediately, there was a policeman by my window.

'Right. Get out of the car.'

Out I got and said, 'Before you say anything, I know you're going to ask me if this is my car.'

'That's right.'

'Then you're going to ask me the number of the car and I'm going to say, "Can't remember!" And you're going to say, "I don't believe you!" And I'm going to say, "It's the truth!"'

'Oh, I see. A smart arse, eh?'

Just then a police sergeant walked over and said, 'Hello, Tony. How are you? What you doing around here at this time of night with a beautiful girl in the car, eh, Tony?'

'Up to no good, of course.' Then I told him where I'd been.

'Oh, been drinking, have you?'

'Yes. But I'm sober now. I'll tell you what, though. I've got a terrific tip for tomorrow.'

'Really?'

'Yes. The leading trainer told me.' And I passed on a tip I'd been given.

'OK, Tony,' the sergeant said. 'I'll tell you what. You get back in the car. We were just about to pack up anyway. So we'll give you an escort to the start of the motorway.'

With one police car in front and another behind – both with their lights flashing – I drove down the middle of the road at about eighty. At the beginning of the motorway, the policemen waved us on our way.

We were almost home when, on the Cromwell Road, the Jaguar ran out of petrol. I hadn't realized the car used it as though it'd gone out of fashion. It was five o'clock in the morning. In the pouring rain and dressed in my evening togs, I tried pushing the Jaguar. It was a fruitless struggle. We had to abandon the car, hail a taxi and go on home.

After rehearsal the next day, I bought a can of petrol and took it to the Jaguar. I then drove to a garage, filled the tank and returned to Hanson Street. When I walked into the pub, who should be sitting at the bar but Jock.

I gave him the keys, bought him a drink and said, 'You'll never guess what happened last night!' Then I told him the story.

'Police! Roadblock!' he said. 'Well you were lucky!'

'Why?'

'Did they ask to look in the boot?'

'No. Why?'

'Did you look in the boot?'

'No. Why?'

'Come outside and I'll show you.'

We walked out to the car and he opened the boot.

I couldn't believe it. Inside, there were two sawn-off shotguns, several fur coats and boxes of jewellery.

'Not only is all that stuff nicked,' he said, 'but so is the car! We just wanted to get it out of the way for a while! See you, Tony. Ta-ta!'

Then he drove off. I never saw him again.

After that, I left Hanson Street and took over a one-bedroom flat in Eton Rise, Hampstead.

I used to drink in a pub called the Richard Steele. All the Hampstead Brigade used to get in there – Leon Griffiths who wrote *Minder*, Peregrine Worsthorne, Hugh McIlvanney of the

Observer. Fred, the landlord, was a smashing Cockney guy. His son – 'My boy Martin' – was bought whatever he wanted and was the height of fashion. Martin was very kind to me. I used to buy for next to nothing his hand-me-downs when after a week they'd gone out of style.

Throughout the sixties, I did a lot of campaigning for the Labour Party and one day, when I was at the BBC working on *Till Death*, I received an invitation from the Prime Minister and Mrs Wilson to attend his birthday party at 10 Downing Street.

'Who's set me up?' I thought. 'Ha, ha, ha! Well there's no way I'm going to fall for this. I'll just hang on until I hear someone mention something about a do at Downing Street and then I'll know who it is.' So I stuck the invitation in my pocket.

About a fortnight later, when I'd forgotten all about it, I was in the Richard Steele with a group including Patrick Wymark, who made his name in *The Power Game*. When someone asked if he'd be in the pub the following Thursday, Patrick, in his deep Churchillian voice said, 'Next Thursday? No, I can't make it, my dear fellow. I shall be at Downing Street. I've been invited to the Prime Minister's birthday party.' And from his pocket he produced an invite which he passed around to gasps of approval.

When it was handed to me, I said, 'Bloody hell! Hang on a second. I've got one of those, but I thought it was a joke.' And from my pocket I pulled out the invitation, the sight of which somewhat deflated poor Patrick.

'Are you going?' I asked him.

'Of course,' he said. 'I have replied. I've been sent a sticker for my car and the arrangements for parking.'

'You mean it's genuine?'

'Of course. And will you be there?'

'I don't know. I'll think about it.'

I thought about it for a couple of days and then I wrote to accept the invitation. It was too late for them to send me a sticker for my car. Not that it mattered to me. There was no way I wanted to drive up to Number 10 in my battered old Ford.

On the Thursday of the party, I'd arranged that the girlfriend I was taking would come round to my place to get ready. When I returned to my flat from rehearsal, she was still in the bath. I put on the stuff I'd hired from Moss Bros and sat there waiting while she dolled herself up.

'Come on,' I said. 'It starts at nine o'clock.'

'What does it matter?' she replied. 'It's a party, for Christ's sake!'

'Oh, perhaps we should take a bottle then!'

'Don't be silly. But parties go on all evening. In any case, it's bad form to be first there.'

She wasn't ready until half past nine and by that time I'd had more than a few drinks. It was peeing down with rain when I rang the taxi rank at Haverstock Hill.

The guy growled, 'Hello.'

'Can I have a taxi?'

'Where from?'

I gave him the address.

'Where you going to?'

'Downing Street.'

'Number fucking ten, of course!'

'As a matter of fact it is.'

'Listen! Don't piss me about, son. Do you want a taxi or don't you?'

'Yes, I do.'

'Well, where are you going?'

'The Whitehall Theatre.'

'That's better. Why didn't you say that in the first place?'

When the taxi arrived, the driver recognized me and fell about laughing. 'Ha, ha, ha,' he went. 'That was a good one, Tone. 10 Downing Street, eh? You would try that one on.'

We got in the taxi and I said, 'Look. Here's the invitation.' And I passed it through to him.

'Bloody hell!' he said. '10 Downing Street. I've never taken anybody there before. Right, you've got it.'

And off we went. Now I'd stuck a ten-pound note into my pocket. When we pulled up outside Number 10, it was raining. I handed the taxi driver the tenner, opened the door and a battery of photographers' lights flashed. My girlfriend and I stood there blinded for a moment. Then I turned and shouted, 'Hey! Come back!' The taxi driver was driving up the road with my tenner! As the fare was only a quid, he must have thought I was the last of the big tippers.

The door of Number 10 opened and a flunkie said, 'You're late! You're late! The Prime Minister was wondering where you were!'

I mumbled an apology and we were taken upstairs into the vast main room on the first floor. It was full of people standing around in evening clothes. I'd come in like a drowned rat.

I was taken over to Harold Wilson, who said, 'Ah! You've arrived, Tony. It did say nine o'clock.'

'Sorry,' I said. 'I thought it was a party.'

The flunkie hissed at me, 'This is the Prime Minister.'

I'd lost my ten quid, I was soaking wet and full of bottled courage. There was no way I was going to be mealy-mouthed. It wasn't my style. 'I know he's the Prime Minister,' I said. 'Me and millions like me made him Prime Minister, didn't we?'

'Oh, you're quite right, Tony,' Harold Wilson said, obviously in the best of humours. 'Ee, you're a lad! I'm sorry you missed the singing of "Happy Birthday".'

'What was that?'

'It was wonderful. Jeremy Thorpe and Harry Secombe sang "Happy Birthday"!' Wilson beamed with pleasure. He was like a schoolkid who'd just been given a new bike.

'Well,' I jibed, 'there's nothing wrong with my timing – is there? – missing that lot?'

This raised a few stifled laughs, but everybody was standing around as though they were in church. And a lot of them had empty hands. So I said, 'Is there any chance of a drink?'

While the flunkie went off to find me a glass of wine, I tried to buttonhole Wilson about his sell out of socialist policies. It was something about which I felt deeply. The Labour Party had carried with it into office the hopes of millions of people who wanted fundamental changes made. But nothing had happened and I told him so.

'Not tonight, Tony,' he said. 'This is a party. It's not the time for politics.'

'But it's the only chance I've had to speak to you since you got into this place. Why are you letting them do this to us? In 1964, before the election, I heard you going on about the changes you were going to make. So what happened, Harold?'

'It's not as simple as you think, Tony.'

We were having quite a ding-dong, when a waiter walked up wearing a Ministry of Works badge on the lapel of his evening coat. This guy was legless and as the tray he was holding lurched in front of one face after another he grabbed a glass, thrust it into a hand and said, "Ere you are! 'Ere you are!'

Then he spied me standing next to Wilson and he slurred, 'Fuck me! Look who it is? The Scouse git! How are you, Tone?' He put his arm round me, and went on, 'Bloody hell! This is the place, eh? The Labour Party, eh? We're 'ere now, aren't we?'

Each time I reached for a glass, his tray lurched out of my grasp. 'Here, pal,' I said, dying of thirst. 'Give us a drink, will you?'

He grabbed me tighter. 'Don't 'ave none of this rubbish. This is Ministry of Works rubbish. A good socialist like you, Tone, doesn't want to drink this shit. This is for that lot, isn't it?' he said, thrusting a glass into Wilson's hand. Then pointing at him, he went on, ''E, 'im there, 'as got in the back some very nice Cognac. I'll go and get some. 'Ere, cop 'old of this!' He gave me a glassful of cigarettes and staggered off.

I expected Wilson to say, 'Get rid of him!' but he acted as though nothing had happened. We continued with our conversation. I told him I couldn't understand why he was so delighted that Thorpe, the Liberal Leader, had come to his party.

'Your trouble is, Tony,' Wilson said, 'you take things far too seriously.'

'You're kidding! It is serious. We're standing here at Number 10. How can you tell me not to take things seriously?'

Back came the waiter with two tumblers full of brandy. He gave me one, raised the other and barked out, 'To the Labour Party!'

Everybody looked round and sheepishly said, 'To the Labour Party!'

I loved it! I took another swig and said, 'To the Revolution!'

The waiter thought this was great. 'To the Revolution!' he bellowed.

From there on in it was all downhill.

I was then accosted by Marcia Williams, the doyenne of Harold's kitchen cabinet and his closest confidante. Obviously bent on prising Wilson out of my clutches, she said, 'Would you like to see the Cabinet Room?'

'Why?'

'I've taken everybody else on a tour. Would you like to see it?'

'Why? Is the Cabinet sitting?'

'Of course not. Most of them are here.'

'So why do I want to see it? It's just a room, isn't it? With chairs and a table?'

'But it's where some of the most important decisions affecting our country are made.'

'I'll tell you what. None of the decisions taken in there has improved my life or anybody like me. That's the place where you carve it all up between you.'

'Ho, ho,' she laughed. 'They were right. You really are a rebel,' she said and left me so she could attend to Harold Wilson.

I looked around and, through the crowd of well-known faces, saw Mary Wilson standing alone in a corner of the room. I'd met her several times and so I went over to have a word with her. We chatted away. I was standing, with a hand pressed against the wall above her shoulder, when a fellow came over and smiled at us. He was wearing evening dress and so I said to him, 'Instead of just standing there, why don't you go over to the bar and fill up our glasses?'

I handed him the two glasses and away he went.

'What have you done?' Mary said nervously.

'What have I done?'

'That's the guest of honour. He's the Prime Minister of Luxembourg!'

I'll say this for the guy – he came back with two full glasses. He had style!

Mary Wilson and I both laughed. I took a step back and bumped into Harry Secombe, who hissed at me, 'For God's sake, boy, don't make a show of the profession in Number 10!'

'Why, Harry?' I said. 'It's our house. It belongs to the people, doesn't it?'

To this day, I don't know how I got home from the Downing Street party. I've been told that I was taken home in a police car! That was just as well. As the taxi driver had gone off with my tenner, I didn't have a penny in my pocket!

15

. . . Us Do Part

At irregular intervals over a ten-year period, the BBC reluctantly commissioned further series of *Till Death Us Do Part*. Most of the rest of the time I was unemployed. So I agreed to take part – much against my better judgement. As the years went by, working on the series became less and less pleasurable. The moguls of the BBC Light Entertainment Department continued to be hostile to the show and we were continually shunted round from one grotty rehearsal room to another.

For one particular episode, we were exiled to the Hammersmith Gaelic Club – a long Nissen hut on the large central traffic island. There was a stage at one end of the hall that was usually hired out for Irish dancing and wedding receptions.

We were rehearsing at the far end. Just after we'd started, we heard the clomp, clomp, clomp of someone marching up the centre of the long hall. It was a huge Irishman, who stopped at the table and announced, 'I want to book the hall for a week on Saturday!' He was told the way to the office, which was back out of the hall, turn right, round the corner and along to the end of an alley.

Warren hated having rehearsals interrupted. If a pin dropped, he'd lose his concentration. So he demanded that a notice be put up informing people where the office was. But that made no difference. At regular intervals, people still came in wanting to book the hall. A barricade of chairs was then erected with a blackboard on which was written, 'No admission beyond this point under any circumstances.' But still they came. The barricade was then built up with more chairs. Getting into rehearsals in the morning was like running an obstacle course. But still the people marched up the hall and every one of them seemed to be wearing hobnailed boots.

Eventually there were notices everywhere, inside and outside the building. We were getting to the end of rehearsals, playing a scene in which Warren sat in his armchair with his back to the doorway of the hall and I lay on the settee facing him. Again we were interrupted and Warren said, 'I've had it! I've totally and utterly had it! This part is difficult enough to cope with without having this army of people constantly parading through the place.'

Brain-drain tried to console him and sent his assistant out to find a set of the flashing lights they place round roadworks. After these had been installed, Warren said, 'I'll tell you what. The next person who comes through that door, I'm personally going to tell them their fortune. I don't care who they are.'

We went on with the scene. Suddenly there was a bang and a wallop. A few chairs went crashing over and I saw somebody come into the rehearsal room. Wearing heavy boots, he slowly clomped towards us. I looked at Warren and started to giggle.

Warren stopped half-way through his speech. Still with his back to the hall door, he leaned towards me and said, 'Why are you laughing?'

'Are you going to keep your promise?' I said.

'Whoever this is I'm going to tear his effing head off.'

'This I've got to see, Warren!'

'Big is he?'

'No, about your height.'

'Well, I'm going to murder whoever it is.'

The footsteps came nearer and nearer and nearer. Then the person stopped behind Warren's chair. Because I was laughing and giggling, Warren was apoplectic. He leapt to his feet and in his full Alf Garnett way, turned round and bellowed, 'Can't you. . .' He saw who it was, stopped midstream and then in the most polite of voices asked, 'Can I help you?'

The Indian postman who'd walked in said, 'Yes. Are you the manager of this hall?'

'No, no, no,' Warren said pleasantly. 'The manager is in the office. To find him, go out of that door, turn right, go round the corner, down an alleyway and the office is on the right.'

The postman then said, 'Thank you very much. You are most kind. Tell me. Are you not the Alf Garnett?'

'Yes I am. We're rehearsing here.'

'I am very sorry to be interrupting you.'

'That's all right.'

'Can I have your autograph, Mr Garnett?'

'Of course,' Warren said, and signed the piece of paper he was proffered.

He was all sweetness and light. So I said to the Indian, 'Ask him what he was going to say to you when you came through the door.'

'What?' Warren said.

'Go on, Warren. Tell him.'

Warren was put out. 'What do you mean?' he asked.

'No, no,' I said. 'Carry on with what you were going to say.'

The postman looked at me and said, 'What is it he was going to say?'

'No, he'll tell you,' I replied. 'Go on, Warren. Tell him.'

'You're a troublemaker, you are,' Warren said to me.

'No, I'm not. Come on. Fair dos.' Then I said to the postman, 'OK. I'll tell you. He said that the next person who came through that door and ignored the notices he was going to tear off his head. And you, my dear friend, were the next person to come in.'

The Indian fell about laughing and said, 'What fun you must have at these rehearsals. Thank you very much. You are most funny people.' Then he wandered off.

Warren sat down, shaking all over. 'What did you want to do that for?' he asked.

'Well, I'll tell you. You're a racist. That was racism of the worst kind. You were going to knock his head off whoever he was and you didn't. Why? Because he was an Indian!'

We then spent the next half an hour arguing about what racism was and whether either of us was a racist.

And that's how rehearsals went on. We were all finding the strain of rehearsals difficult to cope with. I was having lunch one day with Dandy Nichols and she was complaining about what was going on. So I said to her, 'I don't know how you manage to control yourself.'

'That's easy, dear,' she said. 'I take tranquillizers!'

Dandy was a terrific lady, who had a fund of stories that kept you in fits of laughter. She'd worked with everybody, but she was in her seventies and the strain of rehearsals did get to her. Once, she opened her handbag to show me her collection of pills. There

147

were more in there than at Boots the Chemist! Whatever was wrong with you, Dandy would have the appropriate medicine for you in her handbag.

While we were working on a series, the four of us were stuck together in a draughty room for ten hours day after day. In such an environment, it was inevitable that tensions would be created between us that spilled over into the shows and, I think, they contributed greatly to their success.

I cannot claim that I wasn't responsible for some of the aggression. Coming from my background, I didn't respond very well to the difficult working relationship with Warren and I gave as good as I got.

Up unto the mid-sixties I rarely drank – I couldn't afford it, I didn't like the taste, and I got drunk very easily and then behaved in a ridiculous fashion. Although the rest of the cast didn't drink, as soon as I started working on *Till Death*, I found myself in the company of drinkers and I readily joined them. I never touched any alcohol before or during a rehearsal or show, but I made up for it afterwards. Perhaps, like many other people, I drank because I was unhappy – both in my private life and in the show.

I'm sure, too, that Warren wasn't a happy guy at the time and, as I've mentioned, Dandy Nichols was physically unwell. It was Una Stubbs, with her equable temperament and ability always to see the other person's point of view, who provided the stable rock on which the show was built. As an actress, she has been desperately underrated. I admired her enormously and we got on well, although she often used to say to me, 'Sober, you're a lovely fellow, but drunk you're a severe pain in the arse!'

Despite the disagreements between members of the cast, the show increased in popularity with each series. Tickets for the recordings were at a premium. At the beginning, we could get as many as we wanted, but then they cut us down and we were rationed to half a dozen each.

On one occasion, we had an episode that was largely concerned with racism and religion. Unknown to the rest of the cast, Warren had just given an interview to the *Jewish Chronicle* and had arranged for two hundred and fifty of their readers to come along to the recording.

At that time, Warren did the warm-up before the show began and he was always a great success. The audience loved his one-man act. When it was over, he'd introduce the three of us. On this particular occasion, as I walked on to the set I looked out at the audience and couldn't believe it. A goodly number of the seats were occupied by Orthodox Jews.

'Oh, I see,' I said. 'Got all your relatives in tonight.'

'That's right,' he said. 'I'm well supported here tonight!'

And the audience cheered.

Then we started the show. Eventually we got to the lines that we'd had to fight very hard to retain. Warren walked to the front of the set. I followed him and said, 'Come on. Everybody knows your grandfather was a Jew.'

He turned round and said to me, 'Lies, lies, lies!'

'It's nothing to be ashamed of. Why should you be ashamed?'

'Well, you're a Paddy.'

'That's all right.'

'Mick! Mick! Mick!'

'OK. Jew! Jew! Jew!'

The audience were loving it and once he heard everybody laughing Warren started ad-libbing. He grabbed hold of my hands and said, 'Look, look at those hands. Look at those hands! Big Mick, Paddy!' He let go of my hands, waved his arms in the air and said, 'Just look at those hands!'

I pointed at his waving arms and said, 'Just look at yours. What a give-away!'

At this, the audience roared with laughter. Warren went purple and started shouting, 'I'm not Jewish! I'm not Jewish!' The more he roared, the more the audience fell about laughing.

We went on like this for a couple of minutes and then completed the section. The recording stopped and there was a long pause. Johnny Speight came rushing down from the box. 'Marvellous,' he said. 'Bloody fantastic! They want to cut it. I told them n-n-no way. They've got to keep it in.' He rushed out to the audience and said, 'L-L-Look. A l-l-lot of you are Jews. Did you f-f-find that offensive? Did you f-f-find that anti-Semitic?'

'No, no,' the audience shouted.

'W-W-Well, they w-w-want to cut it.'

'Shame! Shame!' they shouted back.

So the power of the audience overcame the objections and the ad-libs were retained for the show that was scheduled to be transmitted in two days' time.

After the recording, Johnny, in his euphoria, said to me, 'Come on. Let's go to the White Elephant.'

The White Elephant was a restaurant on Curzon Street that had originally started as a dining club for actors, who could go there after shows without being hassled by the public. It was always full of faces, although, as is the way with such places, the rich bought their way in and so not all the customers were involved with the theatre.

The place was always packed, but Johnny was one of their best punters and so we were immediately given a table and proceeded to get nobly pissed. On the way back from the lavatory, Johnny espied Bernard Levin and Milton Shulman sitting at a nearby table. He staggered over to them and said, 'Did you couple of Jews miss a scene tonight! I'm telling you it was f-f-fantastic. Who says you Jews don't have a sense of humour?'

That seemed rather like a slap in the face with a wet fish and not the kind of thing you should say to influential critics. I quickly went over to the table, mumbled an apology and dragged Johnny away.

The show went out uncut on Wednesday night. The next day we were at rehearsal. After lunch, Dennis Main Wilson arrived back late and said, 'I'm sorry, but somebody told me I had to read the *Evening Standard* and so I went to buy one. Have you read Milton Shulman's column? My God, I've never read anything like it!'

Johnny and I looked at each other and our hearts sank. 'Why didn't you stop me?' he said to me.

'I tried. I tried.'

'What did I say?'

'I can't remember!'

Pushing Warren out of the way, Johnny grabbed the paper from Main Wilson. He and I read through Shulman's column and discovered he'd given us a rave. He said never before on the television screen had there been seen two people saying to each other the kind of things that were usually only kept among the secrets in men's hearts. I'm certain it was that review which was largely responsible for *Till Death* winning the BAFTA award for best TV comedy that year.

After he'd received the award, Johnny became a celebrity and our relationship rapidly deteriorated. We'd started off the best of mates and ended up barely talking to each other.

In the early days, he would ring me up all the time, often in the middle of the night, to discuss the script. He'd try the Alf Garnett bits on me and I'd respond.

When the script arrived, he always asked me what I thought of it. In the first few series everyone was terrific. He maintained a fantastically high standard.

Then I received a script that I thought was a mish-mash of all the pieces cut out of previous episodes. It wasn't a good script.

Johnny rang me up and said, 'Well what d'you think of the s-s-script?'

'Well, I'm sorry, Johnny,' I said. 'I've got to be honest with you. It's not up to your usual standard. Honest to God, you should take it back and rework it.'

'B-B-But everybody else likes it,' he said.

'Yes,' I said, 'but I'm your friend and I'm telling you I know you can do much better. I know you're under pressure, but what the hell? We've got four days before we start rehearsing it and so rewrite it. Then you'll turn out the quality of script that everybody expects of you. If you don't, you're bloody well going to lose the high standard you've set for yourself.'

'You can't talk to me like that!' he said and hung up.

After that, things deteriorated rapidly. I found it difficult to talk to the guy. I was sad that we were no longer friends, because I thought we'd really been close. We'd had a lot of fun together – going to football matches, meals and having quite a few boozing sessions! But all that came to an end.

There's no doubt that Johnny Speight pushed forward the barriers of television comedy and that he and Warren Mitchell were responsible for creating one of the great comic monsters of the twentieth century. But at the time I thought that this particular script could have been better and that it was my duty to tell my friend to pull himself together. It was a mistake!

16

Oh! Calcutta!

At the end of the fourth series of *Till Death*, I began yet another period of unemployment. Then in 1970 I read in the *Observer* that Kenneth Tynan's review *Oh! Calcutta!* was going to be staged in London. I'd always admired Tynan, who I thought was the best British theatre critic since the war. I asked my agent to put me up for it. He did and I was sent a script.

I don't care what subsequently the critics said or what other people thought. Yes, the sketches involved simulated sex and nudity, but most of them were hilariously funny and extremely well written. Clifford Williams, an Associate Director of the Royal Shakespeare Company, was directing it and Michael White was the producer. So I knew it wasn't going to be crap and the furore it was going to cause was bound to make theatrical history. I was delighted to be asked to join the company.

Four Americans from the original New York production were coming over. Bill Macy, who played the lead, was staying for only a month and it was agreed that when he left I would take over all his parts. Until then, I was offered the pick of the rest and they were terrific, despite the challenge of appearing naked on stage and still making the audience listen, rather than just being voyeurs. It proved to be not impossible, but bloody difficult!

Before we opened, we had six weeks of rehearsal. When we first arrived, Kenneth Tynan and Clifford Williams told us that we'd start with exercises, both to get us fit for the dance sequences and to make us gel as a company.

One of these exercises was intended to create trust in each other. At first, we wore long towelling gowns. We closed our eyes, turned round three times and then, still with our eyes closed, walked about till we touched somebody else and then caressed his or her body.

The first time we did it, the only people I came into contact with were other guys. The next day, for the first time, I encountered one of the women in the cast. She had very cold hands and I got very hot and bothered!

After a week, we did the exercise totally naked and – much to my shame – every time a girl touched me I got an erection. Ten days later, there was a meeting of the cast and we were told, 'If an actor has an erection on stage, it may well constitute a breach of the law, leading to prosecution under the Theatres Act of 1968. John Mortimer, QC, is going to come into the rehearsals to give us his opinion.'

Immediately after that meeting, I discovered from another member of the cast that I'd been the only one doing the exercise with eyes closed. Half of the women had deliberately been keeping out of my way, while the others had thought it was a great joke watching me groping around in the dark!

John Mortimer, the great writer and advocate of whom I stood in awe, turned up to a rehearsal to watch my uncontrollable body movements! Now it was a totally different proposition doing the exercise with my eyes open and watched by the producer, the director, the choreographer, and a barrister. Naturally, I didn't get an erection – nor did I throughout the entire run of the show.

During rehearsals, another problem arose concerning a sketch Ken Tynan had written about a girls' school. Only the women were involved. But, one morning, I was called into rehearsal half an hour before the others. Only Ken and Clifford were there. Clifford said, 'We've tried every female member of the cast in the role of the headmistress. Frankly, none of them is getting it.'

'That's terrible,' I said. 'What are you going to do – cut the sketch?'

'No. Ken has come up with this marvellous idea.'

'OK, Ken,' I said. 'Let's hear your marvellous idea.'

'Why don't you play it?' Ken Tynan said.

'Pardon!'

Ken, Clifford and I sat and talked about it. Up to then, I'd never played a woman, but Ken threw down the gauntlet and, always one for a challenge, I picked it up.

Shortly afterwards, the girls turned up and were told I was going to play the headmistress. They'd been rehearsing the sketch for a couple of weeks and knew all the moves. I didn't. So, as we ran through it, Clifford led me by the arm. I was shaking with terror.

I was then faced with the problem of playing a woman – and it wasn't easy. I am six foot one tall and my shoes are size nine. The whole costume had to be specially made for me. As for the character, I figured that I should play her as a butch lesbian – it seemed the only way I might get away with it.

When it came to the dress rehearsal, I had all kinds of problems. I'd never before worn a skirt or high-heels. Trying to pull them on, I laddered four pairs of tights. Then I put on the wig and by God did I look ugly! Even a sailor who'd been at sea for six months wouldn't have cast me a lecherous glance.

I walked on stage for the sketch and all the male members of the cast and the technicians pissed themselves with laughter. 'Golly gee!' I thought. 'They think I'm funny!' So I played it for the laughs. When the sketch was over, the lads cheered and stamped their feet. It'd been a great success.

In the dressing-room, I was taking off the costume when in burst Ken Tynan. 'What the f-f-f-f-fuck do you think you're doing?' he stammered.

'What d'you mean?'

'My God! I can't tell you how a-a-a-a-appalled I am.'

'Why?'

'You just threw the whole thing away. You played it like every f-f-f-f-fucking drag queen I've ever had the m-m-m-m-misfortune to see. Don't you realize that in rehearsals you were giving the most devastating of performances? You *were* a lesbian on stage. It confused everybody. Nobody knew it was you. Go back to doing that. It was beautiful.'

'If I go back to doing that, Ken,' I said, 'we won't get a single laugh.'

'I don't care if no one laughs throughout the whole sketch. Your performance will carry it. You must do it. I'd sooner pull the sketch out than have you play it as you did.'

As I admired the man and was flattered by his comments, I said, 'OK, Ken. You're right. I'll do it.'

The first night of *Oh! Calcutta!* at the Roundhouse was an incredible experience that only the cast can understand. At the end of the first number, when we dropped our gowns and stood there naked, we could feel a wave of shock flood over the audience and then, after what seemed like an eternity and just as the conductor raised his baton for us to carry on, a roar went through the theatre. People stood up, applauded and cheered. We knew then that, naked and alone, we'd overcome semi-hostility and created a smash hit. It was a fantastic moment.

As the evening progressed, the audience clearly loved the show, laughing at all the jokes and being wildly appreciative. Then it came to the school sketch. I played the part of the headmistress right down the middle. For ten minutes there was stony silence. At the end, there wasn't a single clap. Every other sketch was applauded and cheered.

After the show, Ken came backstage and said to the cast, 'The best part of the show was the magic moment at the end of the f-f-first sketch. But for me, almost as impressive, was the ten minutes of silence during which the bedazzled audience tried to work out what the hell was happening in the school sketch. They all wanted to know where this dyke had suddenly come from to terrify the girls the audience had already grown to love.'

No matter what Ken thought about the sketch, the director and the producer hated it and wanted it taken out. But Ken had devised the show and it was his sketch. So it stayed in.

The reaction of the audience to the sketch was the same at every show and, after the sixth night, Ken was persuaded to pull it out. He was very upset and said to me, 'I wish I was able to review the show, because I've got to tell you that its one great moment was your performance as the headmistress. I don't know how you did it.'

'Fear, Kenneth. Fear!'

After a month at the Roundhouse, *Oh! Calcutta!* transferred to the West End. At last I was earning very good, regular money. Now I was the sort of guy that, if I'd got a hundred quid in my hip pocket, nothing phased me. If I knew I was going to receive another hundred the next week, I had the strength of a giant! As a result, while I was in *Oh! Calcutta!* I was on top of the world.

So when I was told that the BBC were going to do another series of *Till Death*, I didn't want to renew all the unhappy memories. I turned it down. A month passed – I heard nothing. 'At last,' I thought. 'I've thrown off the chains!'

One night, I was doing the show and the manager came round to see me during the interval. 'Guess who's out front?' he said.

'I don't know.'

'Warren Mitchell.'

155

'Oh, I see,' I said. 'Can't be he wants to see me without my clothes on. What does he want?'

The manager gave me a note, which said: 'Enjoying the show. Like to see you for a drink or possibly a meal afterwards. Then we can talk. Warren Mitchell.'

I thought, 'What the hell! He's going to buy me a meal.' Besides, I never drank during the show and when we finished there was only a quarter of an hour till the pubs closed. But if we went to a restaurant, I could drink on Warren for at least another hour. So I agreed to go out to dinner with him.

After the show, Warren came backstage and met the rest of the cast. Then we went out to dinner. Knowing that *Oh! Calcutta!* still had at least six months to run and with the courage born of several large brandies, I was ready to tell him just why I'd no intention of ever returning to *Till Death*.

So after the meal, when he broached the subject, I started: 'We can't work together, Warren. I'm sorry. And I don't like my part, because I feel that Johnny has no sympathy for the young or for women. At first I thought the show was attacking the bigoted ideas of Alf Garnett, but now it's become a vehicle for expressing those ideas. Even I was fooled at the beginning, but what seemed to be a revolutionary left-wing show is really subversive right-wing propaganda.'

Warren then said, 'I'm here to ask you if you want more money.'

'No, it isn't money, Warren. I'm working now and for once I don't need the money. I just don't need the hassle. That's why I want to break free.'

'OK,' he said. 'I'm going to do something I've never done before. I'm going to plead with you to come back. I won't go down on my knees, but I want you in the show.'

'Why, Warren? Why?'

Then, in the middle of the restaurant, he suddenly went straight into Alf Garnett and said, 'Because you are the only fucker in the world that I've just got to look at and I lose my mind, don't I? You drive me crazy. I 'ate everything about you. I 'ate everything you stand for. I 'ate your ideas. I 'ate what you say. I 'ate the way you look. That's why you've got to be in the show. Without you, I can't play the part. As soon as I walk in and see you, I'm there, aren't I?'

I was so taken aback, so full of drunken bonhomie and so flattered that I said, 'Well if that's the only reason why you want me back, you've got it. We've got ourselves a show. But can you

156

keep your voice down? Everybody's staring and the head waiter's just coming over to stop you throttling me.'

So I went back to *Till Death*. By this time, the show was a huge success and Warren had become a big name. All sorts of people wanted to be at the recording. After the second show, Warren knocked on my dressing-room door and said, 'I want to introduce you to somebody.'

He presented the wife of a famous rock star, who told me that she and her husband were great fans of the show and asked if I'd like to go back to their place for dinner. I had to say no because I'd already made other arrangements. So off she went with Warren.

The next show, she turned up. And the next. After the fifth show, I happened to be leaving the dressing-room when Warren dashed by after the dresser, shouting, 'Bring back my costume. Bring back my costume. I'm taking it with me.' He collected his things together, packed them into a holdall and left with the rock star's wife.

Two days later, I'd arranged for Warren to give me a lift to rehearsal because my car had broken down. His costume was on the back seat. So I said, 'What's that all about?'

'Well,' he said. 'That woman wanted to take a picture of me in my costume.'

'Oh, really,' I said.

'Yes.'

'Sounds a bit kinky to me.'

'Well, you don't know the half of it.'

Then he proceeded to tell me the story of what had happened. She'd taken him back to their house in Fulham and he'd changed into his costume, because she'd said she wanted to have dinner with Alf Garnett. Warren played the part all the way through the candlelit dinner. Afterwards, she took him down into the lounge area and announced that she wanted to make love to him.

'I couldn't believe it,' Warren said.

She kissed him and then said, 'Would you mind moving to this side?'

'What do you mean?' Warren asked.

'We can't get a decent shot if you're that side and it's you we want to see.'

'What do you mean?'

She said, 'Well, we've videoed the dinner and now we're videoing this – me making love to Alf Garnett!'

'What the hell did you do?' I asked.

157

'What do you think I did?' Warren said. 'I didn't even make an excuse. I just left!'

'But didn't you see the camera?' I asked.

'Of course I did,' he said. 'But I just thought it was one of those security jobs.'

Poor old Warren! For once I really felt sorry for him! But not for long. I was finding that working with him was just as much of a strain as it had always been.

I wasn't particularly into being interviewed by the press, but the following week I was told that the BBC had fixed up for me to speak to a guy from the *Evening Standard*. We met and had lunch. I gave my usual guarded interview and answered all his daft questions. We finished and he said, 'Great. I've just got to phone it in. What time are you due back at rehearsal?'

'I'm not due back till three-thirty,' I said. 'Then I've just got to sit on a settee while Warren rattles on and on.'

'Well stick around and have a drink,' he said.

That seemed like a great idea. I'd only got one line that afternoon. I knew that even if I was half-cut I could sleep it off on the settee. And after the rehearsal Warren was giving me a lift at least part of the way home.

The reporter rang in his copy, returned and bought more drink. Then he said, 'Between you and me, what really happens on *Till Death*?'

'Between you and me?'

'Yes.'

'Off the record?'

'Yes.'

'Well, I'll tell you. It's agony. Every day is agony.' I went into how I was feeling about the way the series was developing, about how difficult the rehearsals were and about my deteriorating relationship with Johnny and Warren. And I told some funny, private stories about what had happened at rehearsals.

Suddenly he said, 'Oh, look. It's two-thirty. I must get back. You stay here. I'll sign the bill.'

Off he went and I had a few more drinks with the landlord. Then I staggered back to the rehearsal at Maida Vale. I had a kip on the settee and said my one line. We stayed late, because Warren wanted to work on his long speeches.

Then Warren gave me a lift. He was happy to do that, providing he didn't have to go out of his way. That night, he'd agreed to drop me off at Chalk Farm underground station.

We arrived there at about half-past six. As I stepped out of his car, I saw the *Evening Standard* billboard announcing, 'GARNETT FAMILY ROW ERUPTS'. 'Oh my God!' I thought, and quickly turned round to face the car, holding my coat open in the hope of obscuring the blazing headline.

'Thank you, Warren,' I said. 'See you tomorrow!'

'Are you all right?' he asked.

'Fine,' I replied, standing there like a lemon in the rain with my coat held wide open. And off he went.

I bought a paper and there on the front page was everything I'd said off the record to the reporter – all about the terrible rows and how we couldn't stand each other.

The next morning, I made my own way to rehearsal. I arrived a quarter of an hour early, but as I approached the door I could hear Warren in full flood at the other end of the hall. He was ranting on to Main Wilson about – guess what? – the exclusive interview with me plastered across the front page of the *Evening Standard*: 'Something's got to be done about it. Have you read it? I ought to sue him!'

Main Wilson chipped in, 'Suing is a bad move. Can't you leave it until after this series?'

In my soft shoes, I walked across the hall towards them.

Warren was saying, 'I'll kill him. When he comes in 'ere, I shall tear his fucking 'ead off!'

At that point, I tapped him on the shoulder and said, 'Good morning, Warren. How are you?'

He nearly choked himself! Then he said, 'I am not talking to you and that's that!'

The rehearsal was very interesting. Warren sulked all day and so, for once, we finished early. Dandy Nichols's response was, 'You should give interviews like that every day. Then we'd all have some decent peace and quiet!'

17

By Appointment

Till Death continued to be an extraordinary success. Wherever any of the cast went, a crowd gathered. It was difficult for any of us even to walk down the road. People wanted to talk to us and have us sign old bus tickets and the backs of cigarette packets.

We were also approached to make public appearances. I thought it was a ludicrous idea that we should be paid for just cutting a ribbon or presenting a cup. But as I was perpetually short of funds, I often succumbed to the offer.

On one occasion, I was invited to open a new men's shop at John Lewis's department store in Leeds. I was told that afterwards I'd have dinner with the manager, be paid my hundred-quid fee, and have time to be back in London for the pubs opening.

I didn't know what I was expected to wear, but I washed my hair, had a shave and put on a shirt, trousers and my one decent jacket.

It was a beautiful spring day when I arrived in Leeds. I went straight into the bar at the station hotel, where I'd been told I'd be met and then taken to the store.

There were about half a dozen punters in the bar when I arrived. I ordered a gin and tonic. Nobody showed up and so I ordered another. I'd just started on it, when a boy walked through the bar carrying a message-board on a stick. 'Mr Booth. Mr Booth,' he was calling. I asked the boy what the message was and he told me I was wanted on the telephone.

I picked up the phone at reception and said, 'Yes.'

A sharp voice said, 'Anthony Booth?'

'Yes. Speaking.'

'I am the Assistant Chief Constable.'

'Oh, yes.'

'Unless you arrive at Lewis's within the next ten minutes I am going to charge you with causing a breach of the peace. Don't you know what's going on down here? The place is like a madhouse. We've got the mounted police out.'

'What are you talking about?'

'You are Anthony Booth, aren't you?'

'Yes, I am.'

'And you're appearing at Lewis's store today?'

'Yes, I am.'

'Well, it's been advertised on the radio and in the papers. The traffic is at a standstill. It's down to you. Either get down there or we'll come and get you.'

By this time I was a shade put out. 'Who the hell did you say you are?' I asked.

'I'm the Assistant Chief Constable.'

'Oh, my arse!' I said and hung up, thinking it was a joke.

I went back to the bar and said to the barman, 'Do you know? I've just had a phone call from some joker claiming to be the Assistant Chief Constable who said Leeds is blocked with traffic and it's all my fault.'

A bloke sitting by the bar said, 'It's true. I had to get out of my taxi and walk to the station. All the roads are blocked by screaming women. Is it your fault?'

'Oh, come on,' I said.

'No, I'm not kidding,' he said. 'It's total chaos out there.'

I couldn't see it had anything to do with me and assumed that the crowds must be there for the start of the spring sales.

Just then, a man rushed in and said, 'Thank God you're here, Tony. I had a hell of a job getting through. They've blocked off the roads. I've been told by the. . .'

'Don't tell me – the Assistant Chief Constable!'

'Right! Unless we get you there, they're going to use the mounted police to clear the streets because the traffic's all stopped. Come on, we've got a car outside.'

I followed him out of the hotel bar. Outside the sun was blinding so I pulled out a pair of shades, put them on and got in the car.

161

A hundred yards up the road we were stopped by the police and into the front of the car jumped a bloke wearing a uniform with salad dressing on the epaulettes. Around us was a mammoth crowd, through which mounted policemen were trying to clear a way. With two horses in front, one on either side, and two behind, the car slowly edged its way through this heaving throng. Lewis's was just up the road, but it took us three-quarters of an hour to get there. People were hammering on the roof, banging on the windows and demanding autographs.

Meanwhile, I was getting an ear-wigging from the man with the salad dressing – 'How dare you speak to the Assistant Chief Constable like that? You're lucky you're not being arrested here and now!'

Eventually, we pulled up in the road outside Lewis's. There was a line of policemen right up to the main entrance, where, standing behind the locked doors, were terrified members of the staff.

'You'll have to run,' the bloke in the front of the car said.

I did – and it was a gauntlet. I'd covered three-quarters of the way when I was tripped up. As I tried to get to my feet, hands started ripping off my clothes. My only jacket was literally torn from me, off went my shirt and my shades. Then I was bundled by half a dozen burly policemen into the shop. I was scratched and bleeding. The only clothes I had left were my trousers. I looked like something the cat'd brought in.

The manager then started to berate me: 'This is all your fault! We've had to clear the store. It was a riot. We haven't sold a thing since ten o'clock this morning! People wouldn't buy anything – they just wanted to gawp at you. Until you've gone, we won't be able to sell anything. You'd better cut the ribbon quickly and we'll get you out of here!'

'Dressed like this!'

'Oh, no. Right! Well, you'd better get something. OK.'

We went into the men's department and I was given a shirt, tie and jacket. In the gents, I washed the blood off my face and got dressed.

I cut the ribbon. They rushed me to the boardroom and only then did they open the doors to let the crowd in. I was stuck in the building for hours, because the punters were clamouring outside for autographs.

At last the time came when they decided it was safe for me to be smuggled out of the building. I asked for my cheque and was given fifty quid in cash. The manager said it was impossible to get to the accounts department and so I'd be sent a cheque for the other half of my fee.

A few days later, I received a cheque from Lewis's. It was for fifteen quid. They'd deducted thirty-five pounds for the jacket, tie and shirt! But they had given me a discount!

In 1972, *Till Death Us Do Part* was selected to appear in the *Royal Variety Show*. Johnny Speight wrote a very funny fifteen-minute sketch about the family watching the *Variety Show* on television and criticizing all the acts. Because of the concern voiced by the media, the script had to be submitted a fortnight before so that a check could be made on the language used. It became headline news that the sketch would include three 'bloodies'!

At the time, we weren't working on *Till Death* and so I was signing on at the Social Security in Lisson Grove, a place so popular with the theatrical profession that it was called 'The Actors' Club'. As luck would have it, the show was on a Monday and that was my signing-on day. Knowing that I'd be seen in the *Royal Variety*, I asked them if it would be all right to appear because, as it was a charity, I wouldn't be paid. I received a letter to say that as long as I signed on and didn't receive a fee it would be all right. I'd still be paid my dole money.

My mother wanted to see the show. So I inquired if there were any complimentary tickets, but was told that as it was the *Royal Variety Show* there was no such thing as comps. Each performer was allowed to buy four tickets and they were fifty pounds each. Two hundred quid out of my dole money was totally out of the question! I asked if there was anything cheaper. After prolonged negotiations it was agreed on the day before the performance that I could buy two twenty-five quid tickets for the price of one. 'But that will mean,' I was told, 'that your mother and girlfriend will be in one of the tiers, while everybody else's relatives will be sitting in the stalls.'

'That's all right,' I said. 'It's going to take a month's dole money to pay for the tickets I've got!'

There was a rehearsal on the Sunday and we were asked to pay for our own coffee and sandwiches. I didn't eat or drink that day!

On Sunday evening I was contacted by a reporter from the *Daily Mirror* who told me he was doing a piece on the Royal Variety Show. 'Liberace,' he said, 'is staying at the Savoy and he's being picked up from there in a Rolls and taken to the Palladium. How are you getting there?'

'I've got to be there at midday,' I said. 'What I'm going to do is catch a bus to St John's Wood, walk to Lisson Grove and sign on. Then I'll walk to Marylebone Station, get the tube and walk to the theatre from there.'

'You're kidding,' he said.

'No, I'm bloody not!'

'You're actually signing on?'

'Sure,' I said. 'I need the money! I had to get special permission from the Social both to sign on early and to do the show.'

'What time are you signing on?'

'Eleven o'clock.'

On Monday morning, I walked round the corner of Lisson Grove and saw a gang of photographers standing outside the dole office door. As soon as they saw me, they started taking pictures. They caused total confusion inside, flashing away while I signed on. They followed me to the station, piled into the tube with me, and I arrived at the Palladium with this gaggle of pressmen, just as Liberace drove up in the Rolls. He clambered out beaming, but the photographers ignored him – they were too busy taking shots of me walking into the theatre.

All 'English acts – males' were in one dressing-room. All 'English acts – females' were in another and so on for the American acts. Only Liberace and Elton John were given special treatment. They shared the stars' dressing-room. So Warren Mitchell and I were crammed into a dressing-room with a score of others, including Arthur Askey, Dickie Henderson, Ken Dodd, Mike Yarwood, and Rod Hull. There wasn't room to turn round.

After we'd done the runthrough, somebody arrived in the dressing-room and handed out souvenir programmes. My mother had come down to stay with me for the show and before I left she'd said, 'I want you to do one thing for me, Tony.'

'What's that?' I said.

'Will you get me Liberace's autograph?'

When I opened the programme, I saw Liberace's photograph and foolishly said, 'Oh, my God! I've got to get Liberace's autograph for my mother.'

Mike Yarwood then said, 'Oh, yes. I promised my mum, too. Will you get one for me?' And he handed me his programme.

Then all the artists said, 'I've got to get it for my daughter, my aunt, my granny or somebody else.'

I ended up with a huge pile of programmes and was despatched down the corridor to Liberace's dressing-room. When I arrived there, I looked back and from Arthur Askey to Rod Hull there was a column of faces peering at me round our dressing-room door.

I knocked and heard Liberace's much-imitated voice say, 'Who is it?'

'Excuse me, Liberace,' I said. 'I am in the cast.'

'Come in.'

I opened the door and there he was lying on a chaise-longue, wearing a dressing-gown decorated to look like a piano and covered in musical motifs. Around the collar and the cuffs was pink tulle. In his hand was a glass of champagne.

'Oh, my God!' he said. 'You're that guy from that show. I watched the rehearsal. I love it. I love it. Come in. Come in.'

'I just wondered if you'd sign these,' I said, proffering him the pile of programmes.

'Oh, my, you do want a lot of autographs.'

'Well, yes,' I said. 'I happened to say that my mother wanted your autograph and everybody in the dressing-room asked me to get one for them as well.'

'Oh, I see. The cowards sent you, did they?'

'No, no,' I protested.

'That's all right,' he said. 'You drew the short straw, eh? Well, never mind. Now which is your programme?'

'It doesn't matter. They're all the same.'

'Well I'll leave yours to last.'

And he signed all the programmes, bar one, just with his name – 'Liberace'.

Then he said, 'What's your mother's name?'

'Vera.'

He proceeded to create the most extraordinary autograph I've even seen in my life. His name and my mother's were drawn in the shape of a piano with a candelabra on top. He spent a good five minutes doing it and underneath he wrote, 'You have a very brave son!' It was a beautiful work of art.

'That's fantastic,' I said. 'Thank you very much.'

I gathered together all the programmes and was about to go when Elton John, who was lying on another chaise longue on the other side of the room said, 'Doesn't your mother want my autograph?'

'Yes, of course,' I said quickly. 'Sorry. I forgot.' I went over and said, 'Do you want to sign them all?'

'No,' he replied. 'Just your mother's.'

He did a sketch of himself on the opposite page. Then off I went. The heads were still peeping round the dressing-room door and there was a chorus of, 'You've been a long time in there. What have you been doing?'

When I showed them what Liberace had written for my mother, there was uproar and they started bawling me out for not getting them all one like it. Such is the gratitude of fellow artistes!

The *Till Death* sketch wasn't on until the second half of the show. Now Warren was a stickler for detail. If he had to read a newspaper, it had to be that day's newspaper.

We went on stage to do the sketch, the lights came up and Warren was sitting there looking at the back page of the *Evening Standard* that had been placed on the table. I was sitting facing him and there on the front page was a photograph of me signing on!

We were two or three minutes into the show, when Dandy and Una had a little bit to say. Warren turned the paper over, gripped it tight and almost fell out of the chair. Then he started to read the article. Suddenly, up came his cue and there was silence on stage. He looked up and stared around in panic.

There was no way we were going to be given a prompt. We were on a little tiny set in the middle of the stage, miles from anywhere. We were on our own. I knew straightaway what had happened. As usual that day, he'd been impossible and for a split second I thought about leaving him to stew in his own juice. But, of course, there's no way any actor can do that. We were all in it together. So I said, 'You've lost your thread, haven't you?'

'Yes, I 'ave,' he said. 'I 'ave lost my thread.'

'Was it something you read in the paper?'

'Yes it was. It bloody well was something I read in the paper! Disgusting things they put in the paper!'

We ad-libbed for a couple of minutes and gradually I got him back into the script.

After the show, it was line-up time. The whole cast was lined up along the stairs, all the way down to the stars who were in the foyer. We were on the landing next to a group known as the Jackson Five. Actually standing beside me was a young kid called Michael Jackson.

The Queen Mother started with Liberace and moved up the stairs. As she was an extremely sociable lady, she spent a lot of time talking to everybody and so, by the time she approached us, her allotted time was nearly over. After she'd finished shaking hands with Michael Jackson, Bernard Delfont said to her, 'I'm sorry, Your Majesty, but there are many artistes still to see.'

'Oh, yes, of course!' she said.

By this time, having finished the six half-bottles of champagne given to me by the management, I was a fearless man. The Queen Mother shook my hand and said, 'Congratulations!'

Before she'd let go of my hand, I said, 'No, no, ma'am. Congratulations to you!'

She went to move on, then stopped, turned and said, 'Pardon!'

I said, 'Congratulations to you!'

She said, 'What on?'

'The horse winning on Saturday!'

Two days before the *Royal Variety Show*, there'd been a steeple-chase meeting at Sandown Park and the Queen Mother's horse, Inch Arran, had run. I'd been watching the races on television and when I saw her horse I thought, 'I fancy that. I think it's got a chance.' I put twenty pounds on it and it dutifully won at 9–2.

The Queen Mother said, 'Inch Arran?'

'Yes!'

'Were you there?'

'No. I watched it on television. I think it was great!'

'Oh, yes, it was magnificent.'

'Are you going to run it in the Grand National?'

'I might do.'

'Well, it's a two-and-a-half-mile horse, it'll be good for the Grand National.'

'Did you back it?'

'Yes.'

'What price did you get?'

'9–2.'

'Did you? I only got 7–2!'

Then she remembered that two years previously I'd literally bumped into her at the races. I'd just been told by a jockey friend of mine that he thought his horse would win and when I saw an opening in the crowd I ran through to place my bet, nearly knocking down this sweet little old lady. I danced round with her, saying, 'I'm terribly sorry. I'm terribly sorry.'

She said, 'My, you're in a hurry!'

I said, 'Yes, I've got a tip. I've got to go.'

'What is it?' she asked and I told her.

So, as we were standing there on the steps of the Palladium, she said, 'I remember meeting you at Sandown. You gave me a tip and it won!'

She had a fantastic interest in horses and we stood there chatting happily about racing, while the rest of the retinue was jammed on to the staircase. As we laughed and joked, Bernard Delfont was getting himself into a terrible tizz. His whole schedule was up the creek. Eventually he leaned across and said, 'Excuse me, ma'am. We must get on.'

'Yes, yes,' she said. Then she turned back to me and said, 'I have to go. But I do so like talking about horses. Why don't you call on me at Kensington Palace and we can have tea together? By the way,' she added confidentially, 'I'm not supposed to tell you this, because I was advised not to spend any time with you terrible people from the show, but I always watch your programme and I love it!'

Then she moved on, shaking hands with the others and saying, 'Congratulations! Congratulations! Congratulations!' as she sped rapidly up the stairs and then disappeared into the night.

The next person in the royal retinue was Princess Margaret, who'd been left standing on the stairs tapping her fingers. 'What was all that about?' she asked.

'Oh, we were just talking about horses,' I said.

'Oh, I see,' she said. 'That explains it. Well I'm glad to meet you at last.'

'Yes. I've always wanted to meet you.'

'Oh, really. Why?'

'Ever since I saw that picture of you in your Girl Guide's uniform! You haven't still got it, have you?'

She laughed and said, 'Oh, they told me you were terrible.' Then she leaned closer and added, 'Yes, I do still have it, as a matter of fact!'

As everybody else came along, they all wanted to know what both the Queen Mother and Princess Margaret were laughing about.

We'd been told by the press officer that immediately after the occasion we shouldn't tell anybody what the Royals had said to us. So when I got back to the dressing-room and all the other artistes asked, 'What was going on?' I answered, 'Nothing!'

Mike Yarwood said to me, 'Come on. What were you talking about to the Queen Mum?'

'Just something we had in common,' I replied.

As quick as a flash, Dickie Henderson said, 'Oh, you mean the fact that neither of you carry any bloody money!'

18

Life After Death

Although I'm sure it had nothing directly to do with the *Royal Variety Show*, in the period that followed I was offered several parts in films and in the theatre.

One day, I received a call asking me to go and see Douglas Hickox, who was directing *Brannigan*, a film John Wayne was going to make in London. When I went along, I was told that there were three parts I could play and that I could have my pick. I selected one and Hickox said, 'No, no. I'd prefer you to play one of the other parts.'

'So why did you offer me the choice?'

'We want you in the picture. But the character you picked has a fight with John Wayne and we've already got somebody else in mind. If you insist, you can have it. But if you take the part we have in mind, we'll build it up for you.'

Still having green eyes, I agreed. I hadn't yet learned to distrust the promises of film directors!

In the final script, the part was still only a minor one and I was only in one scene. I was told this would take three days' filming at the studio. When my turn came to be called on to the film, it was running so far behind that I was told I might be there for as long as three weeks. That was great! I needed the money!

On the first morning, I was taken to the dilapidated offices at the studio where the scene was to be shot. There, the director introduced me to Richard Attenborough, who was also in the scene. Eventually, John Wayne made his entrance, doing the most appalling imitation of a John Wayne walk. He was so over the top that it was ridiculous!

'Hi,' he said. 'I'm Duke.'

I had to stop myself laughing. Tenth-rate impressionists in back-street clubs did it better.

He was a big man – at least six foot four – but he had the worst wig I'd even seen. Everybody had told me, 'Don't look at the rug! Don't look at the rug!' The first thing I did was look straight at the rug! It didn't fit. It didn't match! I would have thought with all the money they were spending, the producers would at least have gone to the trouble of getting the guy a decent wig! Instead, he had a second-hand Weaver-to-Wearer job stuck on the top of his head!

But he turned out to be a hell-of-a-nice guy and easy to work with.

We started on the scene and flew through it. Long before lunch-time, we'd almost completed it and we were supposed to take three days!

At the end of the scene, John Wayne had to bang me up against a wall that had shots of suspects being projected on to it. These were flashing on my face as he was talking to me – that kind of arty-farty shot that goes down well with the punters! Attenborough had gone off to answer the phone, and John Wayne had to say to me, 'If I were you, I'd tell him what he wants to know, because last night, in a pub, he bit off someone's ear.' I'm not impressed. So he adds, 'And that isn't all. . . ' Then he whispers something in my ear.

'No,' I had to say.

'Oh, yes,' he replied.

Then, as Attenborough returns, I say, 'OK, OK, I'll tell you.'

When we came to play the scene, John Wayne spoke so slowly that his short speech seemed to last for at least five minutes. I was banged up against the wall wondering what was going on. The only way I could play the scene was to forget it was John Wayne. He was an American burk called Brannigan who was wearing a stupid wig, had a beer gut and was acting tough, thinking he was frightening me. No way!

When he finished, he leaned across and went 'Psss, psss, psss,' in my ear.

I fell about laughing.

'Cut,' they shouted.

'Sorry,' I said, wiping the spit out of my ear.

'What's the matter?' John Wayne drawled laboriously.

'Well, Duke, you're supposed to say something to me.'

'There's nothin' in the script!'

'I know. But I'm the type of actor who needs to have something said. I'm really that dumb. So would you help me? If you just go "Pssst" in my ear, I'm going to break up. But if you actually say something to me, it'll be OK.'

'There's nothin' in the script!'

'I know. But if he bit a guy's ear off in the pub last night and that doesn't impress me. . . '

'Right!'

'Well, what do you think would impress me?'

'I've no idea.'

'Well, I'd be pretty impressed if he'd bit a guy's balls off, I can tell you!'

There was a terrible silence on the set. John Wayne went bright red, towered over me and said, 'What?'

'If he bit a guy's balls off, I'd be doubly impressed!'

'Hell, kid,' he said in slow motion. 'The Duke can't say a line like that!'

'Why not?'

'My fans wouldn't stand for it! But never let it be said the Duke hasn't helped a fellow actor when he needed it. You leave it to me. I'll think of somethin'. Can we take a break while I think of somethin'?'

A few minutes passed and John Wayne came back.

We started again. He gave his speech, leaned across and whispered in my ear, 'He hit this guy in a place where a guy shouldn't hit a guy!'

I fell about laughing.

They shouted, 'Cut!'

We went twelve takes. John Wayne progressed through, 'A guy shouldn't do what that guy did!' to 'And he bit this guy somewhere he didn't ought to have done!' Sweat was pouring off him.

I was in hysterics. Lunch was coming up and the director was getting steamed up.

John Wayne said, 'Goddamnit! Leave it to me.'

We started take thirteen – the last one before lunch. John Wayne leaned across to me and whispered, 'He chewed this guy's conkers off!'

I stifled a laugh, which turned into a strangulated scream. 'All right. All right,' I screeched through clenched teeth, 'I'll tell you anything you want to know!'

'Cut! Print!'

When the film was shown, the noise of a passing car had been added to the soundtrack to cover John Wayne's embarrassed whisper!

Afterwards, John Wayne took me back to his caravan for a drink. 'You know what?' he said to me. 'It's been a long time since an actor made a horse's ass out of me on the set!'

'I'm sorry, Duke. I really am.'

'No, it was great,' he said, seeming to take a pause between every word. 'You ought to come to Hollywood. You'd be a big star.'

'Yes,' I said. 'Why?'

'Because you've got those mad eyes!'

At the end of the film, he invited me to his party and presented me with a mug and a special Duke's cowboy belt. He was a great guy.

In the same year, while we were doing a series of *Till Death*, Dandy Nichols said to me, 'I've been offered a part in a film called *Confessions of a Window Cleaner*. But I'm not sure about it. You're good at scripts. Have a look at it and tell me what you think.'

She gave me the script. I read it overnight and knew it was going to be a hit. It was very, very funny.

At rehearsal the next day, I said to Dandy, 'You should take it. It's a winner.'

'Do you think so?' she said. 'They're talking about it being the first of a series.'

'If the rest are like the first, you're on a cert. Who's doing it?'

'Greg Smith and Norman Cohen.'

I knew Norman Cohen well. He'd directed the film of *Till Death* and so I asked how he was.

'Funnily enough,' she said. 'I spoke to him on the phone last night and told him I'd asked you to read the script for me. He said, "My God. Tony would be perfect for Syd Nogget." I'm talking to him tonight. Shall I say you're interested?'

'Yes. If he's desperate, I'd love to see him.'

Later that evening, Norman rang me at home and said, 'Isn't it funny? When you're casting, you never think of somebody who's been a friend for years. But I mentioned you to Greg Smith and Val Guest and they both think you're right for the part. So would you like to read the script?'

'There's no need. I've read it.'

'And what do you think?'

'You've got a hit on your hands.'

'Would you like to play in it?'

'I'd love to.'

And that's how I got into the four films made in the *Confessions* series.

I also received an invitation to spend a season with the Welsh National Theatre, playing Brutus in *Julius Caesar*. There were to be six weeks at Clywd, two weeks at Cardiff and a week at Aberystwyth. I was really looking forward to it. Brutus is one of the most complex yet most satisfying parts in Shakespeare. It was a great challenge for me, because it was unlike so much of the work I'd been doing. The guy is so pure. He does everything for the benefit of the Republic and never for himself.

The theatre at Clwyd is in the middle of nowhere. It's just stuck on the side of a hill. On the first night, the curtain didn't go up until seven-thirty, but when I arrived at four-thirty in the afternoon there was a monsoon. It was unbelievable. At six o'clock in the evening, I was sitting with the director in the tea bar. There was nobody else there, apart from the tea-girl. We sat looking out at the rain sheeting down.

'Are you going backstage?' he asked.

'Is there any point?' I said. 'Who's going to come and see us? Who in their right mind would leave their homes on a night like this? I got drenched just running from the cab to the theatre.'

But that night was packed and so was every other in the eight-week season.

We took this smash hit from Clywd to Cardiff. I arrived on Monday afternoon and, rather than going to my digs first, I decided to go straight to the Sherman Theatre, which backs on to a railway line. I walked down the alley behind the theatre and at the end there were two huge guys with snarling Alsatian dogs.

When they saw me, they said, 'Oh, it's you, Tony. How are you? Come on. It's all right!'

'Oh thanks,' I said. 'What's all this about?'

'Never played the Sherman before?'

'No.'

'It's the university theatre, you know.'

'So what?'

'It's full of bloody hooligans.'

'Come on!'

'No, no. If you've never played the Sherman before, you're in for an experience, I'll tell you. You're in for a bloody treat! We

173

have guard-dogs here and security patrols wandering around. It's a real rough bunch you're going to face tonight.'

Having just played for six weeks to silent appreciation in Clywd, we were about to open in Cardiff where, apparently, audiences were used to having punch-ups.

Curtain up was at seven-thirty. I was ready at seven. At the quarter, the director came in and told me, 'There'll be a bit of a delay with the curtain. Apparently, there's some students in with forged tickets.'

Half-past seven came and went; quarter to eight came and went; eight o'clock came. Over the Tannoy we could hear backstage the sound of something like a football match in progress. There was chanting and screaming and the odd loud thud. At a quarter-past eight, there was still pandemonium. Audiences don't usually like waiting for even a few minutes, never mind three-quarters of an hour. So the director decided that we had to start or otherwise there really would be a riot.

The curtain opened and the lights went up. The guys in the opening scene were playing in loincloths. Before the first line was spoken, a voice bellowed: 'Get 'em fuckin' off!'

Steven Yardley, who was playing Cassius, turned to me and said, 'Beautiful, isn't it. The first line of Shakespeare's immortal *Caesar* is "Get 'em fuckin' off!".'

In the auditorium, there was uproar. I knew it was a night we were going to remember.

'What you going to do if they keep this up when we're on?' Steven said.

'Nothing,' I replied. 'I'm Brutus and as far as I'm concerned they have freedom to do what they want.'

'Don't talk daft.'

'I'm not. You'll see.'

The first scene passed for nothing. Not a word could be heard. It was just like being in a fairground.

The second scene started and it was like playing in a madhouse. The actors were shouting and getting red in the face. They were staring out into the audience and getting raspberries blown back at them.

After thirty or so lines, all the characters leave the stage, apart from Cassius and Brutus. There was still uproar in the house and so I just sat on the edge of a rostrum – and I sat and sat and sat. I was getting paid for sitting there and they had paid to watch me do nothing. Eventually, the audience began to hush and I started to speak softly. The noise died down and then they were listening.

174

The conspiracy scene went well. Then Portia entered. There was silence in the theatre.

After a few lines, she said:

'Is Brutus sick?'

Then from the wings came the loudest fart I've ever heard. The audience was lost. There was hysterical laughter. Portia put her head on my chest and hissed, 'I can't go on. I can't go on.'

'It's all right,' I whispered. 'Whoever it was, I will personally kill. Don't worry about that.'

So Portia said:

> 'and is it physical
> To walk unbraced and suck up the humours
> Of the dank morning?'

Another fart – more uproar.

Portia continued:

> 'What, is Brutus sick,
> And will he steal out of his wholesome bed
> To dare the vile contagion of the night .
> And tempt the rheumy and unpurged air
> To add unto his sickness?'

Then yet another, even louder, trumpeting fart. The audience's laughter was uncontrollable.

We managed to finish the scene and came off into the wings. Standing there was the stage manager, who whispered, 'Sorry, Tony.'

'You bastard,' I said. 'It was you, wasn't it?'

'No, no, Tony. It was a loose floorboard.'

'Oh, yes,' I said. 'Come here!' And I dragged him off through the pass doors. I was really pissed off. 'Who was it?' I demanded. 'Who farted?'

'I swear to you, Tony,' he whimpered. 'It was a loose floorboard. We forgot about it. It's down by the prop table and when the conspirators came back with their daggers they stood on it and that's what it sounded like.'

'You're trying to tell me I don't know the difference between a loose floorboard and a fart? You're talking to the wrong bloke. Now get back in there and find out who it was.'

Still protesting, he went off. As I stormed back in, I almost knocked over a little Welsh stagehand. 'Hey, you, Taff,' I said to him. 'Was it you that farted?'

'Oh, no, Tony. It was a loose floorboard. Honest to goodness.'

Eventually, I calmed down. The play was continuing and the audience had begun to quieten again. The theatre manager, the stage manager and the director were standing by the prop table warning everybody about the loose floorboard.

Everything went well, until just before the assassination of Caesar – a part played by an actor who, even if he'd played it a hundred years, would still be going over his lines. He was pacing up and down, mouthing the words and ignoring everybody.

In the scene immediately before the assassination, as Portia said to Lucius: 'Hark, boy! What noise is that?' Julius Caesar trod on the loose floorboard and there was the sound of a loud wet fart. The audience erupted into laughter. Caesar froze on to the board, one foot in the air, not knowing what to do. Everybody offstage was hissing to him that he wasn't to move.

The laughter began to die down. Lucius said:
'I hear none, madam.'
The audience tittered.
Portia continued:

'Prithee, listen well;
I heard a bustling rumour, like a fray,
And the wind brings it from the Capitol.'

At this, Caesar suddenly hopped on to his other foot and the sound of an enormous fart reverberated again across the stage. After that, nothing could stop the audience laughing. They kept it up until the interval, when the loose floorboard was repaired.

The director came up to the dressing-room afterwards to explain why the start had been delayed. Apparently, three of the students who had got in on forged tickets had been so pissed that they'd thrown up over people in the stalls below. As a result, fights had broken out and chaos had ensued until the troublemakers had been thrown out.

I've appeared in many Shakespearian productions, but that's the only time I've seen *Julius Caesar* turned into a comedy!

After the last series of *Till Death*, in the intervals when I wasn't acting, I turned my hand – as I had done since the early sixties – to scriptwriting. In a pub one day, I met a guy who'd been involved in an incident that brought him in close contact with Carlos, the Jackal. He told me the whole story and I developed it into a screenplay. I gave it to Greg Smith, who'd produced the *Confession* pictures. He'd got Robert Aldridge interested in it, but it was likely to be some time before a decision was made. So Greg said to me,

'While we're waiting, why don't you turn it into a novel? If it's published in paperback, it'll help the film.'

I started work. Because of the more detailed description I had to write, I needed to do far more research. In the screenplay, I could just say somebody was shot; in the novel I had to give details of the gun used. First I went to the police, but they were no help. They obviously thought that I was intending to shoot the Prime Minister or somebody like that!

Immediately after this, I dropped into a pub by the New Theatre in the West End. The landlord asked me what I was working on. I told him about the novel and the difficulties I was having.

'Funnily enough,' he said. 'This pub is used by SAS guys when they're in London. A lot of them are heavy drinkers. They get in here and shoot the shit. The next time they're in, I'll give you a call. You can have a chat with them and they'll tell you anything you need to know.'

A week or so later, I called into the pub one lunchtime, and the landlord said, 'You've just missed a couple of SAS guys. They've gone off to the Palace to pick up some medals, but they're coming back this evening. If you get in here about eight, you can have a word.'

I returned that evening and met these two guys. They started to tell me stories about assassination squads in Northern Ireland that made my hair curl. They'd been to a reception, were well pissed and keen to talk. 'Forget the book I'm writing,' I thought. 'If I can get these guys back to my place and tape them, I'm going to have a story and a half.'

I put it to them. They accepted my invitation and just before closing time, we bought a bottle of whisky and went back to my flat in Hampstead.

The woman I was living with at the time was none too pleased that I'd been out all evening drinking and, when the two SAS boys and I arrived back at the flat, I discovered that she'd locked me out. It had happened before and there was no point in hammering on the door.

The flat was at the top of a three-storey block. On the landing was a trapdoor that led into the loft. Because we didn't have much money, the flat was heated with paraffin. In a cupboard on the landing by the front door, there were five five-gallon drums – two full of paraffin and three empty. What I used to do when I was locked out was to stack up the five drums, climb up them into the loft, go along the rafters and then through another trapdoor that led into my flat.

So I said to the SAS guys, 'Don't worry about it. I'll get in and open the front door.' Then I started getting the five drums of paraffin out of the cupboard.

One of the guys said, 'There's no need to do that. This is what we do in Northern Ireland.' He then took some rags out of the cupboard and started ripping them into strips.

'What are you doing?' I said.

He then opened one of the drums and started soaking the torn pieces with paraffin.

'What the hell are you doing?'

'It's OK. We do it in Northern Ireland all the time. I'm just going to jam these rags in all round the door. Then I'll set fire to them. It'll make a hell of a row. All the smoke will go into the flat. The people inside'll think they're going to be burned to death. They come rushing out and then we jump 'em.'

'Hang on! Hang on! You can't do that. My girlfriend's in there. Don't be so bloody stupid. Look, I'll be back in a couple of minutes. Just stay here.'

I left them to wait and with a struggle clambered up into the loft. I started walking along the rafters and was about two-thirds of the way to the trapdoor that led into my flat when I heard an explosion. Flames and smoke shot up through the open hatch into the loft.

'My God,' I thought. 'The fools have done it. The drums have exploded and the whole bloody place is going up.'

I slipped. My foot smashed through the ceiling. I bellowed to my girlfriend to get out. For a moment I didn't know what I should do. But as there were no more flames coming through the open trapdoor, I staggered back to it. Then there was only one thing I could do. I dropped down into the smoke. I landed on one of the drums of paraffin. It exploded as I hit it.

I went up in flames.

Films of people on fire rushing out of buildings look horrific. Being on the inside looking out is a million times worse.

I screamed in panic. All my life I've known that panic kills. Within seconds, I'd stopped panicking. I felt beside myself, as though I'd jumped out of my body. I saw the two SAS guys pissing themselves with laughter. I grabbed a fire extinguisher off the wall and smashed it on the floor. Nothing happened. I hammered on the door of the neighbouring flat. A man opened it and saw me burning like a torch. He sprang back. I grabbed a coat, rolled over and over in it, falling down the stairs. Then I passed out.

19

Through the Valley

A young man was leaning over me, saying, 'Wake up! Wake up!'
I slowly came to and said, 'Yes.'
'Look,' he said. 'We've got to do an emergency operation.'
'Why?'
'Because you've been badly hurt. All I'm going to do is make
an incision from here,' he said, pointing to my right ankle. He
went up my calf, past my knee, right up to my groin. He was a
third of the way down my left leg when it opened up like a flower
and I realized that he was actually doing the operation there and
then. I couldn't stand it and I fainted.

I went in and out of a coma, not knowing where I was, but
experiencing the most appalling pain. Forty-three per cent of my
body – the whole lower part – had third-degree burns. Another
ten per cent was affected by first- and second-degree burns. My
feet had actually boiled in my boots.

I don't know how many days later it was when I next came
round, but a doctor was sitting by the bed. 'How do you feel?' he
asked.
'What day is it?' I asked.
'Thursday.'
'Will I be out by Saturday?'
'Why?'

'Liverpool are playing Arsenal. If we beat them, we'll win the League!'

He laughed and I passed out.

During the weeks that I was in intensive care, the only way that I could cope was to continually leave my body.

It is highly unfashionable now to talk about the soul or spirit of a person, but I know it exists and is immortal. It is the body that decays, but the spirit cannot be destroyed. Whatever happens, you have the strength of knowing that nothing or nobody can break your spirit – and that includes the highest powers of darkness or the most appalling visions. So you can laugh at death.

In any out-of-body experiences, there are no such things as space or time. You might only leave the body for a second, but it might seem as though you were away years. Or you could be away several hours and it would seem like a flash.

In my spirit travels, to make sure that I would be close to my body, I would stay in the London area so that I could return quickly – before they carted off my body and stuck it in the oven! I was convinced that I would survive, although every time I returned to my body it was in bad shape!

Having made several films at the ABPC studios at Elstree, I often used to go there during my out-of-body journeys. I thought that I would never be able to prove to anybody else that, while I was fighting for my life, I was watching a film being made. So, on one occasion, I decided to look around and check whether there was anybody I knew. The only person I recognized was Sian Phillips, the former wife of Peter O'Toole. The set was a Grecian temple and I was on top by one of the columns. I memorized what she was saying, because I knew that when I left the hospital I would find out that the scene had been shot on a day when I was in intensive care. That would be proof enough for me – I didn't care about anybody else.

I came back to my body as a doctor was shaking my shoulder and saying, 'Would you like a drink?'

'I'd love a drink.'

'What would you like?'

I said, 'I would like mango juice, pineapple juice, orange juice, ice, a dash of lemon – stirred, not shaken.'

'No,' he said. 'I mean a drink drink.'

'Are you kidding? I'll never drink again as long as I live.'

'No, no. What do you want? Beer? Whisky? Champagne? Whatever you want.'

180

'I can't get through to you, can I? I'll never ever take another drink of alcohol as long as I live.'

'Please,' he said. 'I'm asking you as a personal favour.'

'Why?'

He whispered into my ear: 'Because you're driving us all crazy with your shouting and screaming! Please have a drink!'

'Yes. I want mango, pineapple and orange!'

He came back a little later and said, 'I'm sorry. We can't find any mango, but here's some pineapple and orange.'

It was the sweetest, most delicious drink I've ever tasted!

Contrary to popular belief, when a patient suffers a severe relapse, it's not like it is in the films, with doctors and nurses all calm and collected. Everybody panics! During one of my out-of-body experiences, I came back and looking down on my bed in the intensive care unit witnessed all this panic down below. Doctors and nurses were dashing around.

'What's happening?' I thought.

Then a doctor suddenly jumped on my body and – from where I was high above – it looked as though he was beating the hell out of it.

'Why is he doing that?' I thought. 'What have I done to deserve all this?'

'God! He's going!' somebody called out.

'So why don't you let the poor sod go?' I thought. Then I realized that they were convinced I was dying. 'Look! I'm up here. Can't you see me?'

Nobody took any notice. There was only one thing I could do. I had to get back inside my body. How could I do it? They were all in the way. But if I could get through the ceiling, I could get through the wall. So I went out of the room again, came through the wall, straight into my head, and screamed. The doctor was flung clear off me!

That, I was told later, was one of the three occasions when I'd been declared clinically dead. Fortunately, each time, I managed to get back from one of my trips to the film studios before it was too late! Who said the cinema wasn't pure escapism?

Every four hours I was given morphine. The half hour before the injection and the quarter afterwards were the worst times of the lot. Once given, the morphine for a while heightened the pain, rather than relieving it.

I remember one of the doctors telling me, 'There is one drawback to the morphine. It will ease the pain but, should you pull through this, you may have become addicted.'

'Great,' I said, before I passed out. 'I survive the burns and become a drug addict!'

One day, I opened my eyes and said, 'What's the date?'

The nurse said, 'The twenty-seventh of December.'

'My God,' I said. 'I've been in here a month.'

'What do you mean?'

'I came in here on the twenty-seventh of November.'

'No, you didn't. You came in on the seventeenth of November.'

Not only had I lost ten days, but Christmas had been and gone! I was told that at first they'd stuck the telegrams and cards I'd been sent all round the room, but then they had to take them down. There were so many of them they'd become a fire hazard. Apparently, two sackfuls of mail were collected and then destroyed. So I'm afraid I do not know who wrote to me and I've never been able to reply – but, to whoever the kind people were, I now say thank you.

On New Year's Eve, I was the only patient in the burns unit. Both my arms were suspended in the air and my hands were in bags of Savlon. I was lying on my back, unable to do anything and not knowing what had happened to my body from the waist downwards. I couldn't feel anything and didn't dare even think about it.

A night nurse gave me my injection at ten o'clock in the evening. She was a sweet, gentle Irish girl. Like everybody who came into my room, she was wearing a surgical mask. I was waiting for her to go, because I was happy to drift off into one of my out-of-body experiences. But she sat there talking. She told me there was a party for the staff in the pub across the road and that they were all having a great time. Some of them had come back and given her a bottle of champagne. She asked me if I'd mind if she opened it.

'It's fine with me,' I said. 'But why don't you go to the party?'

'I can't leave you here by yourself,' she said.

'Look. As long as you're back here by one-thirty, it'll be all right. That's when I'll start screaming for my next shot. Then if you give it to me at a quarter to two, instead of two o'clock, I'll have a great time and you'll have a great time.'

We hummed and hawed for about a quarter of an hour before she agreed to go off to the party. She put the cord with the buzzer for emergencies at the top of my chest and saw that I was able to push it with my chin. 'If you ring that,' she said, 'there's a male member of staff down the corridor and he'll come straightaway.' Then off she went to the party and I drifted away.

True to her word, she came back at half-past one, but she brought with her a couple of other people – carrying bottles of champagne and smashed out of their heads. That was all I needed – a party! They gabbled on about having loved *Till Death Us Do Part* while they knocked back the champagne.

By five to two, I was going crazy with the pain and I needed them chatting away like a hole in the head. I screamed out, the other two left and the night nurse gave me my injection. I knew there was going to be fifteen minutes of heightened pain, but I'd learnt to cope with that.

The night nurse sat down beside me and said, 'Is it all right if I open another bottle of champagne?'

I told her to go ahead and, as she drank, she talked to me about her life and her ambitions. I was happy to listen – it took my mind off the pain.

She was obviously really drunk. Suddenly, she emptied her glass, put it down, looked at me and burst into tears.

'What's the matter?' I asked.

'Oh, God,' she sobbed. 'I think you're lovely. I used to watch you on the television. I really think you're lovely.'

'I don't believe this. You're having me on.'

'No, I'm not,' she said. 'Do you mind if I get into bed with you, darling?'

'Don't be ridiculous,' I said, but before I'd got the words out she was taking off her uniform. In her underclothes, she pushed me over and jumped into bed.

With my arms trapped, I was lying on one side like a goalkeeper diving to save a penalty in a freeze-frame. She started to kiss me and tell me how much she loved me. Then she passed out!

I couldn't rouse her. She was lying on my right arm and she was a dead weight. It was bloody uncomfortable.

'Come on!' I was saying. 'Don't be daft! This is bloody ridiculous! You're hurting my arm! Wake up! Wake up!'

Then the morphine took effect and I passed out. I came to at five-thirty in the morning. I felt as though I'd been crucified. One of the arm supports was across the bed and the nurse was snoring in my arms. I was in agony. The only thing I could do was bite her on her nose.

She yelled and woke up. She looked at me and her face screwed up in horror. 'Oh my God!' she exclaimed. 'What have I done?'

'You haven't done anything,' I said. 'Just get off my arm. You're killing me. You've been lying on me for hours!'

She jumped out of bed, saw she was in her underclothes, grabbed her uniform and fled!

'The injection!' I was shouting after her. 'The injection! The inject. . . !'

About five minutes later, she came back, gave me the morphine and walked out without saying a word, even though I kept on telling her that I was all right and nothing had happened.

During the day, I thought, 'This is all surreal. It's every patient's dream. A nurse declared undying love for me and then climbed into my bed. I wonder when she's next on! God, it's weeks since I thought about sex. With my hands tied up, I can't even feel my penis. I don't know what's left down there. But I can ask her. She'll soon find out.'

That evening, I asked the night staff when the nurse who'd been on duty on New Year's Eve would next be working. I was told she wouldn't be back until the fifth of January. Right, I thought. That gives me something to aim for. On the fifth of January, I shall get the Irish beauty back into my bed and ask her to tell me what I have from the waist downwards.

On the fourth of January, I said to the night nurse, 'Tomorrow night, the Irish girl's on duty, isn't she?'

'Oh,' she said. 'You mean Mary. Didn't you hear? She's left. She's going to nurse the lepers in Africa! I don't know what happened to her on New Year's Eve, but she left straightaway and hasn't been back since!'

A few days later, I woke up in the morning and even though it was January the sun was shining. I felt great. For the first time, I knew not only was I going to live but I was going to get better.

My specialist was always called by the nurses 'Young Mr Harrison', because his father also worked in the hospital. That day, young Dougie Harrison came in during his rounds and sat on the bed.

'How are you?' he asked.

'Dougie,' I replied. 'I'm going to make it. I'm really going to make it.'

'Are you?'

'Yes. I feel great.'

'Well, I hope you've got the strength to take what I'm going to tell you.'

'What's that?'

'I have to tell you that, if you don't do exactly as you're told, you will be dead in five days.'

'Nonsense,' I said. 'I feel great.'

'No, you don't. Do you know how much weight you've lost?'

'I've no idea. Why? Have I lost weight?'

'You are now under six stone. At the rate you're losing weight, you have five more days to live. You must save yourself. You've got to eat.'

'Have you tried eating hospital food, Dougie? I know it's not the hospital's fault, but it's terrible. I love spicy food and they serve up bland stodge.'

'Well, you've got to eat it if you want to live.'

'You're kidding me.'

'Would I kid you about a thing like this?'

'No,' I said. 'You wouldn't, actually.'

'I do mean it. This lunchtime, you've got to decide whether you're going to live or die.'

When the food came, it wasn't any better, but I made myself eat it. I'd been forced to accept how bad my condition was. Up to then, I hadn't known. I'd been in and out of consciousness all the time and, when my relatives had visited for the few moments they were allowed, they'd spent all their time in tears. I had seen the state of my legs, but – drugged as I was with morphine – I'd assumed that something would be done about them and that the mess would simply wash off!

Twice a week, I was being taken down for operations. But most of the time, I didn't have a clue what was going on.

One day in the middle of February, I suddenly woke up and wanted a pee. I called for a nurse and eventually one came.

'I need a bottle,' I said. It had never occurred to me why I hadn't needed one before in the three months I'd been in hospital.

'No,' she said. 'It's all right.'

'What do you mean?' I asked.

Then she showed me the bag beside the bed. I was on a catheter and had been since being admitted into hospital. I hadn't realized, but then it dawned on me that I hadn't any feeling in my penis. I resolved that the next time Dougie Harrison visited me on his rounds I'd ask him if it was still, shall we say, functional.

When he came, I said, 'Now I'm feeling a bit better, I'd like to talk to you. When am I getting out of your magnificent emporium?'

'It'll be several more months,' he said. 'You need many more operations.'

'I see. Well, what about my sex life?'

'What sex life?'

'You know. My sex life!'

'I'm afraid that's a thing of the past!'

I gulped. 'What do you mean? I haven't lost my. . . '

'No, no, no. The heat was so intense that your testicles retracted into your body. They've only just descended again. That's why you now feel like passing water. When the flames shot up your body, you instinctively covered your private parts. That's why your hands are badly burnt. Your penis is undamaged. However, you will be impotent.'

'For how long?'

'For ever.'

I couldn't believe it.

I discovered that this shattering news had already been given to the girl with whom I'd been living. It seemed to be an explanation of why she'd moved an eighteen-year-old boy into the flat and had stopped visiting me.

I went into a deep depression and spent a lot of time crying and bemoaning my fate. For much of the time, I was still in agony. To make the skin grafts on my legs, the surgeons removed donor skin from my back and shoulders. After they'd done that, I had to lie five days on my front, with my hands hanging out of the bed. My back was covered with muslin, soaked in honey and glycerine to help it heal. Just moving my head from one side to the other took me all of three minutes. It was such an effort.

On the fifth day, Dougie Harrison came to inspect my back. He squatted at the end of the bed, where my head was, and said, 'Tony, we're now going to give you the biggest dose of morphine you've ever had. I'm sure you think that the pain you now feel is bad enough, but I have to tell you that what you are about to feel is the worst pain any human being can inflict on another. It appears you're a quick healer and sadly the muslin has actually attached itself to your back. We've got to strip it away. You may scream as much as you wish. The burns unit will be empty. We're moving out the staff and the rest of the patients from their rooms.'

'So who's going to do it?' I asked.

'A couple of special nurses.'

I was given an injection and told that these nurses would start in half an hour. An hour later, a man and a woman arrived. The man squatted on the floor at the foot of the bed, put his feet on the two bed legs and said, 'Give me your arms.' He grabbed hold of them, braced himself and hung on to me.

From off a tray, the woman took a wire-brush, like the ones used to untangle a dog's matted hair. She climbed on to the bed and sat astride me. Then she started to strip my back. My scream went straight through the man. By the time she'd completed my left shoulder, I'd passed out twice with the pain. And so it went on. Each time they had to bring me round because, unless the patient was conscious, they wouldn't know whether or not he was dead or alive. When I was conscious, I was screaming. When they finished, I passed out.

An hour or so later I came round and a nurse was sitting by the bed.

'What happened?' I said. 'Why was there so much pain?'

'That's the way it is,' she said. 'Nobody could stand it. That's why the staff and patients had to go away. They couldn't bear to hear the screams.'

I hadn't had a bath since being admitted to the hospital. But the very next day, I was taken down to the washroom. I was lain face-downwards on a rubber bed and then the nurse played warm water from a shower attachment on to my back.

I have never experienced such sensuous pleasure! It was unbelievable. Four layers of skin had been taken off my back and warm water was being sprayed on the most sensitive of flesh. I was having mental orgasms all over the place! The nurse kept on telling me to stop calling out – but experiencing such ecstasy it was impossible to keep quiet!

The threat of impotency continued to be more than a trifle worrying, but there had been nothing I could do about it. I couldn't even examine myself, because my hands were imprisoned. Then came the great and glorious day when my right hand was taken out of the bag and I was told it was all right. After they'd left me, the first thing I did was to gently ease up the covers and search to see if the doctor had lied to me! He hadn't! But the poor thing had all but disappeared! I had great difficulty in finding it!

I determined to prove the doctors wrong. I was going to make a complete recovery, but first I had to leave the hospital. So I asked Dougie Harrison when I could get out of bed and start walking again.

'You can try next week,' he said.

The day arrived when two nurses came to take me for my first walk across the room. As soon as they put my feet on the floor, they burst open. I felt it happen.

'My feet have split,' I said.

'Don't be ridiculous,' they said. 'Come on. Put one foot in front of the other.'

Because I had to learn again how to walk, they held on to me and frogmarched me towards the wall. As they turned me round, I saw a trail of bloody footprints across the room. As I walked back, I left another trail. They put me on the bed and left to get the stuff to clean up the floor.

While they were away, the jolly Philippino woman who brought the food entered with my lunch. She slipped on the blood and began a spectacular slide that would have brought applause at any ice-skating rink. The tray flew up into the air and crashed on to the floor in front of her as she fell. She looked up at me and grinned. Her big round face was covered in food. It was pure slapstick.

But I lay there and didn't laugh. 'My God,' I thought. 'I may as well be dead. I've lost my sense of humour.' Then suddenly, welling up from nowhere, came a great belly laugh. I owe a lot to that Philippino woman!

There was a young night nurse I told about the problem that worried me most. She said that many burns patients suffered in the same way. The shock to the nervous system made some men impotent for life, but there were others who eventually recovered.

We spoke freely to each other during the long nights. I told her theatrical stories and she related her nursing experiences. We formed a pleasant easy-going relationship and she agreed that, as part of my therapy, she would try to help me with my problem. She put as much time, manual effort and patience into it as I did. Lo and behold, one magic evening, I had an orgasm. I knew I was no longer impotent. The only difficulty was that I ejaculated blood!

She told me not to worry. I went to sleep. The next morning when I woke up, I saw that the end of my penis was caked with blood. Very gently, I squeezed it. Blood shot out all over my stomach. I thought, 'The brothers were right! That's God's punishment on you, Tony. You're going to bleed to death through your penis and you deserve it!'

I panicked and called for a nurse. When she arrived, I said, 'I want to see a doctor.'

She told me there'd been a bad fire and that all the doctors in the unit were busy and so I'd have to wait. I was then wheeled down to the washroom. As I had the use of my right hand and because the nurses found my cries of ecstasy so embarrassing, I was expected to shower myself.

As soon as the water was switched on, the nurse left. I gently showered around my penis, squeezed it and more blood appeared.

Working in the burns unit was an Indian doctor – a terrific guy, but his accent made Peter Sellers as the Indian doctor in *The Millionairess* sound distinctly underplayed.

As I was contemplating my penis, the door of the washroom opened and in walked this Indian doctor.

'Where is the sister?' he said.

'She's not here,' I replied. 'But could I have a word with you?'

'Not now! Not now! I am in a great hurry.'

'I must talk to a doctor,' I insisted.

'Well not now! Not now!'

'But I must talk to a doctor!'

'Is it a matter of life and death?'

'It is to me! It is a matter of life and death!'

'Oh, my goodness. Well what is it?'

I explained what had happened and said, 'You see. When I squeeze the end of my penis, blood comes out.'

'What is that?'

'Look,' I said. I squeezed the end of my penis and blood came out. 'What shall I do, doctor?'

'Don't squeeze the end of the penis!' he said and walked out.

And, do you know, he was right!

20

Though I Walk

If it had not been for the attention I received from the National Health Service and, in particular, the doctors and nurses at Mount Vernon Hospital, I would have died. I owe them my life. They were magnificent and did everything they could to help me. Theirs is an awful job – working in a burns unit means constantly hearing the agonizing screams of people forced to endure the unendurable.

Patiently, the nurses helped me begin the slow and painful process of learning to walk again. In time, I was able to have the most desirable of luxuries – going to the toilet by myself. The walk down the corridor took as long as three-quarters of an hour, but it was worth it to escape the indignity of being sat on a bedpan.

Dougie Harrison promised me that after my last operation he would try to get me into Farnham Park, a rehabilitation centre outside Slough. He said he'd have a great deal of difficulty, because most of the people who went there were athletes suffering from relatively minor ailments. In any case, before I could be accepted, I had to be mobile and be able to dress myself.

The night before the final operation, I became very anxious. When Dougie came to see me, I said, 'I've had a premonition. I'm sure that this will be once too often for me to go to the operating theatre. This time, I know something is going to go wrong.'

'Don't be ridiculous,' he said. 'This is the last operation. It's very minor – just folding over a piece of skin and trimming off. It's nothing compared with the other operations you've had.'

'I don't care. I can't go through with it.'

On the morning of the operation, I refused to have it and Dougie was sent for. When he arrived, he said, 'I will be there. You have my word.'

'But I know I'm going to die,' I said.

Eventually, he talked me into it and I was taken down to the operating theatre. I was such a regular that the anaesthetist and I were old friends. I'd made more appearances there than Laurence Olivier had at the National.

When I came round from the operation, I opened my eyes and tried to speak. The only sound I made was an horrific gurgle. I tried again – another gurgle. Then I knew that something had gone wrong.

A nurse came to the bed and said, 'Lie still. You've got a collapsed lung.'

My premonition had been right. I'd damned near died.

With a collapsed lung, a tube is put into the lung to drain away the liquid into a bottle by the bed.

Because I'd been in the hospital so long and was hailed as the star survivor, I had a television in my room. Five days after my operation, I was lying in bed, watching a live broadcast of England playing at Wembley. Beside me was the bottle, gurgling away like something out of *Quatermass and the Pit*.

The match had only just started, when in walked a West African nurse. She was a large, jovial, charming, cack-handed woman who would have been great at anything, other than nursing. She was a walking disaster – a menace to life and limb. People used to scream when she entered a room intent on giving an injection. She was the most heavy-handed person I've ever met. With her was a young Chinese trainee who came up to her navel. They said they were going to sit me up and rearrange my pillows. I looked at them and knew there was no way this disparate pair would be able to handle it.

'No, no, no,' I pleaded. 'How can you two do anything together?'

'Don't be silly,' the West African nurse said. 'I know what I'm doing. I'll do it by myself.'

While I was still protesting, she lifted me and flung me up the bed. Out came the tube from my chest and a stream of blood spurted into the air.

'You cack-handed idiot,' I shouted. 'Look what you've done now.'

'Don't worry about that,' she said, picking up the tube. She rubbed the end of it and tried to push it back into my chest!

'What the hell do you think you're doing?' I screamed. 'Get a doctor! Get a doctor!'

While the two of them went off to find a doctor, I sat watching the match on television with my finger staunching the blood.

After about five minutes, in walked my friend, the Indian doctor. He looked at my chest and said, 'You'll have to be taken down to the operating theatre.'

'Why?' I said. 'What are you going to do?'

'Put in the stitches.'

'How many stitches?'

'Three or four,' he said, inspecting the hole.

'But why in the operating theatre?'

'Why not?'

'Because I'm watching the football.'

'I also watch the football.'

'So why can't you put the stitches in here? Then we can both watch the rest of the match.'

'Why not indeed.'

Off he went and soon returned with his gear. Then he got me ready and put in the first stitch. I was looking over his shoulder at the television. He started the next stitch.

'Come on,' I shouted at the set.

He turned round to watch, still holding the needle in his hand and as Keegan scored he shouted, 'It's a goal!' He jumped up in his excitement, yanking on the thread and nearly pulling me out of the bed.

He had to put in a dozen stitches to sew up the wound. But we both saw the rest of the match!

Having recovered from my collapsed lung and knowing that I'd had the last of my operations, I began to feel much better and was looking forward to my release from hospital.

I was eternally grateful to Dougie Harrison, but I loved ragging him. The next time he visited me on his rounds, I said to him, 'Can I have a word with you in private?'

'What do you mean?' he asked.

'I want to speak to you alone,' I said, 'without anybody else here.'

'All right,' he said. 'Go ahead.'

'But the room's full of people!'

'Oh, yes,' he said, and waved his entourage outside. He came and sat on the edge of the bed. 'Well? What is it?' he asked.

'I want to prove to you that I'm not impotent. I've been in here five months and now I feel the need for a woman!'

He blushed and said, 'Well, what do you want me to do?'

'It's all right,' I said. 'I'm not asking you to procure for me. I know certain telephone numbers. If I ring, one of my friends will come round and help me out. All I want is your permission to bring into this intensive care ward a woman who will service me!'

'You mean you want to turn this hospital into a brothel?'

'If you want to put it that way – yes!'

'And you're asking my permission?'

'Sure. Because if it works, according to you it'll have been a miracle. So what's your answer?'

'Let me think about it.'

'How long do you want to think about it?'

'Till my next visit.'

'OK, Dougie. Think about it.'

He came on his rounds twice a week. On Friday, I saw through the window that he'd arrived at my door. He went to push it open, looked at me in the bed, I smiled, he let the door swing back and walked on.

'Come back, you coward,' I shouted.

He didn't come to see me for two weeks! He'd believed me! That really made me feel that I was getting better.

As part of the preparations for my departure from the hospital, I was taken for physiotherapy. I was pushed down to a place which was so far away that, as my mother would have said, it was in the middle of next week.

In the physiotherapy unit, there was a walk with bars at either side. My wheelchair was taken to the start of it. I was helped out and I grasped the bars. Then I began the long walk. I was so slow and it was so painful that I thought I'd never get to the end. I said I wanted to stop, but the physiotherapists urged me on.

All the time, I'd been keeping my eyes downwards as I forced one foot after the other. I paused and looked up to see how far I'd still got to go. Ahead, facing me was an old man. I stared at his white hair, at his pain-crevassed face and his frail body. 'What bastards these people are,' I thought, 'trying to make that crippled old man walk!'

I took a step towards him as he took a step towards me. I stopped. He stopped. Then I knew I was looking at myself. In the five months I'd been in hospital, I'd never once seen myself in a mirror. But there I was. My hair had turned white, my sunken face was deeply lined and my body was emaciated. Then I began to cry.

Afterwards, alone in my bed, I cried again. It occurred to me that I was often crying. I didn't know why. I just assumed that it was because my girlfriend had left me and I'd no home to go back to. Then one Sunday night, a nurse who'd been away on holiday came in to give me my pills. 'Why are you taking Valium?' she said.

'I didn't know I was taking Valium,' I said.

'Well you are. They're these pills here.'

'Right,' I thought. 'No wonder I'm so depressed. Well, there's no way I'm going to take any more.'

The next Friday, when Dougie Harrison called, I said, 'What do you think you're doing, putting me on Valium?'

'It was thought you were depressed,' he said.

'I was, but I'm not any longer – now I've stopped taking these things,' I said and handed him the phial of pills I'd collected during the week.

Quickly changing the subject, Dougie told me that with the work I'd been doing in physiotherapy and my own exercises, I might be able to go to the rehabilitation centre in nine days' time. But there would be no chance of me being accepted unless I'd learnt to dress myself by the following Friday.

As all my clothes had been burnt in the fire, a relative brought me some things to wear, including a pair of girl's jeans. I'd lost so much weight that they were the only trousers that fitted me!

I practised for hours, but dressing was hell. My feet were still so swollen that I'd had to have special felt shoes made. My left foot was size seventeen, and my right foot was size fifteen! The skin on my legs had little elasticity and so I could hardly bend them. To put on my underpants, I had to swing them round and round before trying to lasso one of my enormous feet. Even when I'd managed that, I still had the problem of trying to slide my other foot through the hole and then pulling the underpants up. But by the time Dougie Harrison came back a week later, I was able to demonstrate that, even though it took an age, I could dress myself.

Dougie then announced that I had been given a place at Farnham Park and that I'd be taken there on Monday. I'd promised myself that when I was given this news I would kneel down and thank God for all He had done for me. So when Dougie and the nurses had left my room, I slowly eased myself out of bed and went to kneel beside it. As my knees touched the floor, the skin burst open and I watched in horror as a pool of blood formed.

I got back into bed as quickly as I could and rang for a nurse. I knew that if I had to be given another operation I'd lose my place at the rehabilitation centre. I began to panic, thinking I'd never be able to leave the hospital.

When the nurse arrived and saw what had happened, she immediately called a doctor. After some hesitation, he agreed that my knees could be bandaged, rather than my having to endure another operation. I was overwhelmed with relief. However, it took two months before my knees were healed.

On Monday morning, when I awoke, I was suddenly terrified. Despite my desperation to leave the hospital, I started shaking with fear. It had been nearly six months since I'd seen anything of the outside world. To all intents and purposes, I'd become institutionalized.

After an early breakfast, I was wheeled down to the hospital entrance and put into a car. 'Do you want to go to Slough by the motorway or by the scenic route?' the driver asked.

'I'm in no hurry,' I said. 'Take the scenic route.'

After we'd driven off, I kept glancing at the speedometer. It seemed as though he was driving like a lunatic. In fact, he never went faster than thirty miles an hour.

Shortly after we'd left the built-up area, the car crested a hill. It was a beautiful sunny morning in June. Ahead of us, the road dipped down into a beautiful wooded valley through which a small stream meandered. Nestling in a hollow was a pretty little cottage. Beside it was a field where sheep were grazing. Looking at this unspoilt country scene, lit by the early morning sunshine, it suddenly struck me how readily and unthinkingly man spoils the environment in which he lives. Then I burst into tears, overwhelmed by the sheer beauty of what I saw.

'Are you all right?' the driver asked.

'Fine,' I replied. 'It's just been a long time since I've been aware of anything so beautiful.'

'Yes,' he said. 'Six months is a long time.'

'It's been a hell of a lot longer than that!'

The regime at Farnham Park had been designed for athletes. As soon as I booked in on Monday morning, I was sent to the first class of exercises – violent exercises to pop music. I could barely stand up and stagger a few feet. And there they were, putting me in a gymnasium asking me to do push-ups and squat-jumps. It was ridiculous.

195

A group of us who'd just arrived were unable to participate. I discovered later that we were the first batch of incurables sent to the rehabilitation centre. As a result of the pressure put on the National Health Service by Mrs Thatcher's new Tory government, Farnham Park had ceased to have its specialist role. They'd been too successful looking after athletes, like Paul Mariner, the footballer, and Jillian Jilkes, the badminton player – both of whom were there at the same time as me. So they'd been instructed to deal with the really halt and lame – like us.

And they were a great bunch. Before I'd arrived, I'd been really sorry for myself. But then I met men and women who with great fortitude and good humour were coping with hideous injuries. One I shall never forget was David, a chap from Lancashire. He'd been in his car at some traffic lights, when a lorry had run into the back, causing him severe spinal injuries. When I arrived, he was able to take three steps in his walking-frame before he fell over. He'd get up, smile and take another three steps. Shortly afterwards, he could take only two steps at a time. And he knew that it wouldn't be long before it was only one step and then eventually he'd be imprisoned in his wheelchair. Yet he was not only a courageous but a joyful man.

In addition to physiotherapy, we were also given occupational therapy. It consisted of making what they termed salad bowls, but which appeared disturbingly like begging bowls. It was no good to me. If I was going to have occupational therapy, I wanted to occupy myself in a way that would be useful to me.

What I wanted was a typewriter, so I could put on paper my experiences and describe the pain I'd felt. I'd no intention of publishing or of showing it to anybody. I just wanted to expurgate this thing from my life. What I had to say was that no one, but no one, other than a burns sufferer, can ever understand the pain we have been through. We – and we alone – share this hell in common.

The head doctor told me it couldn't be done. The regime was geared to making salad bowls, not to typing. I threatened to go on strike and refused to leave his office.

'If I can't clear my head,' I told him. 'I'm going to go crazy. And I don't fancy that. It means you'll have to lock me up again and I've been locked up long enough, thank you. I can't handle a pen, because I haven't got the manual dexterity. That's why I need a typewriter!'

He told me to get out and I did. For two days, I didn't attend occupational therapy. Then I was given a typewriter and I began the process of purging the hate that lay deep within me.

Although I was exhausted by the exercises and my feet had split open again, my new-found friends and I had a great deal of fun. We organized an escape committee. We forced the staff to hold elections for the spokesperson of the patients. It was good being back in a situation where I could be as disruptive as I'd always been!

At the end of a fortnight, I was given permission to go up to London so that I could – as the doctor put it – 'effect a reconciliation' with my girlfriend. We met in a Hampstead pub and started talking. Then her young man turned up. They left. I tried to walk after them. She turned and in her anger kicked me on the shins and stamped on both my feet.

Blood oozed through my felt shoes. I was taken back to Mount Vernon Hospital and put in a short-term unit. Dougie Harrison came to see me and examined my feet.

'They're in bad shape,' he pronounced. 'I don't know if I can save your feet, but you're going to lose both little toes.'

He worked a miracle and I lost only one of them, but then an infection took hold of the other one and the foot was left deformed.

After four weeks, I was sent back to Farnham Park. Having already spent a fortnight there, I was like an old lag. I knew precisely what I wanted to do and what I didn't. When I'd first arrived there, it was run like a military establishment. By the end of my six weeks, it was more like a fun palace – for some of us.

There were others whose whole world had caved in. One of them was a well-known jazz pianist. He'd had a severe stroke that affected his memory. He used to shuffle around not knowing who he was. But there was nothing wrong with him physically. So we used to encourage him to play the piano. He would start playing. A beautiful melody would fill the whole room and everybody would go silent. Then suddenly he'd stop, burst into tears and say, 'I can't remember. I can't remember.' It would end up with half the people there crying with him.

A group of us used to spend a lot of time together, especially at the weekends when most of the other patients and the staff went home. There was a young Army officer who'd had a stroke, a Marine sergeant armourer who'd also had a stroke, a policeman who'd come off his motorbike and smashed his legs, David, and myself. Apart from a skeleton staff, we had Farnham Park to ourselves from three o'clock on Friday afternoon to nine o'clock on Monday morning.

197

To amuse ourselves, we used to have dances in our wheelchairs. We'd sit around, play games and tell stories. Like naughty children, we'd break the rules and stay up until one or two in the morning. One Friday, however, the senior nurse told us that we all had to stay in our rooms on Saturday night 'because the Friends of Farnham Park are holding a dance here and they don't want to see any of you people!'

We held a meeting to work out our strategy. With a good deal of effort and cunning, we rigged up our own sound system that not only worked independently but could also cut out the system in the hall. During the dinner for the Friends of Farnham Park, we had amplified screams coming from all parts of the building. When the disc jockey put on the first record, it wasn't one that any of them expected. It was one of ours – the Sex Pistols with Johnny Rotten singing, 'Bollocks! Bollocks!' Then, as a finale, we all appeared on the balcony in our wheelchairs to harangue the dancers.

As part of my rehabilitation, I tried with the help of relatives to track down the two SAS men who'd been responsible for my accident. I really wanted to find out the full truth of what had happened. But we got nowhere. When we pointed out that the two men had been at Buckingham Palace on the fateful day, we were told that they hadn't received the awards themselves. They'd both been in Germany at the time and somebody else had collected the awards on their behalf. It was even claimed that there hadn't been a fire at my flat – even though it'd been reported on television and in the newspapers. For a time, this apparent conspiracy of silence made me even more bitter than the accident itself. But in a strange way, it also made me more determined to get better and stand on my own feet.

After my six-week stay, my weight had gone up to eight stone seven and so I was sufficiently fit to hit the road. Farnham Park, frankly, had seen enough of me. I decided that, as I'd nowhere to go, rather than to my mother's, I'd throw myself on the mercy of Mother Church. I asked the senior doctor if I could see a Catholic priest, preferably a Jesuit.

On the Saturday, a Jesuit came down to see me. I was in my wheelchair and he pushed me out into the grounds. We sat in the gazebo and he said, 'What is it you want to talk to me about?'

'I want to embrace Mother Church and I want Mother Church to embrace me. I want to join a closed community.'

He said, 'You can't be serious!'

'Of course I am.'

'No, you're joking! I was warned that you would joke!'

'No, I'm not joking, father. I would like to enter a closed community. I think it is best for me.'

He stared at me and said, 'No way! No way! We want nothing to do with you. We know all about you, Tony Booth! There's no way the church wants anything more to do with you!'

He fumed on like that for a while and then stormed off, leaving me alone in the gazebo. I might have died there if a friendly nurse hadn't found me and pushed me back into the house!

So the Church's loss was my mother's gain!

Before I left the rehabilitation centre, I was given seventeen pounds in cash, the gloves that I had to wear and a Job garment – an elasticated body stocking intended to smooth down my scars from vivid scarlet, puckered weals to something more socially acceptable. I was to wear it for a year. Every day, I was supposed to have a bath in oil and water to help the elasticity of the skin. I used to flake like mad. Every time I took off the Job garment, there was a veritable snow shower.

My sister came down to Farnham Park and drove me to my mother's house in Liverpool – back where I started. I'd only visited my mother at irregular intervals and, though she'd been brought to see me in hospital, I'd been unconscious and hadn't seen her. My sister told me that my mother was inclined to be confused and so it would require patience on both our parts if we were to learn to live together again. She explained that my mother was in the early stages of senility, which wasn't helped by the Valium tablets she was taking. She was popping them as though they were going out of fashion – because she could never remember how many she'd taken. I knew that I'd have to get her off the drugs and myself straightened out at the same time.

We arrived in the early evening. My sister had to leave straightaway, because she had her own family to look after. My mother and I sat looking at each other for a while.

Eventually, I said, 'Are we going to eat?'

'Have we?' my mother replied.

'No. I'm asking *are* we going to eat?'

'When?'

'That's what I'm asking.'

'Yes.'

'Yes, we are going to eat?'

'When?'

'Well, when you're ready.'

'Who?'

'You.'

'Me?'

'Yes.'

'What?'

'Eat!'

'I'd like to.'

'So would I!'

'When?'

'Whenever you're ready.'

'Good,' she said and just sat there.

'I can't do anything, mother.'

'What?'

'Make a meal!'

'I'd like one.'

'So would I.'

'Good.'

'When?'

'Whenever you want?'

'Well, will you get it?'

'I don't get it. . . I can't remember when. . . They bring them in, you know!'

'Do they?'

'Yes, a woman comes.'

'Oh no,' I thought. 'My mother gets meals on wheels. She's eaten today, but I'm going to starve.'

Part of me wanted to cry, because it was so sad that my mother's mind was in such a state. Another part of me wanted to kill her! At least she was mobile. I could only walk fifty yards and then I was done for.

Yet the only way I could get any cooked food was to go to the fish and chip shop – and that was a hundred and fifty yards away. It took me nearly an hour to get there and then another hour to get back. By then, the food was congealed and barely edible!

Welcome home, Tony!

21

The Phoenix Rises

It was now September. In the last nine months, I'd totally changed as a person. Nobody can go through a major traumatic experience, during which they face death, without being changed. It turned me back to my childhood and the fundamental beliefs that I had held. I knew they were right and the beliefs current in society that I'd so readily accepted were wrong. I knew that it was wrong to be cynical, to lie and cheat and measure success only by material standards. I knew that the most important commandment was 'To your own self be true.' For a long time, I had been untrue to myself, both in my private and my professional life. I was determined it would never happen again.

Within a matter of days after returning home, I pulled myself violently together, knowing I was in a sink or swim situation. As it was the only way I was going to be fed, I took over the cooking, although my mother – under close supervision – had to wash and peel the potatoes. I didn't have sufficient movement in my hands to do it myself.

I began to wean my mother off Valium. She improved a bit, but she didn't do much more than watch television – morning, noon and night. After I'd been home about five days, we were watching *Granada Reports* after the lunchtime news. A man was sitting at a desk, giving information about local events. Behind him was a coloured photograph of an office.

My mother suddenly said, 'I hate that girl!'

'It's a man, mother.'

'No. I don't mean him.'

'Well what girl are you talking about?'

'That girl!'

'What girl?'

'That girl! Can't you see? There's a girl sitting behind him.'

I looked and on the still there was a girl behind a desk. 'Oh, yes,' I said. 'But why do you hate her?'

'Do you know? I watch this programme every day and she never does anything. She never even taps that typewriter. It's disgraceful paying her money just to sit there doing nothing!'

I didn't have the heart to tell her it was a photograph. But at least she was showing some response!

In the evenings, having made the meal, I used to stagger up to my room and, while my mother watched television downstairs, I studied racing form. As the only money I was receiving was the seventeen pounds from the Social Security, I found it very difficult to survive. The only way I could think of to get my hands on extra cash was by gambling. But I couldn't afford to place a bet on a horse that would lose. So I spent hours going through the current form books.

On the Monday, a week after I'd returned to Liverpool, I was in my room when I heard the music of *Coronation Street*. I knew it was half-past seven and it was time for me to make my mother a cup of tea. I made my way downstairs and arrived just before the commercial break. There on the screen was Pat Phoenix. It was a strange experience – like going back in time.

'Of course, yes,' I thought. 'Pat's in *Coronation Street*. I wonder how she is? I would love to see her again. I must give her a ring some time when I get a bit better.'

Not only did I remember her with fondness, but I'd always looked upon her as one of the best and certainly the most under-rated actresses I knew. Twenty-odd years before, we'd spent many pleasurable hours discussing the anatomy of good acting.

And the need to act was still a vital part of my life. While I'd been in hospital, at the moment when I reached the very pit of pain, what bounced me back up again was the thought that some day I'd be able, through my work, to express what was happening to me so that people could understand what real pain was. Both inside my head and in my soul, my experiences had made an enormous difference to me as an actor. But for the time being, I was physically in such bad shape that there was no way I was ready to start acting again. Stuck as I was in my mother's home in Liverpool, I was hungry for contact with another, sympathetic fellow artist.

Three weeks later, my gambling had been successful enough for me to salt away thirty quid. I rang Granada and was put through to the rehearsal room. As luck would have it, Pat answered the phone. She recognized my voice straightaway. We chatted for a while and she told me that she'd once almost visited me. She'd been driving with a friend and they were very close to Mount Vernon Hospital. She'd said, 'Let's go and see Tony.'

But the friend had replied, 'You don't know how bad the guy is. His face may be badly burnt. He's maybe too ill to see you.'

And so they drove on. I wish she hadn't.

During the nine months I was hospitalized, the only visitors I had from the profession were Greg Smith, the producer of the *Confessions* films, Brian 'Blind Pugh' Elvin, our cameraman and Una Stubbs. They were tremendous and offered me their help and friendship.

I said to Pat, 'I wonder if I could come to see you.'

'Yes, of course,' she said.

'Could we have lunch together?'

'Fine. What about tomorrow? I'll meet you at the Film Exchange in Manchester at one.'

My feet had become somewhat smaller. I was taking size eleven on one foot and size nine on the other. So I didn't look as though I was wearing seven-league boots. The only clothes I had were things I'd left at my mother's years before. But among them was a jacket that more or less fitted.

So, dressed as well as I could manage, I took myself over to Manchester with my thirty quid of accumulated winnings in my pocket. Naturally, I was uncertain about the meeting. How different would Pat be? Would there be any contact between us?

I walked into the Film Exchange and it was like going back twenty-odd years. Pat and I embraced. She burst into tears. I'd forgotten how much I'd changed. I'd got used to the way I looked!

Because of the compassion she showed me, I knew I'd found what I most needed – somebody I could relate to spiritually. I had to talk to someone about what I was going to do with the rest of my life. I was nearly fifty. My original personal, political and professional beliefs had been reaffirmed – and for me there was no going back to the way I had been living.

What I didn't know at that time was that, running parallel with my own difficulties, Pat had been going through an appalling time, in both her private and working life. She was facing similar problems, and she had nobody else to talk to. So for both of us, amidst the general darkness, a light appeared.

We spent a couple of hours talking animatedly to each other, until the time came for her to return to the rehearsal. Before she left, she invited me to spend a weekend with her at 'Sunny Place', her cottage near Glossop.

I went back to Liverpool and had ten days in which to pick another winner before I went to stay with Pat. For the first time in over a year, I had a little hope. I'd met someone who'd not only forgiven me for what happened in the past but who was compassionate enough to be able to counsel me. And I did need to be able to talk to somebody on a different level to that of my mother or my sister.

Unfortunately, I broke down again – the scars on my feet reopened. But I'd got it into my head that, if ever I returned to hospital, I'd never get out again. So I kept quiet about the bleeding during my weekly visit to Walton Hospital and dressed my own wounds.

Fortunately, as a result of my studies, I had a successful double and made over eighty pounds. Thanks to William Hill, I was wealthy beyond my wildest dreams!

On Friday, I went over to Manchester and met Pat after rehearsal. She took me in her car to 'Sunny Place'. Because of the difficulty I had in walking, my eyes never left the ground. If I looked up, I was certain to stumble. It was not until we'd entered Pat's cottage that I really became aware of it. But as soon as the door was opened, it was like being embraced. The atmosphere was so welcoming. A fire was blazing in the hearth. All around the walls were paintings and books. The place summed up Pat. It was warm, serene and everything she was. It had an ambience of love.

Pat's elderly housekeeper couldn't cook and so that evening I took Pat out to dinner at the pub just down the hill. I told her what had happened to me and she described the ups and downs of her life, including her marriage to Alan Browning, whose severe drink problem caused his premature death. When we returned to the cottage, we stayed up late talking. We talked all the next day.

On Sunday evening, I lay on the settee, because I had to rest my feet. Pat lay on another settee, and we spoke to each other about the tragedies in our lives.

'What are you going to do now?' she asked.

It was a question I'd faced. I knew I couldn't return to acting until I was fit enough. A fifty-yard walk still exhausted me. So I said, 'I've a portable typewriter at my mother's. I'm adapting a novel I started before the fire.'

Then I described what it was like working at my mother's. She'd given me permission to use the front parlour. Up to then, it'd only ever been used on Sundays and for funerals. I'd no sooner sit down to start typing, when my mother would walk in and say, 'Are you all right?'

'Yes. I'm fine, mother. Thank you.'

'I thought something was wrong.'

'Why's that, mother?'

'I heard a funny noise.'

'That was me typing.'

'Well, nobody's ever done it in here before!'

She would leave, but in five minutes she'd come back again to ask if I was all right. After an hour and a half, I'd end up screaming at her! It was very, very difficult.

Pat laughed and said, 'Why don't you come and stay here for a while? Then you can work uninterrupted in the study upstairs. Please come. I'd really like to help.'

I was overwhelmed by the offer, but I had a problem – I couldn't leave my mother for any length of time. I'd almost weaned her off Valium and I didn't want her to revert back to the state she'd been in when I returned home. I explained this to Pat and she understood.

I saw Pat the next weekend. Then fate intervened. My brother rang to say that his marriage had got into difficulties and, as he'd nowhere else to go, he wanted to come home to my mother's. When he arrived, I told him about the state of my mother's health and explained my system of care. It was obvious that he was going to be at home for some time. So I took up Pat's offer and moved with my typewriter into the guest room of her cottage.

I had explained to Pat that it would be difficult for me to live in her house, because I was supposed to have a bath every day and I couldn't manage it unaided. I'd nearly drowned my poor mother and myself several times!

I'd asked Pat if her driver could help me into the bath. 'Don't be silly,' she'd said. 'I will.'

Apart from my mother and the nurses in hospital, no woman had seen my scarred body. When I looked at myself naked, I was revolted. Michael Crawford in *The Phantom of the Opera* was a raging beauty compared with my appearance from the waist downwards.

So, not unnaturally, I was rather wary of Pat finding out the state I was in. That's how unsure I was of anything at that stage.

When the time for my first bath came, Pat helped me undress and take off my Job garment. She cried with compassion, not with pity, as she helped me into the bath.

Every day she bathed me. The elasticity in my legs was so poor that I could barely bend them and so I couldn't reach my own feet. Now Pat hadn't had much experience of getting a fully-grown man in and out of the bath. Several times, she sat on the edge of the bath to tackle my feet and unbeknown to her my head had slipped down under the water. I'd be splashing about frantically, while she was saying, 'Stop buggering about, Booth!'

Each evening, when Pat came home from rehearsing, we sat in front of the fire and talked. As the bond between us strengthened, I was able to tell Pat about all my secret fears – about being told by the doctors that I would always be impotent, that I might be unable to resume my acting career. She was the most considerate and supportive of counsellors.

A few weeks later, Pat went with friends for a fortnight's holiday in Cornwall. I returned to my mother's house. Every night, she phoned me and the calls grew longer and longer. While we were apart, both of us became aware of our love's second flowering.

When we were reunited, we told each other of our love and embraced. I toppled backwards on to the settee and Pat fell on top of me. We both burst out laughing.

'Anybody would have thought,' Pat said, 'that we were both old enough to have managed our first kiss without collapsing in a heap.'

It was late in October and the nights were cold. Pat got into bed with me, we made love and I really knew I was no longer impotent. Her tenderness and her love had made me whole again.

Pat guided me back into life. She encouraged me to finish my novel, which I never let anybody read. On the day that I typed the last line, I went downstairs and put every page on the fire. It was the only blaze that I could watch with pleasure! The novel was rubbish and I knew it – but it had enabled me to purge myself of all that had happened before I was reunited with Pat.

Of course, I still bore some visible and invisible scars. I'd screamed so much that my vocal cords had been damaged and I couldn't scream any more. There was a time I thought that, after all the tears I'd shed in hospital, I'd never ever be able to cry again. Little did I know. It was true that I'd no tears of self-pity left; the tears I was later to shed were of a very different kind.

I'd been told by my doctor that I had to increase my weight from nine and a half stone to over ten. It proved to be a real struggle. I'd never had a sweet tooth, but the only way I could put on the necessary weight was to eat cream buns and cakes. Every day when Pat was at work, I used to struggle down to the village baker's to buy a batch of goodies for teatime.

One particular day, I walked into the shop just before closing time. The elderly lady serving behind the counter told me that all the cream cakes had gone and that she was about to lock up the shop. Just then the baker came in. He knew about my need to put on weight and so he said he'd fill a couple of cakes with cream for me. At this, his assistant seemed to be none too pleased.

The baker covered a cake with a small mountain of cream, put it on the counter and went off to get another one. The assistant picked up the cake and looked at me. I looked at the cake and then at her and smiled.

'You'd really love to push that straight into my face, wouldn't you?' I said.

She blushed and said, 'No, I wouldn't.'

'Oh, yes, you would!'

The baker returned and said, 'What's going on?'

'Because I'm keeping her late,' I said, 'she would really love to throw that cake at my face.'

'No. I bet she wouldn't,' the baker said.

'No, I wouldn't,' the assistant said.

'I'll tell you what,' I said to her. 'I'll give you a pound if you've got the nerve to do it.'

'You what?' she said.

'I'll give you a quid if you throw it. You know how they do it in films? Well, have you ever done it to anybody?'

'No.'

'Well, you'd really love to do it now to me, wouldn't you?'

'All right. Yes, I would.'

'I knew I was right,' I said. 'OK, you can do it.'

'And you'll give me a quid?'

'Yes.'

I had every intention of ducking as she threw the cream cake so it'd go splat on to the back wall. Just as she was picking up the cake, the shop door opened and in came two diminutive Lancashire ladies who stopped immediately behind me. If I did duck, one of them was likely to end up with a face covered in cream! I quickly stood back between the two old ladies and put an arm around each of them.

As they stood either side of me, I said to them, 'Now I want you to watch this very carefully. I think you'll find it very interesting.'

'What's going on?' one of them asked.

'She,' I said, pointing to the assistant, 'is going to throw a cream cake right into my face!'

'Never!'

'Yes. Right now!'

The assistant picked up the cake and threw it. I ducked and it hit the wall. I laughed, the baker laughed, but the assistant became furious. She picked up the other bun and pushed it – whoosh! – straight into the baker's face.

The two old ladies were looking on in amazement and I was falling about with laughter. The baker staggered back, picked up the bag of cream and shot some right into his assistant's face. She staggered back, picked up a blackcurrant tart and threw it at him. It missed and splattered against the wall. The baker dashed into the back and returned with a huge Christmas cake.

'Think of the money!' I shouted. I couldn't think of anything else to say that might stop him!

He paused, put the cake down and said, 'Yes. You're right. The money!'

I put my quid on the counter and said, 'Forget the cream cakes. I'll see you tomorrow!' Then I fled.

For New Year's Eve, a friend of Pat's chartered a plane to fly a party to Robert Carrier's restaurant at Hintlesham Hall in Suffolk. I'd been secretly training to build up my strength. When we arrived at the airport, it was raining and so it was sensible to run across the tarmac to the plane. Pat said she would walk with me.

'No. Come on,' I said. 'Let's run.'

For the first time in a year, I ran. It was much more of a canter than a gallop, but it was a marvellous end to the year. All the way down to Suffolk, Pat and I sang because we were so happy.

After a fantastic meal, Pat decided that she had to go to the loo. While she was still away, we suddenly realized it was just before midnight. The three men and the two other ladies dashed to stand outside the loo. The men decided that as a joke, we'd drop our trousers as Pat walked out and shout, 'Happy New Year!'

We stood there with our trousers round our ankles. The door opened and out walked another woman! She was horrified at the sight!

When Pat came out, we discovered we'd been premature and that there was still time to return to our table before midnight.

The others toasted in 1981 with champagne. I toasted it in with water!

Throughout the winter, my health continued to improve. One day, I was walking to the village post office when I met a fellow client of the Social Security. He told me he'd written a play based on the experiences he'd had during his nervous breakdown. It was a one-hander that lasted three-quarters of an hour and was set in a pyschiatric hospital.

I read it and thought that it was very interesting. I worked on it and in April, for one week, I presented it in a Manchester pub at lunchtime. I wasn't paid a fee, because it was a try out. That was my theatrical comeback – a reformed drunkard playing for free in a pub!

In the summer, Pat took all her holidays from *Coronation Street* in a block: She wanted to work for a while in the theatre. We accepted the offer of an eight-week season at Eastbourne, appearing in *The Unexpected Guest*, a play by Agatha Christie.

Occasionally, when we had a matinee and a second house, I would really get tired. But I never missed a performance. It was a great experience. On stage, Pat crackled with an energy and excitement that in her maturity had been honed into something very special. Even though the play was not particularly challenging, both of us obtained enormous satisfaction from working together.

At the end of the season, Pat returned to *Coronation Street* and once again I went back to being on the dole. But this time it was very different – I was in love and extremely happy. With Pat, at last I'd found contentment. It was such a pleasure being with her.

She was a highly intelligent, articulate woman who had a mind of her own. I've never met anybody who was prepared to work so hard or so long. Because she was so exceptionally generous and never wanted to let anybody down, she'd be prepared to set off after work in the evening to present the prizes at some charity do which could be a hundred and fifty miles away. Every night she'd be out at some function or other. We were constantly on the run.

I managed to make her cut down a little and, after her chauffeur retired, I did all the driving for her. But we'd still be setting off for Scotland on a Friday evening so she could do a charity show on Saturday night, then driving down to Sheffield for another one on Sunday. I used to drive her about thirty thousand miles a year!

With so many engagements, it's hardly surprising that Pat was for ever getting things mixed up. One weekend, she told me that she had a personal appearance in Newcastle on a Friday night.

That meant we'd have to drive straight there as soon as she'd finished at the Granada studios. She said that the next morning she had to be in Carlisle.

'Will you be able to make it?' she said. 'I'll finish in Newcastle at about two in the morning and then you'll have to drive over the Pennines to be in Carlisle by nine o'clock.'

'That's seven hours,' I said. 'It's a doddle. I'll grab a couple of hours kip while you're on stage at Newcastle.'

At six-thirty on Friday, I picked her up at the studio and set off for Newcastle, where she was due to appear at midnight to present the awards in a gay club. Halfway there, I said, 'Where are we staying tomorrow night?'

'The Arms Park Hotel.'

'Is there an Arms Park Hotel in Carlisle?'

'Yes. We've been there.'

'We've been to the Arms Park Hotel in Cardiff, but not in Carlisle.'

'Did I say Carlisle? Well, it's wherever the Arms Park Hotel is.'

'But that's Cardiff.'

'What's the difference? When we get to Newcastle, I'll check whether it's Cardiff or Carlisle.'

'Christ! It does make a bit of a difference. Still, with seven hours I could make it to Cardiff. You'll just have to go to sleep in the back of the car and I'll drive through the night. Don't worry about it.'

When we got to Newcastle, Pat rang up and discovered that she was supposed to be in Cardiff, and not Carlisle.

The gig at the gay club didn't finish until three in the morning. When we came out, Pat climbed into the back of the car and fell fast asleep as soon as we'd set off.

I had the radio on and I'd just hit the A1 when I heard an announcement: 'The motorways are closed to all traffic because of dense fog covering much of the country. Motorists are strongly advised to stay at home.'

Then we ran into a pea-souper.

I drove down the A1, onto the M1. It was supposed to be closed, but nobody stopped me. I didn't see a sodding thing – not even another car. So I drove as fast as I dared down the middle of the road, just praying that I wouldn't hit anything. Despite driving blind, I managed to make my way onto the deserted M5 and headed for Wales.

It was eight o'clock in the morning and about ten miles from

Cardiff before I could see a hand in front of me. Just then, Pat woke up and said, 'Aren't we there yet?'

When we were not spending our evenings at a function, Pat and I used to sit in front of the fire at home and watch videos. She preferred fantasy films; I liked political thrillers.

One day, on the way to pick up Pat from Granada studios, I called in at an excellent video shop in Ashton-under-Lyne run by a friend of mine called Cyril. I asked him if he'd got anything suitable for Pat. He chose two which he thought she'd love.

Later that evening, Pat picked up one of the videos and said, 'I want to watch this. It sounds great.'

'What is it?' I asked.

'It's called *Clash of the Titans*.'

I groaned, but put it on and sat back in the chair. As soon as it started, I recognized the film. It was the one with the scene I'd watched being made while I was having an out-of-body experience in hospital. I dashed over and stopped the video machine.

'This is the film,' I said to Pat. 'The one I told you about. The one with Sian Phillips in a Grecian temple. I saw her making it at Elstree.'

When it came to the temple scene, I switched off the video again and told Pat exactly what happened next. I'd memorized all the lines, including one which went, 'After this, your love will arise like a phoenix out of the ashes.'

Pat later contacted her agent, who also happened to represent Sian Phillips, to find out more about the film. We were told that the temple scene had been shot in late November 1979 – at precisely the time that I was in the intensive care unit of Mount Vernon Hospital.

22

I Have a Rendezvous

Pat and I always had great fun together and we laughed a lot. Crazy things happened all the time that tickled our sense of humour.

I was a long-term devotee of Chinese food, and Pat came to share my enthusiasm. To vary the monotony of driving Pat backwards and forwards to the studio, I'd try to find a different route home. One night, as we were passing a Chinese takeaway in Stalybridge, we stopped to buy a meal. It was a small family concern, run by a couple and their two daughters. The food turned out to be excellent. So, at irregular intervals, we'd buy takeaways there.

As Pat's housekeeper didn't cook and was of an age when she should retire, we started looking for a replacement. I suggested that we find a Chinese woman or couple who could become our cook and housekeeper.

'But how are we going to find a Chinese cook?' she said.

'Well, you ask, of course.'

'Who?'

'The Chinese! You ask if they know anybody.'

The next time we stopped outside the Stalybridge takeaway, I said to Pat, 'I'll ask them in there.'

'Are you crazy?' she said. 'You can't go into a Chinese takeaway and ask if they can provide you with a housekeeper!'

'Just watch me,' I said.

I was the only customer and so, after one of the daughters had taken my order, I said to her, 'Do you speak English?'

'Oh, yes.'

'Forgive me, but what I mean is, do you really understand English well?'

'I was born in Stalybridge.'

'Great. I wonder if you can help me?'

'You tell me what it is.'

'Well, I'm looking for a woman. . . '

Before I could go on, she said, 'You want woman?'

'Yes. Well, no! What I mean is, do you know of a Chinese lady who would be willing to come and live in with me and my wife and housekeep for us.'

'You want Chinese woman to live with you?'

'Well, yes. But as a housekeeper.'

'What you mean?'

'To keep house.'

'You want Chinese woman to keep house for you?'

'Yes.'

'How old you want this Chinese woman?'

'It doesn't matter, really. I mean, do you know of a single woman or a couple who. . . '

'Ah. You want couple of women,' she interrupted.

'No. I want a Chinese couple or a single woman,' I said, sensing that I wasn't making myself understood at all. 'You see, our housekeeper is about to retire.'

'Ah, you already have woman?'

'Yes.'

'Why you want to change woman?'

'She is old.'

'Ah, you want to be rid of old woman!'

'No. It's not that. She wants to retire – stop working.'

'Ah, so. But you have wife?'

'Yes. I have a wife.'

'And wife not mind you having Chinese woman?'

'No, no. It's our idea. My wife hasn't time to do the cooking.'

The shop door opened and a couple of customers came in. She served them and then came back. 'Now, let me see I understand,' she said. 'You want Chinese girl come your house because your wife no look after you?'

213

'No,' I said, glancing around at the couple who were taking a great deal of interest in the conversation. 'My wife goes out to work.'

'Ah. You have wife go out to work and when she away you want young Chinese girl to come and look after you?'

I could see that I was getting nowhere fast so I said to the girl, 'It doesn't matter. Don't worry about it.'

'No, no,' she said. 'Please. I am very interested.'

I didn't want to go on, because it was teatime and the shop was getting very crowded. Not only that, but the young Chinese girl was saying everything in a very loud voice and I was getting more and more embarrassed.

I took a few steps back. The customers had obviously never heard anything like it in their lives. There was Pat outside in the car, while I was in the takeaway propositioning a young Chinese girl!

I was totally flustered. Her mother had a few words with her and then shouted out something in Cantonese. Suddenly, the father arrived from out the back with my order. He was obviously in high dudgeon.

'Where is this man?' he said to his daughter.

'This one here,' she said, pointing to me.

He pulled a knife from his overalls and said to me, 'You come here looking for Chinese girl?'

'No, no,' I said. 'I came here for this takeaway.'

He stared at me and then said, 'Ahhh. I know you.'

'Yes?' I replied nervously.

He smiled. 'You come here for Chinese girl. You naughty man. *Confessions of Window Cleaner*! I have seen picture five times. You are dirty man!' He started shouting: 'Get out of my shop! You go now! You no come back ever again! Go now!'

I grabbed the carrier-bag and rushed out to the car. Pat fell about when I told her what had happened.

Many moons passed and the incident was forgotten. Then one night, I was driving home and decided to buy a Chinese takeaway. I was in the shop before I realized it was the one in Stalybridge. Behind the counter was the same girl. I prayed that she wouldn't recognize me. I gave my order and hid behind a copy of the *Sporting Life*. The girl came over to me and tapped the paper. I lowered it.

'What is it?' I said.

'Why you not come back?' she asked.

'Pardon?'

'You man from *Confessions of Window Cleaner* my father chased out of shop?'

'Yes.'

'And you ask me about Chinese girl?'

'Yes, but it was. . . '

'You wanted Chinese girl to service you?'

'No, no. You got it all wrong.'

'That is great pity!' she said. 'I ask my friend and she say she would be delighted!'

'It's all right,' I said, waiting anxiously for her father to come dashing out with a knife. 'We're fixed up, thank you!'

We never did find a Chinese housekeeper!

After the enjoyable experience of our first summer season working together, Pat and I did another couple – one in Eastbourne and the other in Bournemouth – for the same management, John Newman and Daphne Palmer, who became close friends of ours.

Apart from these summer seasons, Pat worked most days on *Coronation Street*. But she was very unhappy with the direction the writers were taking and what was happening to her own part. Her story lines were getting thinner and increasingly unlikely. The truth of the matter was that they didn't know how to cope with the show's sex symbol who'd passed her fifty-fifth birthday. It was a very difficult nettle to grasp. Should she still carry on as before or should she abdicate and become resigned to old age?

Also she felt that the *Street* had failed to adapt to the radical changes taking place in society. Its corner shop was not being run, as it was everywhere else, by an Asian couple. There was very rarely a non-Caucasian in the show. There was no attempt to deal with the changing role of women and the problems of unemployment. *Coronation Street* was like a time warp that still reflected working-class mores of the fifties and the production side seemed incapable of doing anything about it.

By the spring of 1984, Pat had become so disillusioned with the show that she decided to leave. Much as I admired her spirit, I tried to persuade her that throwing up professional security at her age was at best impracticable and at worst suicidal. If she was going to leave, she should have done so much earlier, when she was being offered some of the best parts available in both films and plays. I knew that being out in the cold was not a fun trip. I also felt that, because of her twenty-year association with one character, she might find it difficult to find new parts, especially in television.

The management assumed, however, that Pat's decision to leave

Coronation Street had been influenced by me. In fact, she'd been thinking about it seriously for at least five years. The security of the love we had for each other was what helped her to make the final decision.

As soon as Pat's decision was made public, the press went crazy. We were beseiged at the cottage by reporters and television crews. A fictional character was leaving a fictional street and it was being treated as though it was for real. Pat couldn't go anywhere without somebody rushing up to her in tears and saying, 'Don't do it! What are we going to do without you?' For the first time I understood that some people believed that when a character left a serial that person was actually dead. They sent wreaths offering their commiserations!

The British media seemed obsessed with what Pat was doing and one of their major preoccupations was when we were going to get married. We both found it amusing that although we were both in our fifties, I was constantly referred to as Pat's 'live-in lover'. It suited us fine to carry on in this way. We intended to get married in our own time and in our own place. In 1982, when we spent eight days sailing up the Mississippi on a riverboat, we discussed the feasibility of marrying on board, but the captain told us he didn't have the authority. I'd been told that British couples could be married when abroad by their country's ambassador. That appealed to Pat and she thought it would be a great idea to marry in some obscure place, well away from prying journalists. But the more we were questioned about the subject, the more we rebelled and put off the event until another year. On Pat's sixtieth birthday, we got engaged – but that only increased speculation as to the date of the wedding.

My health continued to improve by leaps and bounds. I'd broken the ten-stone barrier, quickly arrived at eleven and in a wild gallop touched twelve! I was having the devil's own job pulling up at twelve and a half stone!

At the same time, unbeknownst to me, Pat's health was gradually deteriorating. Without saying anything to me, she went to see her doctor. He told her she must see a specialist, because there was a possibility that she had a spot on her lung. She'd had TB as a child and it was suggested that it might be the result of that.

We were very much in love. Although we trusted each other implicitly, in no way would either of us inflict pain on each other. Thinking that I had enough problems, she took the decision not to tell me. It may also have helped her cope, because by not having to talk about it she could pretend that it wasn't actually happening.

216

Perhaps too she didn't want anything to change, however subtly, the relationship which had become so important to us both.

So I knew nothing of the state of Pat's health when we accepted an offer from John Newman and Daphne Palmer, the management that had presented our three summer seasons, to take another Agatha Christie play on a twenty-six week tour of the country.

It was only towards the end of the tour that I realized that Pat's vibrant energy seemed to be ebbing away. She was famous for her outbursts as Elsie Tanner on screen – she was equally famous for the outbursts in her private life. She had a wild, exciting Irish temperament that shot like a bolt of lightning through a situation she found unacceptable. Once the lightning had passed, it was gone for ever. But now, I realized, the lightning was no longer gone in a flash. It was leaving behind a dull, lingering ache.

At first, I thought this was merely because she'd lost the security of *Coronation Street* and was facing an uncertain future. Although she was earning more money than she'd ever done in her life, she still didn't know where the next job was coming from and, when we finished the tour, both of us would be unemployed.

But then I noticed that Pat was sometimes breathless and tired at the end of a performance, so I asked her what was the matter and for the first time she told me what her doctor had said. Straightaway, I went with her to see the specialist.

I waited for her in the ante-room. When she came out, she put on a wonderful performance for me, saying that everything was fine, except that she had a hiatus hernia. I believed her. I didn't know until much later that she'd actually been told that the early stages of lung cancer had been discovered.

Although Pat was in many ways a free and adventurous spirit, she had a strict professional discipline, believing the show must go on and that she must fulfil her commitments no matter what. So we finished the tour. It may not have aggravated her condition, but it certainly didn't help.

We finished in October. Both of us were offered other work – Pat was to appear in a situation comedy on television called *Constant Hot Water* and I was acting in *Albion Market*.

In the spring of 1986, I went with Pat to the Alexander Hospital in Manchester. She was away for hours. I sat waiting. When the specialist came to see me, he told me gently that the tests had shown that Pat had a cancerous growth on one of her lungs. They would, however, be able to do something about it. She would be given radiation treatment at Christie's Hospital. After that, she would be well enough to do the summer season we'd planned.

I wanted to throw up and dashed into the bathroom. While poor Pat was still coming round from the anaesthetic, the nurses were having to fuss around me, offering medication.

The terrible news gave our relationship a new dimension, because we were fighting together for her life. We convinced each other that she would be cured.

Pat went in to Christie's Hospital. The staff were extremely kind and concerned. I knew the place well, because during the previous couple of years, my sister had been back and forth receiving treatment there for cancer of the lymph glands.

While Pat was in hospital, I worked daily on *Albion Market*. In the evenings, I'd drive like a bat out of hell to Fazackerly Hospital in Liverpool, where my mother was seriously ill. Then I'd return to Manchester to visit Pat's housekeeper, who was in the eye hospital after a cataract operation, and then drive on to see Pat.

At the end of her treatment, Pat told me that she'd been given a clean bill of health. We went out for a celebration dinner. In fact, I now know that Pat had been told that she had but a short time to live. But she put up the greatest performance of her life and I believed her.

We started rehearsing the play that I'd written for our summer season. It wasn't very good – I dearly wish it had been better. But it had been written while Pat was in hospital and then I'd had other, more important things on my mind.

She was not her old self, but the specialist had warned me that the radiation treatment would sap her strength. Her bright blaze of energy had been dimmed. But I was too blind to see it – possibly because I didn't want to believe that her light was fading.

The play opened in Scarborough. How she got through it, where she found the energy, I do not know. But she did – for a fortnight. Then one evening, after I'd driven her to the theatre, I heard her coughing in the dressing-room. I went in and she was leaning over a sink that was full of blood.

We had a hell of a row, because she wanted to go on, but I said, 'No way!'

'Well what are we going to do?' she asked.

'We're going to cancel the show. That's what we're going to do. I'm putting you straight in the car and driving you back to Manchester. You've got to see a doctor.'

Fortunately, my will prevailed. There was no way I could allow her to go on. The performance was cancelled and we left the theatre at a quarter-past seven.

The following morning, I took her to the doctor. He said to her,

218

'Go home. Put your feet up. You're going to be all right. The radiation treatment has probably caused a flare-up in the lung.'

The play was taken off for a week. Then the understudy went on and I had to return to finish the two weeks of the season.

Pat stayed at home. I rang her every night. At the end of the first week, I drove to 'Sunny Place' on Saturday night and spent Sunday and Monday morning with her.

When I returned the second Saturday night, I could see that Pat was seriously ill.

She was admitted to the Alexandria Hospital. Even then, the doctors persisted in telling me that she was going to be all right. They said they were putting her on new drugs. After a couple of weeks' rest and attention, she'd be able to return home, although she wouldn't be able to work again until after Christmas. I believed them.

There was enormous media interest in Pat's illness. At first, I used to drive backwards and forwards daily from 'Sunny Place' to the hospital. Each time, I had to run the gauntlet of the reporters. It became impossible and after ten days the staff suggested that it would be much better for me to stay at the hospital. I was given a room next to Pat's and virtually became an inmate, even though I'd sworn I'd never again stay in a hospital.

For the next ten days, I didn't leave the corridor where Pat's room was. Then the Senior Nursing Officer came to see me and said, 'You must go out and have a walk in the fresh air.' It was a strange experience to step outside the hospital again. The evening was dark and damp. It was early September and everywhere had gone cold. I couldn't wait to get back inside.

Pat's room was like a theatrical dressing-room – full of flowers, cards and telegrams. The response from the public was magnificent and heartfelt.

I genuinely didn't believe that Pat was dying. It's incredible that I didn't know, but I still clung to the hope that I'd been in a similar situation and recovered. So, of course Pat would get better. I spent most of my time assuring her that she'd soon be up and about. We made plans for what we would do when she left hospital. She chose the clothes she was going to wear. The whole of my mind was preoccupied not with the present but with the future.

Yet all the time, I now know, Pat was aware that she didn't have long to live. She was sinking slowly and I was oblivious to it. Every time I was in the room, she pulled herself together. We laughed and we talked. We had great fun. She went to the trouble of making herself up. The doctors and nurses would all say how well she was looking. Everybody spoke of her being able to leave the hospital in a fortnight or so. I was living in a fool's paradise.

On Saturday, 6 September 1986, two specialists visited Pat in the late evening. They came out of her room and said to me, 'We've never seen such a marked improvement in a patient. We're now thinking of her being able to leave here in a matter of about ten days.'

I went in to see Pat. She told me the specialists had given her the same good news. We were both deliriously happy. When Pat went to sleep I went to the nurses' room to have a cup of tea before I went to bed.

There were two nurses there. 'Isn't it great?' I said to them. 'The specialists have just told me that in ten days Pat will be able to go home and that she's going to make a full recovery.'

One of the nurses burst into tears.

I thought she was crying because she was happy for Pat and me. So I said, 'It's all right. There's no need to cry.'

The other nurse said, 'We can't let you go on like this.'

'What d'you mean?' I asked.

She looked at me and said, 'You genuinely don't know, do you?'

'Know what?'

'Pat is not going to recover. In ten days, she will be dead.'

I was devastated.

After consoling me for some time, one of the nurses said, 'Here's a sleeping-pill. Take it and have a good night's sleep before you see Pat in the morning.'

I could no longer think for myself and so I did as I was told. They took me to my room next to Pat's, I swallowed the pill and went out like a light.

As soon as I woke up on Sunday morning, I went in to see Pat. When she saw me, she knew that I knew.

'I asked them not to tell you,' she said, and started to cry.

I cried with her. Only then did I understand that she didn't have long to live.

'I want to die as Mrs Booth,' she said. 'Can you arrange that for me?'

'Of course – if that's what you want,' I replied.

'It is,' she said. 'But both of us have to be brave. We have to pretend to everybody else that I am going to get better.'

Sunday passed. Visitors came and went.

I prayed that a miracle would happen. I prayed more than I had during my own illness.

I spoke about the wedding to my cousin, the priest, who told me it would take a week to make the arrangements.

Pat began to deteriorate. The doctors informed me there was little chance that she would survive after Wednesday. With the help of relatives and friends, special permission was given for us to marry on Wednesday, 10 September.

It was a simple, moving ceremony. Some eighteen months later, I met by accident the registrar's assistant who'd been there that day. 'I've officiated at thousands of weddings,' she said, 'but that was the only one where everybody cried, including the priest and the registrar.'

Although it had been thought that Pat might not survive for long after the ceremony, she perked up and pressed the button for a nurse so that she could order champagne.

When the nurse came and said, 'Yes, Mrs Booth,' Pat cried with happiness.

She looked at me and said, 'We made it, Booth. We made it.'

So, after all, we were married in an unusual situation – but it wasn't one that either of us would ever have wished for.

Pat survived a week. During that time, I could barely sleep. I asked friends to bring in books of poetry which I spent hours reading to Pat, even when she went into a coma. She had asked me what had been the greatest comfort to me when I was seriously ill and I told her it had been the twenty-third psalm. It became her favourite passage. We relearned it and often said it together.

At nights, a wonderfully kind young nurse sat with Pat. Once when I went off for a break, I returned to hear her reading Pat some poetry. It was beautiful. On the night of Monday the fifteenth, I walked into Pat's room and there was a nurse I'd never seen before, sitting silently and solemnly by the bed. It was a terrifying moment – the death watch had started.

At about eight o'clock on the morning of the seventeenth, I was called into Pat's room. No, she didn't die in my arms. I was kneeling by the side of her bed, holding her hand.

I cannot remember what I did or said – only the words that were going through my head:

'Yea, though I walk through the valley of the shadow of death, I will fear no evil: for thou art with me, thy rod and thy staff they comfort me.'

Postscript

Death brings out the best in most people. It also brings out the worst in a few. One of Pat's colleagues sent a bill for £876 for coming to the funeral, claiming that it would help me with my tax problems! Other acquaintances clamoured for mementoes and lay claim to possessions.

If it hadn't been for the support of my immediate family and my friends, I don't think I would have pulled through after Pat's death. And so for their help and friendship I should like to thank Keith Pollitt, Kim and Nigel Tinkler, Vi and Bert Farrow, Harry Shelton and Carol Taylor.

Seven months later, my sister died in the same hospital as Pat had done. Shortly afterwards, my mother also died. In one heartbreaking year, I lost my wife, my mother and my sister. There were times when I thought I'd never come through the experience.

Although the words are trite, I found it true that 'Time is the great healer'. It takes a hell of a long time, but time does heal. That isn't to say that you forget – I shall never forget.

Somebody said to me, 'One day you'll turn a corner and, when you're not even thinking about the possibility, you'll find love again.' One day, I walked into a restaurant and met someone with whom I fell in love. I started to live again – but that's another story.